PASTORAL CARE MATTERS
IN PRIMARY AND MIDDLE SCHOOLS

This wide-ranging book, challenging in many aspects, offers a fresh survey of the pastoral needs of primary age pupils and pupils in early adolescence:

- **Principles** considers the future needs of children, learning processes, planning and implementing a pastoral programme, and the co-ordination of personal and social education.
- **Aspects of Pastoral Care** develops six specific pastoral approaches: welfare and liaison, health and medical services, life crises and counselling, managing behaviour, bullying, and starting secondary school.
- **Viewpoints** has three personal statements on: television viewing, core values for teachers and parents, and the professionalism of teachers.
- In **An Agenda for Discussion** the editors comment on the previous chapters of the book and add extra material on pastoral care and social and personal education.

The material contained here can be used by both the trainee-teacher and practising primary teacher. It will also interest all professionals working in this area.

Kenneth David and Professor **Tony Charlton** are both at Cheltenham and Gloucester College of Higher Education. They are experienced educational editors and writers who see pastoral care as an issue pervading all aspects of education, strengthening and supporting learning as well as providing welfare, care and personal and social development.

PASTORAL CARE MATTERS IN PRIMARY AND MIDDLE SCHOOLS

Edited by Kenneth David and Tony Charlton

London and New York

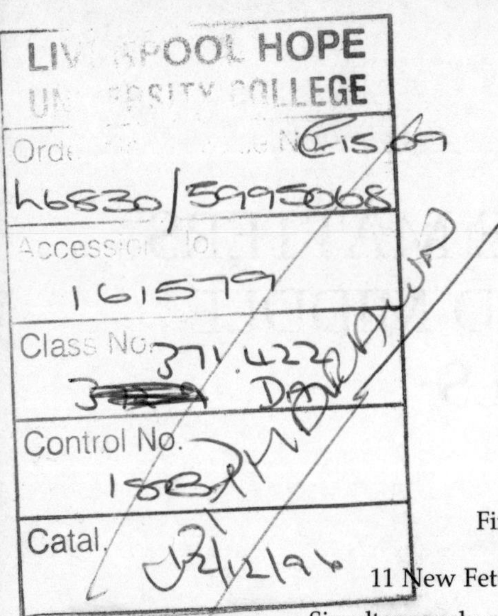

First published 1996
by Routledge
11 New Fetter Lane, London EC4P 4EE

Simultaneously published in the USA and Canada
by Routledge
29 West 35th Street, New York, NY 10001

Typeset in Palatino by Keystroke, Jacaranda Lodge, Wolverhampton
Printed and bound in Great Britain by
Clays Ltd, St Ives PLC

British Library Cataloguing in Publication Data
A catalogue record for this book is available from the British Library

Library of Congress Cataloguing in Publication Data
Pastoral care matters in primary and middle schools / edited by
Kenneth David and Tony Charlton.
p. cm.
Includes bibliographical references and index.
1. Children–Pastoral counseling of. 2. Teenagers–Pastoral counseling of. 3. Church work with children. 4. Church work with teenagers. I. David, Kenneth. II. Charlton, Tony.
BV639.C4P37 1996 96–33799
259′.22–dc20

ISBN 0-415-13279-7

CONTENTS

ILLUSTRATIONS

FIGURES

TABLES

BOXES

CONTRIBUTORS

Mick Abrahams gained a degree and teaching certificate from the University of Exeter in 1975. He has since worked in all phases of education as a teacher, a member of a county advisory service and a lecturer in higher education. While a teacher he held the position of Senior Pastoral Head of House in a large urban mixed comprehensive school, and on moving into higher education has lectured on personal, social and careers education with initial teacher training students. He is at present Head of the Department of Professional Education at Cheltenham and Gloucester College of Higher Education.

Philip Carey worked as a researcher from 1989 to 1995 for the Cancer Research Campaign, Education and Child Studies Research Group, at the University of Manchester. Although the research initially concentrated on cancer education in the formal curriculum, there was an increasing emphasis on the hidden curriculum and the pastoral care system. The culmination of this work was the development of a counselling and communication skills training programme for teachers. This is currently being evaluated at the University of Manchester. Having completed a Master's degree in Health Promotion, Philip Carey has now taken a post as Lecturer in Health Studies at the University of East London.

Tony Charlton was a Director of English Studies and Head of Pastoral Care in a large comprehensive school and taught in primary and special schools before becoming a part-time tutor at University College, Cardiff. He was then Principal Lecturer and Head of Special Needs at the College of St Paul and St Mary, Cheltenham. This became the Cheltenham and Gloucester College of Higher Education where he is currently Professor of Behaviour Studies in the Faculty of Arts and Education. He has published widely on a range of subjects concerned with children's and adults' emotional and behaviour problems, and is co-editor with Kenneth David of *The Caring Role of the Primary School* (1987), *Supportive Schools* (1990), *Managing Misbehaviour* (1989, 2nd edn 1993). He is also the Director of the St Helena project which is monitoring the effects of the inception of broadcast television upon youngsters' social behaviour.

Kenneth David was an army education officer and taught in primary education before becoming principal of a teacher training college and an administrator of schools in Uganda. He then taught in secondary and further education before becoming tutor-advisor in personal relationships in Gloucestershire, and a general adviser with special responsibility for personal relationships in Lancashire. In recent years he has been a free-lance writer and lecturer, with special links with Cheltenham and Gloucester College of Higher Education, as well as working with teachers in many parts of the country. He has published many books and articles on personal and social education (PSE), pastoral care, health education, personal relationships and counselling.

Ronald Davie, contributing the Preface, was formerly Professor of Educational Psychology at Cardiff and Director of the National Children's Bureau, and is now an independent consultant psychologist. He works in the courts as an expert witness in children's cases; undertakes training on the 1989 Children Act and the 1994 Code of Practice; is Chairman of the Policy Committee of the National Association for Special Educational Needs; and continues to have particular interests in the area of children's behaviour and emotional problems. He is currently a Visiting Professor at Oxford Brookes University, and an Honorary Research Fellow at University College, London.

David Frost is a tutor at the University of Cambridge Institute of Education and was a Principal Lecturer in Education at Canterbury Christ Church College where he played a leading role in the development of continuing professional development programmes. For a number of years he taught the Pastoral Care option course on the PGCE programme, and has retained his interest in this area. His main area of research is in continuing professional development and he has published on such topics as 'mentoring' and 'action research'. He has also been instrumental in establishing the Careers Work Centre at Canterbury and has edited a book, *Careers Education and Guidance*, for Kogan Page.

David Hammond is Head Teacher of Greswell Primary School in Tameside, and was joint author of *Mathematics through Action* (1976) and *Development through Action* (1990) published by Tameside LEA. He was joint author with Jean-Pierre Kirkland of 'The pastoral school at primary stage', in *Pastoral Care in Education* 11 (1) (March 1993).

Kevin Jones is a Senior Lecturer in Education in the National Institute of Education, Nanyang Technological University, Singapore. He was formerly Principal Lecturer in Education at Cheltenham and Gloucester College of Education, where he held responsibility for in-service courses and academic standards. His teaching experience spans primary, secondary and special schools, and he has held advisory and support roles. He has published articles on special educational needs, is co-editor with Tony Charlton of *Learning Difficulties in Primary Classrooms* (1992), and contributed a chapter entitled 'Working with Parents' in *Managing Misbehaviour* (1989, 2nd edn 1993). He is currently working with Tony Charlton on a new book entitled *Overcoming Learning and Behaviour Problems: Partnership with Pupils*. His research interests include assessment and recognition of learning difficulties and problem behaviours, special educational provision in mathematics and co-operative teaching approaches. He carried out a doctoral research project into the special oral language needs of low-attaining mathematicians.

Jean-Pierre Kirkland was a secondary teacher and school counsellor. He was Adviser for Personal and Social Education and Child Protection in Tameside LEA (1990–93) and is now a private education consultant. He is a private counsellor and stress management counsellor, and an Ofsted inspector for primary, secondary and special schools. He has published a number of articles on adolescent friendships, home and school relations, residential and therapeutic community work, psychosynthesis and change, and stress relief. A chapter on 'Restoring spiritual values in abused children' in *Spirituality and the Whole Child* (1995) is shortly to be published, as is an article in *Pastoral Care in Education* on 'Developing child protection policies in schools'.

Jean Price is a community paediatrician. She qualified as a doctor at Durham and then spent ten years in child psychiatry. For the last fourteen years she has been in charge of a community child health department at Southmead Health Trust, Bristol. Specialising in child abuse, she has particular concerns in educational and social issues in children's development, and how they will impact on our future society. She is Chair of the British Association for Study and Prevention of Child Abuse and Neglect.

Mayling Quah is currently Senior Lecturer and Head of the Division of Specialised Education at the School of Education at the National Institute of Education, Nanyang Technological University, Singapore. She was previously a school teacher, a research officer, a lecturer and Head of a Reading Clinic. In 1982 she became Head of the Department of Education for Children with Special Needs at the Institute of Education, and concurrently Project Director at the Curriculum Development Institute of Singapore producing teacher and pupil materials for slow learning children. Her research interests include under-achievement among gifted children, learning difficulties, and language and reading skills in children with developmental delays. Her publications include articles and research monographs dealing with school learning problems. She is currently serving as editorial consultant to two journals, *The International Journal of Disability, Development and Education*, and *Support for Learning*.

Anita Ryall and her colleagues **Gillian Goddard** and **Irene Travis** are senior lecturers at Liverpool Institute of Higher Education and have all been primary teachers. Anita Ryall and Irene Travis were also head teachers. Between them they co-ordinate work with the under-5s, and with Personal and Social Education on the Bachelor of Education course, and undertake in-service work with practising teachers on PSE, curriculum co-ordination and work with under-5s.

Sonia Sharp taught in a special school, and was a teacher of English and Drama in secondary schools, before becoming an educational psychologist in Barnsley, a Research Fellow in the Department of Psychology at the University of Sheffield, a visiting Research Fellow at the Institute of Social Research at the University of South Australia, and now Senior Educational Psychologist in Lincoln. She has written numerous articles on stress in adolescence, on bullying, playground behaviour and peer counselling. She has been a joint author and/or editor of four books on bullying, one a package distributed by the Department of Education in 1994, and the latest *How to Tackle Bullying in Your School: A Practical Handbook for Teachers* (1994).

Kate Wall was a home–school liaison teacher in Gloucestershire, and was seconded for two years to develop parental involvement projects in the county. She is now Head of an Opportunity Group, a unit for pre-school children with special educational needs. She has previously contributed to Charlton and David's *Supportive Schools* (1990).

Richard Whitfield is Emeritus Professor of Education at the University of Aston, Honorary Chair of the National Family Trust and presently Warden of St George's House, Windsor Castle, a study centre concerned with the interfaces between moral, spiritual and practical affairs. He has written extensively on curriculum theory and evaluation, family policy and child welfare. He is principal author and general editor of the *Life Foundations* resource bank for personal and social education for a wide range of abilities and age ranges.

PREFACE

Attitudes towards pastoral care in school are often ambivalent. This can be seen in parliamentary discussions, in the media and at times within the profession itself.

Since the 1988 Education Act, there has been tremendous pressure on schools to raise standards of educational attainment. The National Curriculum, a product of the 1988 Act, laid down quite detailed guidelines about the knowledge, skills and understanding which children were expected to acquire as they progressed through their schooling.

The justification for this statutory framework was in part to achieve a measure of consistency across the country. However, the principal reason was to improve standards in schools and bring the UK into line in this respect with other advanced countries. Furthermore, open enrolment to schools and the publication of external examination results were meant to reinforce the push towards higher standards, cast within a 'market forces' ideology.

The effect of all this was inevitably to alter the balance of priorities given by many schools to the non-academic and non-examinable aspects of the curriculum. Thus, amongst other aspects of school life, pastoral care tended to lose out.

There was one fairly straightforward way of counteracting this effect, namely, to include personal and social education as part of the National Curriculum. As the legislation was going through the House of Lords, a small delegation went to see the then Secretary of State for Education to press this point. I was one of that delegation – as Director of the National Children's Bureau at the time. The others were mostly parliamentarians from both Houses but the Director of the National Society for the Prevention of Cruelty to Children (NSPCC) was also there. He and I stressed that preparation for parenthood (as part of the personal and social education (PSE) curriculum) should have a significant place in any educational programme if the prevention of child abuse and the promotion of sensible, 'good enough' parenting were to be seen as important goals. Further, the delegation pointed out that the mere raising of educational standards was unlikely to be optimally effective unless this was set in a context of pupils' balanced personal and social development.

The delegation conceded that to include PSE – or, with the addition of health education, personal, social and health education (PSHE) – in the National Curriculum would not always or necessarily guarantee such a balance. On the other hand to exclude it would surely carry the message that, whilst the ten conventional subjects were *essential* elements of the curriculum, children's personal and social development was an *optional* extra.

The Secretary of State's response was in effect to accept the substance of our case but to say that if he opened the door to another subject in the National Curriculum, he would be besieged by renewed representations from other subject groups whom he had already turned down. This, it might be thought, was hardly the best or most rational of reasons for declining our suggestion. Unfortunately, however, rationality is not always a feature of political judgement.

The predictions of the delegation were largely confirmed. Although the National Curriculum Council, of which I was also a member in the Council's early years, gave some attention to PSE, the topic became diluted and diffused and was never rigorously defined. It was caught up in a number of overlapping discussions on what were called 'cross-curricular themes'. Thus, PSE was included, for example, in part in guidance on health education and also in guidance on citizenship. It also featured in a consideration of the 'whole curriculum'.

It has to be said that the case for some diffusion of PSE across the curriculum cannot be gainsaid. Indeed, the essence of the argument for the importance of PSE is that it is at the centre of the education process, reinforcing and being reinforced by the study of conventional school subjects. Nevertheless, the failure to give statutory recognition to this centrality served to heighten the 'atomism' of the National Curriculum. The education of the whole child within the context of a whole curriculum became simply a desirable goal rather than an essential feature. Therefore, within the market-place pressures being applied following the 1988 Act, schools understandably gave priority to what they were told were the essentials; the desirables often languished in a mountain of paper awaiting some future unspecified attention.

I have focused above upon the fate of PSE in the context of the Education Reform Act and the National Curriculum. However, the fate of pastoral care was inextricably linked to this. The atomism of the legislation tended to be reflected in the priorities and realities of school life. Staff time and training budgets were given to reviewing and developing National Curriculum subjects. After all, progress and standards in these areas were largely to be the litmus paper for appraising the school's success. Schools' policies and procedures in the area of pastoral care would perhaps at best be 'put on hold'.

The ambivalence towards pastoral care which I referred to at the outset goes beyond simply giving priority to children's cognitive functioning over their emotional and social development. It has also to do with the respective roles of the family and the school in promoting or safeguarding children's personal development.

In some way schools are caught – somewhat like social services in the context of child protection – between the devil and the deep blue sea. If teachers are felt to be going too far in, say, discussions on sex education, contraception or drugs they can be denounced as usurping parents' responsibilities. On the other hand, whenever teenage pregnancies are reported to be rising, or when a child dies as a result of drug-taking, there can be implicit criticism that schools could be doing more, or could be acting more effectively in these areas.

For all these reasons, this book is both important and timely. First, the editors set about unpicking the term and the concept of 'pastoral care' and bring intellectual rigour to that task.

They review its purpose in the light of current trends in society and against the background of education legislation and public policy.

Individual chapter authors then pick up these and other themes, putting flesh on the bones of the editors' earlier analyses and contributing their own analyses and constructions. One point which comes through very clearly is a rejection of the dichotomy between children's learning on the one hand and their emotional and social development on the other. This idea is untenable from two points of view. First, research evidence confirms the commonsense observation that children's cognitive development is affected by emotional and social factors and vice versa. Second, both emotional and social development are themselves learning processes. Like cognition, they are a function of the interaction between biological, genetically determined, maturational factors and environmental forces, the latter providing the opportunity and the context for mental as well as physical growth.

Throughout the book there is an easy relationship between theory and practice. The dichotomy sometimes drawn between these two – for example, by government ministers and assorted 'think tanks' – is a false one. To imagine that one can have a 'practical' book which does not draw on theory is a mistake, unless the book is quite literally a rather facile catalogue of 'tips for teachers'. The moment that one begins to generalise from experience, to explain the assumptions on which the suggested practice is based, to indicate a context or framework within which the practice can be seen, one enters the world of theory.

The framework set out in the present book is both rich and diverse, ranging from the everyday realities and problems of school life – personal crises, discipline, bullying – to the other systems which complement education – notably health and social services – and through to wider contexts such as the effect of the media and the changing role of the family.

Notwithstanding its diversity, the book has a coherence and unity which will, I am sure, commend it to the kind of reader who will anyhow be drawn by its title and subject matter. Teachers interested in pastoral care are essentially people who see children as individuals, as wholes, rather than vessels to be filled with discrete bodies of knowledge. They also see children and staff as part of a wider whole, which is first the school and beyond that society.

The editors in their final chapter draw together the threads, underlining the book's unity and proposing a thoughtful and challenging 'Agenda for Discussion'. This chapter offers, amongst other possibilities, the basis for a productive programme of staff discussions on aspects of pastoral care for as far ahead as most schools will wish even to contemplate.

Professor Ronald Davie

INTRODUCTION

In *The Caring Role of the Primary School* (1987) we attempted one of the first surveys of pastoral care in primary schools, and this was received with reasonable approval in schools. So much has happened in primary education since then that a fresh review is overdue, and we have taken the opportunity to extend the scope of the work into middle schools, adding consideration of lower secondary school pupils and early adolescence.

We see pastoral care as those aspects of a school's work and teaching which particularly contribute to the care, welfare and personal development of the pupils. There cannot sensibly be a clear boundary to pastoral care, however (such as limiting it perhaps to welfare and discipline, as in an unhappy past), for the spirit and ethos of the school, the curriculum, teaching methods and relationships must also inevitably contribute to the development of pupils as whole persons. The cross-curricular themes of the National Curriculum illustrate this point, for example, the NCC (1990) *Curriculum Guidance 3: The Whole Curriculum* refers to a broad and balanced curriculum which:

(a) promotes the spiritual, moral, cultural, mental, and physical development of pupils at the school and of society;
(b) prepares pupils for the opportunities, responsibilities and experiences of adult life.

Pastoral care is about education in its widest sense, therefore. It aims to support successful learning as part of the pupil's development, and in turn the teaching and curriculum can contribute greatly to the personal and social education of the child.

The term 'personal and social education' (PSE) is a label to describe the aspects of the curriculum which are particularly concerned with the health, growth and personal development of a child. Either in cross-curricular themes or in tutorial or teaching periods there is a range of PSE themes which can be introduced to pupils as they grow. This book ranges widely, therefore, as it considers all aspects of pastoral care in primary and middle schools.

In **Part I Principles** we consider four personal views on fundamental issues which appear to us to underpin the study of pastoral care. Kenneth David in Chapter 1 reflects on what we are educating primary and middle school pupils for, and how we do it; and this is followed by personal guesswork as to what the future holds for our pupils. Kevin Jones and Mayling Quah in Chapter 2 emphasise the fact that pastoral care is intended to enhance learning. They discuss the various factors which appear to support or challenge the way children learn, and classroom relationships and approaches are considered, together with relevant research. In Chapter 3 David Hammond and Jean-Pierre Kirkland offer their definition of pastoral care, and consider one approach to the planning of a whole-school policy in a primary school. They consider the development of staff, administration and management factors, and evaluation. They consider the issue of discipline, and also link pastoral care with learning as in the previous chapter. Chapter 4 has been contributed by Anita Ryall and her colleagues Gillian Goddard and Irene Travis, and reviews how they see pastoral care and personal and social education being co-ordinated, again with the purpose of facilitating learning. The National Curriculum is considered, as are case studies of schools' management of pastoral care and personal and social education.

In **Part II Aspects of pastoral care**, having considered the previous four views of basic pastoral care issues, we develop six further important themes, all of which arise inevitably in any discussions of pastoral care. They all follow from and are further aspects of the issues developed in Part I. Kate Wall in Chapter 5 looks at the fundamental task of welfare, and the important theme of liaison with other agencies and with parents is examined, as are the effects of the Children Act and other legislation. A case study involving these issues is presented. Medical and health aspects of pastoral care are examined by Jean Price in Chapter 6. Stress and counselling are the main aspects of Chapter 7 contributed by Philip Carey. He also examines confidentiality and liaison, linking again with Chapter 5. The editors review the management of behaviour in Chapter 8, reinforcing the views of other contributors. They include some of their conclusions from *Managing Misbehaviour* (2nd edn). The difficult subject of bullying is given specific attention in Chapter 9, for this has attracted much public concern. Sonia Sharp offers theoretical and practical ideas from her specialised knowledge on the subject. Finally, David Frost in Chapter 10 looks at the often ignored question of the transition from primary to lower secondary school.

Part III Viewpoints adds three personal considerations of themes which affect education in general and pastoral care in particular. Tony Charlton looks at television viewing in Chapter 11. This is a reflection of the constant debate about the influence of television on morality and violence, and thus on the moral aspects of personal and social education and on the potential conflict between schools and their society.

In Chapter 12 Richard Whitfield deals with the core values which can underpin our educational work, particularly in religious and moral education. He offers what we see as a particularly important contribution, and his work links with ideas first raised by Kenneth David in Chapter 1. He considers education as a concept, the shared responsibilities of school and home, and the phases of moral and social development. He examines a 'pedocratic oath', a 'children's charter' and 'parental promises'.

Chapter 13 by Mick Abrahams usefully reminds us that all the implementation of all the thinking and suggestions in the previous chapters implies demands on teachers and depends on their professionalism. He considers teacher accountability, autonomy and appraisal, as well as initial and in-service training, and challenges what he terms the 'deskilling' of teachers.

In **Part IV An agenda for discussion**, the editors comment on and extend the differing opinions and views from earlier chapters on pastoral care with younger pupils. They discuss other pastoral care themes not dealt with elsewhere and offer additional material that can be used for student discussions and staff in-service training sessions. Throughout the book the intention is to offer not only theoretical views, though these must be presented, but also practical ideas for positive pastoral care work for younger pupils, mostly by offering material for initial and in-service training.

Hopefully, the final impression left by this book will be that pastoral care does matter a great deal, not only for the regular development and welfare of the pupils, but particularly to aid and support their day-to-day learning, and even, ideally, to prepare them for their future lives.

REFERENCES

David, K. and Charlton, T. (1987) *The Caring Role of the Primary School*, Basingstoke: Macmillan Educational.

National Curriculum Council (1990) *Curriculum Guidance 3: The Whole Curriculum*, York: NCC.

Part I
PRINCIPLES

1

EDUCATION IN THE MARKET PLACE

Kenneth David

This chapter attempts a personal reflection on the world our young pupils may be living in as adults. As well as dealing with the immediate horizons of our daily work, teachers have an idealism obligation, and we can perhaps peer ahead to guess at the relevance of what we are teaching now.

INTRODUCTION

We have to sell our educational planning ideas in the market place characterised by a very critical public opinion nowadays, and hopefully those plans are focused on what our children need from us for their future lives. We can reasonably be questioned about what our aims are. A lot of people talk of living one day at a time, coping with the problems of the moment; teachers can argue, 'It's enough to do to deal with the load of this school day, and yes, maybe the week ahead, but that's my lot. Don't expect me to talk about twenty-first century needs'. Memory and attention spans have great limitations, and even among professional workers imaginative planning ahead can be one burden too many. Perhaps planning for the future is the job solely of senior leadership, though that seems a reduction in individual professionalism. When visiting schools I used to worry about head teachers and their staffs who were immersed always in detailed daily chores, and who never seemed able to stop to plan much ahead. Well, someone in every school must keep asking, '*Why* are we doing this?' and '*How*?' and, even more so, '*For what end*?', 'What exactly is this school selling?'

In less developed communities abroad that I once knew there were few such questions. A child learned what was necessary for survival from his or her family, then, after initiation rites, from the peer group and finally from the discussions of the tribal elders. The Why? and How? were obvious – self survival and the preservation of the clan. The future meant a day ahead. I spent absorbing years in Africa introducing education in one such area, and shaping education in neighbouring districts which were far more advanced, some with growing urban development. The purpose of all that education was a constant question. What were the basic necessities for a remote and simple village, and for a sophisticated town setting with growing industry and an increasing demand for university graduates? We were trying, with African colleagues learning to replace us, to forecast the future needs of their people. Was it to be academic, agricultural or technical? Were they heading for farms or factories in twenty years' time? Sadly, what we did not prepare them for was civil war.

In Britain now we have in one primary school class children destined for prosperous professions and others apparently destined to be unskilled and unemployed for at least part of their lives. What are the educational needs of both kinds of children, and how best do we prepare them for life?

FUNDAMENTALS

The fundamental Why? is fairly obvious in a modern society. Children have to be able to read and write and be numerate. There is an obligation in primary schools to teach fundamentals well, better than in the past few years. We have modern resources in the form of well-educated teachers, books, reading schemes, and TV and computer technology. There is no excuse now for failing. There may be difficulties, particularly in family and community support, and in meeting special educational needs, but there is no real excuse for finding many children unable to cope with fundamental skills. And those skills need constant renewal and practice for they fade if left unattended. Included among such skills is speech, a sometimes forgotten part of being literate. To chat about things, to put words together clearly, to discuss an idea, to put a point of view, to give an opinion and to learn to listen are as essential as reading.

With so many passive leisure pursuits, and with democracy disappearing into pressure groups, perhaps being articulate is a fundamental survival skill. The Why?, therefore, is fairly obvious in primary education. We are providing foundation skills, and continuing to practise them well into secondary education, to ensure they last into the adulthood of every child. The How? also seems reasonably obvious, for we surely have competence in imparting such skills, and splendid technology and materials to help in motivating and interesting children, despite the competition that sometimes emanates from their backgrounds. In a parallel competence one thinks of the considerable skills of the armed services in educating recruits, not only improving their literacy but then giving them impressive skills with sophisticated weaponry and apparatus. Surely we must be good at basic teaching? Are teachers not the experts in these matters? When we extend the How? into subjects other than basic literacy skills, the expertise should follow. After the interesting debates over the content of the primary and secondary curriculum we seem to have settled to an acceptable range of selected knowledge, and there should be no difficulties in our methodology in other subject areas in primary and middle schools. The content has been endlessly argued; perhaps more thought has gone into lists of themes than into the fact that good teachers' enthusiasms can usually capture the imagination of most children. Creating enthusiastic learners seems the major task – an enthusiasm for varied interests. I sometimes think it is almost as important to produce an enthusiastic recruit to a lifelong hobby as it is to shine in test results. There is so much knowledge available that our job in schools is to create curiosity about the vastness of information, and to begin to give pupils the skills of managing and gaining access to the particular knowledge they need, as well as remembering the outlines of subjects. We are only offering 'tasters' of different subjects, rather than pretending to equip them with a life's supply of facts.

Setting aside the personal factor of special educational needs, failure in the teaching of the fundamental skills, as in the teaching of the whole area of primary and lower secondary curricula will probably lie in one of three areas: an uninterested family or community background, a lack of commitment and enthusiasm in the teaching, or a failure of the school leadership to provide the right ethos and setting.

FOR WHAT?

For What? takes more thought for we may have to look far ahead. We can deal with the foundation skills and the imposed curriculum of the primary and middle school, but as educationists we will be considering cross-curricular matters, some of them themes listed in this chapter. We can consider other dimensions of our teaching and of the knowledge we are putting over, give children differing emphases and implications of the facts we are using, encourage new or important interests as we range over the classroom lessons, use examples even in the simplest subject teaching which serve more than one purpose. This 'matrix' thinking is the way cross-curricular teaching becomes effective. We are teaching pupils the straightforward curriculum programme, but are always considering the background of cross-curricular demands, with our agenda of ideas of health education, community values, moral and social education, and perhaps some of the following aspects of the future of our pupils.

Passivity

We are seeing the watching generation, the passive cohorts, the couch potatoes of the brave new world, in many of the pupils facing us in the classroom today. Tony Charlton reflects more deeply on this in Chapter 11. This passivity is likely to grow as television expands with satellite choices, and with little likelihood of effective regulation. A headline in my newspaper today reads, '75 per cent of schools skimp on sport', a passivity caused by classroom demands. The following page has an article saying, 'Television has made [children's mental] problems worse by killing communication in the home'. A report from the Henley Centre for Forecasting recently claimed that middle-class families were only (sic) watching twenty-three hours of TV each week, and lower-income families thirty-four. The first TV game show for 3-year-olds, 'Fun Games', is in production in 1995. There are constant reminders, admittedly alarmist at times, which point to some isolation or passivity factor among pupils. In the USA a recent book by Lasch (1995) published posthumously, argues that the lively and intellectually active elites are convinced that they have brains and that ordinary people have none. The new elites are mobile, cosmopolitan, ambitious and contemptuous of Middle America, of home, family and neighbours. The passive majority and the active minority exist in our own classrooms, and our own society perhaps? Presumably some answers lie in lively teaching, though I recall exhausting myself and my primary school class once years ago, with something called, I think, 'Activity Maths', which was a grave mistake. Lively and interesting teaching, trying to fight passivity or tiredness (and not retreating to the enjoyment of concentrating on the brightest pupils) is very hard work, but it is part of our professional task in fighting lazy thinking. So is team teaching, and specialised subject teaching in primary schools, so that the pupils face the challenge of differing personalities. We can challenge children intellectually far more than we do in many schools. We do molly-coddle pupils at times. I knew an educational psychologist once who argued fiercely that it was quite possible to teach philosophy to infants. I am not sure about infants, but I am sure that we often underestimate the capabilities of primary children, and, in passing, one pictures an even more youthful version of Jostein Gaarder's adventure in philosophy, *Sophie's World* (1995).

Violence

Whether there is in fact more violence in our society than in the past is constantly debated, though a recent British crime survey indicates that there is. There has always been city violence and the violence of wars. But the majority of parents and teachers that one meets still appear to think that we live in a harsher world, if we exclude wartime, and one with more assertive and overt crime, and much less respect for authority. There is evidence of this in schools also, and teachers may face violent pupils from the infant school upwards. Christ Church College,

Canterbury, conducting a survey for the government, points to more than 10,000 expulsions a year, for varying reasons, from primary and secondary schools. Some 15 per cent of these are from the primary sector. We also meet with confrontational and sometimes violent parents.

The challenge of drugs in our society and in our schools adds to violence and crime, and reveals an emptiness in the lives of the apathetic and the inadequate, as well as among pupils from more prosperous and intelligent families. *The Economist* in December 1994, under the heading 'There are no children here', suggested that gangs have turned America's inner-city streets into war zones, with the drug trade and the spread of powerful guns commonly blamed, but with teenage nihilism as possibly the most lethal factor of all. One state authority in Germany, alarmed by a sharp increase in classroom violence, plans to send teachers on judo and martial arts courses (including the use of an umbrella in self-defence). The drop-out rates for teachers – once one of the highest rated professions in Germany – are now among the worst in Europe. The complaints procedure of the Children Act (1989) alarms our teachers, who may face more unjust accusations from pupils. Dyfed Education Authority's recent *Stress Report for School Staff* (1984) reveals the authority's anxiety over stress levels among staffs. Jack Dunham (1992) points out in some detail that change has been rapid since 1988, and teachers in primary and secondary schools are now doing what in some ways can be said to be a quite different job. Stress itself is a kind of violence, and surely behind all the other management reasons for teacher stress lies our own unquiet society and its children.

So, we are obliged to warn children they are eventually to manage a potentially violent world? (A world, by the way, in which there are now some 200 disparate states with only twenty or thirty peacefully well-governed.) Or perhaps we just work harder to give them a peaceful school setting as a contrast to the world outside, a peaceful setting in which we actually emphasise for the children how to cope with the violence of others, how to discuss instead of argue, and the drills of conflict resolution. After we have done all that we will constantly fail. Should we persist in trying?

Work

There is an increasing gap between rich and poor in our society, even though the poverty is relative compared with the past. In 1977 the income of the richest 20 per cent of Britons was four times that of the poorest 20 per cent, but by 1991 the multiple increased to seven. At the same time the opportunity to find useful and satisfying work is increasingly unequal; as manual work decreases, the gap between the ill-educated and the well-educated sharpens, and we now face a crudely termed and growing 'underclass' of the inadequate and the ill-educated. Charles Murray of the American Enterprise Institute, an experienced sensation creator, puts it even more bluntly: intelligence, he says, rather than background or social status, is the most powerful determinant of poverty, and of crime and unemployment. Since those who are excluded from success by poor education, limited intelligence, or poor family and community setting may eventually spoil life for the rest of their society, there seems good reason to give much more time and thought to our pupils who seem booked for failure. We do not deal with career education in the primary and middle school, nor can we influence society in major ways. Finding proper answers lies in politics; schools can only work to avoid inequalities in the classroom, in resources, in teacher attention, in searching for potential, in testing and in school ethos.

We can also recognise that the whole nature of work is changing, and it is becoming a scarcer commodity as technology becomes more sophisticated: there are now plenty of downwardly mobile middle-class professionals badly hit by unemployment, and university graduates can be found driving mini-cabs and working in canning factories. Self-employment is one answer we are told, with service industries predominant, though even service jobs are being automated now with cash-dispensing machines, voice-recognising computers and address-reading machines to sort mail. Jeremy Rifkin (1993) argues that within the next century the world's richest economies will have virtually no need of workers, so our older pupils could be pondering on the fact that technology, having eliminated much manual work, will begin to eliminate their chance of traditional middle-class jobs. 'Clerical work of all sorts is already threatened', said the Chief Executive of Barclays Bank recently (*Sunday Times*, 2 April 1995).

Do headmasters brood on the attitudes (and curriculum examples) their staffs can offer even young pupils on the following: the kinds of work that men and women will seek in future, on the unlikely nature of a life of full or unchanging employment, on the kinds of work men and women do nowadays in Taiwan and Singapore and Delhi, on the shortening working lives of their parents, on longer lives of eagerly sought or enforced leisure, on the bleakness of life without daily work, on personal survival skills in a constantly changing world, on the awfulness of not finding enjoyment in books and people, and hobbies and interests?

The Knowledge Age

The teacher's role, it is suggested, changes from 'sage on the stage' to 'guide on the side' with the coming of the computer and video age, and schools are being changed by children themselves who cannot conceive a world without colour television, video games, take-away meals, and now

CD-Roms (see also Chapter 11). Digital technology will greatly change the way children learn, and the way teachers deal with them. On a CD-Rom you could own the entire collection of the National Gallery or a library, and a 'smart card' can carry our personal history for a hospital or bank visit, or can buy a newspaper. Fascinatingly we may even find politics more vulnerable to citizens' information-power, which will upset the present monopolies of knowledge and reliance on poorly informed voting. Peter Drucker (1993) argues that modern society is no longer dominated by communities, nations or families, but increasingly by special-purpose organisations such as businesses. Many organisations, he continues, take up people's time, determine their status and create nearly all wealth. The Yale professor Paul Kennedy (1993), brought up and educated in England, forecasts that with too many people and too few resources, and with the knowledge explosion dizzyingly accelerating technological change, the problems of population, ecology and technology are connected and compound Malthus's theories. To complete this cheering review of futurology we might consider the ideas of President Carter's former national security adviser Zbigniew Brzezinski (1993) where, echoing Solzhenitsyn, he sees a spiritual desolation of unrestrained hedonism and greed. So the concepts of the Knowledge Age, and the Global Village, with technology making the world smaller and better, can be viewed questioningly by primary school children and their teachers. We can continue to concentrate in the primary and middle school world on teaching children how to learn, how to use study skills, how to use their visual and aural memories, how to collect appropriate knowledge for a particular task, how to make judgements and choices, how to question with skill, how to see the whole and select the detail, how to use computers as extensions of their mind, and how to enjoy knowledge. Not unlike the formula for sixth form work really!

A youthful world

We read in tabloid and serious newspapers of the 'ME' generation, where people look after themselves first and last. It is doubtful if the younger generation is, in fact, any more selfish than previous generations, for the instinct for selfishly surviving and stepping on the fingers of the person below you on the ladder is long-standing, but competes with the selflessness, heroism and kindness that we also see around us every day. What is certain is that we are seeing what is termed by the journalist Paul Goodman, 'The greying of Europe'. Longer life expectancy, earlier retirement, fewer births, rising living standards, greater welfare and medical demands, and a feeling that anyone over 45 years of age is ancient, will put great demands on a smaller younger generation to generate the wealth to keep more dependants. Young minds are needed for new technological innovation, and hopefully someone is working out who is going to pay the pensions of an expectant retired generation in the future. One senses that there is greater impatience with the demands of the old, greater family dislike of caring for its own old folk, greater expectation that the state will deal with caring work, and a greater need for teaching about family life and human relationships, as well as about the vitality of youth. Dr Benjamin Spock (1994) follows his earlier works (which sold 40 million copies, second only to the Bible) by appearing to despair of the third generation of post-Spock children and the deterioration in our society. Old age often brings pessimism, but how selfish is the ME generation, and how far can the schooling years offset family and society attitudes? Is the idealism of modest teachers the only conscience of the nation now? Are teachers the role models for our youngsters, or is Woody Harrelson in *Natural Born Killers*, or John Travolta in *Pulp Fiction*? Despite the alarming weight of evidence that can be assembled about the present youthful world one still has careful optimism about the influence of the ordinary decent teachers of primary and middle school age groups. If they could be supported, led and enthused to add more imagination and teaching excitement to this fundamental decency we might start a revolution in primary education.

Family life

Evidence of the massive changes in family life are obvious to every teacher. There can be few teachers who can ignore the effects of divorce and family breakdown on their pupils' learning and behaviour, for the family is clearly the most influential socialising agency in a child's life. In Northern Europe two out of five marriages end in divorce, in America half. One in five children in Britain see their father less than once a month, it is suggested. The number of single-parent families is considerable and, sadly, evidence is mounting that children of divorce often do worse than children whose parents stay married. We know that unhappiness and disruptive behaviour can occur in pupils whose parents are divorcing. Additionally, recent work by McLanahan at Princeton University suggests that children whose parents split up are more likely to leave school early, girls are more likely to have teenage babies, and boys are more likely to be out of work. We can debate how far American figures can be transposed to Britain, but evidence here is adding to this thesis. Divorce appears to lower living standards of children, particularly in middle-class families. Remarriage may add to prosperity but still seems to lead to high drop-out rates in American high-school evidence. Martin Richards of Cambridge University, looking at what happens in adulthood to children brought up in one-parent families, suggests that signs of disruptive and unhappy behaviour in children appear before their parents part, but argues that divorce is worse for children than living in an unhappy marriage, because divorce brings relative poverty as well (Elliott and Richards, 1991).

Divorce does have profound effects on many children, and this affects their learning and our teaching lives. It is as well that there is no evidence that beyond about the age of 12 months alternative types of mother care are harmful to the children of working single mothers, and indeed good child care facilities can improve young children's development. The need for improved and extended nursery education, and improvements in the staff–pupil ratios in infant classes is therefore, obvious to everyone (see Charlton *et al.*, 1995). From the massive rise nowadays in welfare payments for lone parents, society may look ahead to more pupils who will be early leavers and badly educated, low earners or unemployed. We could also be adding in the future to the numbers of the elderly poor.

To ruminate with some pessimism on the trends in family life in society does not mean that schools can provide the cure. Again only politics can manage society, but schools cannot only care for the obviously vulnerable to the best of their overworked ability, but can also be positive by teaching about family life, family relationships and child care. It is not impossible to strengthen even young children's understanding of the importance of friendship, personal relationships and family life in their lives.

The environment

The Environment Secretary recently called for a major national debate on a Green Paper which asks what kind of Britain we would like to see in 2012. This debate clearly deeply concerns the future lives of our present pupils, and presumably we involve them in it. Do we build roads or railways, how do we develop land not now needed for crops, do we have to worry about the chemical and nuclear industries, should we use fewer cars because of global warming, do we limit family sizes? The Green Paper poses fundamental questions on population, global atmosphere, air quality, water resources, acid rain and the use of mineral resources. Children are perfectly capable of debating these aspects of their future, and involving their families as well, as many have done with our health warnings about smoking.

EFFECTIVE AND RELEVANT SCHOOLS

We have reviewed many factors which may affect our society and the lives our pupils are likely to face. Guessing about the future may be incredibly difficult but we are duty bound to keep attempting it, in order to see where we are supposed to be leading our youngsters, and what we should be attempting in our schools. We conclude now with consideration of what makes effective schools, and schools which are attempting to consider the future lives of pupils and the issues considered in this chapter. Peter Mortimer the Director of London University Institute of Education in a useful published lecture (1995) suggests the need for schools to have:

- strong leadership
- shared vision and goals
- orderly atmosphere and attractive environment
- concentration on teaching and learning
- purposeful teaching
- high expectations
- clear discipline
- monitoring progress
- pupil rights and responsibilities
- home–school partnership
- staff development

He adds, 'In the face of growing competition from emerging economies [in the world], supported by literate, numerate and technologically proficient workforces, school improvement has never been more necessary.' He does not specify, but hopefully implies, consideration of cross-curricular issues raised in previous pages. Anita Ryall and colleagues from Liverpool Institute of Higher Education give consideration to cross-curricular themes in Chapter 4. Since the National Curriculum is not marked by coherent guidance on how the skills of social and personal themes are to be managed in primary and early secondary school classrooms, their chapter is fundamental in this book. Additionally Martin Buck and Sally Inman (1992) suggest approaching the planning and delivery of cross-curricular themes by using nine central questions, which can be relevant in primary and middle schools, and should be well within the capabilities of older primary and younger secondary pupils.

What is the nature of our rights and responsibilities in everyday life?
On what basis do people influence and control others?
What is the balance between individual freedom and the constraints necessary for co-operative living?
In what ways do people organise, manage and control their relationships?
In what ways are people different and with what consequences?
How do people learn the requirements of a particular culture?
What constitutes a community, and how are communities organized?
How is the welfare of individuals and societies maintained?
On what basis do people make decisions when faced with particular choices?

Through our basic National Curriculum teaching, by the various cross-curricular themes that schools choose as relevant, and by the general ethos of primary and middle schools we can perhaps prepare some children for their confusing future. Teachers are, after all, professional optimists and idealists as well as pragmatists, are they not?

REFERENCES

Brzezinski, Z. (1993) *Out of Control: Global Turmoil on the Eve of the 21st Century*, New York: Scribner.

Buck, M. and Inman, S. (1992) *Whole-school Provision for Personal and Social Development: The Role of the Cross-curricular Elements*, London: Goldsmith's College.

Charlton, T., Essex, C., Lovemore, T. and Crowie, B. (1995) Teachers' approval and disapproval rates and pupils' on-task levels in first and middle school classrooms on St Helena, *Journal of Social Behaviour and Personality*, 10, 4, 1023–1030.

Department of Health and Social Security (1989) *The Children Act*, London: HMSO.

Drucker, P. (1993) *The Post-capitalist Society*, Oxford: Butterworth-Heinemann.

Dunham, J. (1992) *Stress in Teaching*, London: Routledge.

Dyfed Education Authority (1994) *Stress Support for School Staff*, Carmarthen: Dyfed County Council.

Elliott, B.J. and Richards, M.B.M. (1991) Children and divorce: educational performance and behaviour before and after parental separation, *International Journal of Law and the Family*, 5, 258–278.

Gaarder, J. (1995) *Sophie's World*, London: Phoenix House.

Kennedy, P. (1993) *Preparing for the Twenty-first Century*, London: HarperCollins.

Lasch, C. (1995) *The Revolt of the Elites*, London: W.W. Norton.

Mortimer, P. (1995) Effective schools: current impact and future potential, available from University of London Institute of Education.

Rifkin, J. (1993) *The End of Work*, London: G.P. Putnam.

Spock, B. (1994) *A Better World for Our Children*, New York: National Press Books.

2

HOW CHILDREN LEARN

Kevin Jones and Mayling Quah

GAVIN

Gavin, aged 11 years, seems to have a fairly good idea about some of the things which affect learning. On the surface he appears to have a 'couldn't care less' attitude about school, but deep down he really wants to succeed in his studies. He is willing, with the right kind of support, to work hard in class and on follow-up activities at home. He expresses considerable unhappiness about his experiences at school, some of which appear to be blocking, rather than enhancing, learning.

When asked about school, his initial reactions are very negative. His choice of expressions, such as, 'I hate it', 'They pick on me', 'They nag me', 'I don't know what to do', reflect the unhappiness which he feels from the beginning of the school day until he is 'released' (his words) in the evening. However, further probing shows that Gavin, like many pupils, experiences a mixture of positive and negative learning experiences, as will be shown below. Unfortunately, the negative experiences leave such a marked impression upon him that they overshadow and therefore 'block out' (Charlton, 1992) the positive ones, leaving him with a poor impression of schooling which seems to have a detrimental effect upon his learning.

When Gavin is encouraged to talk about his experiences at more length it becomes apparent that, for him, the most significant factor affecting learning is the quality of relationships which he has with certain teachers. After listening to him, it was possible to 'map' those settings which facilitate learning and those which militate against it (see Jones, 1992, p. 12). This process of 'ecological mapping' (Laten and Katz, 1975) allows teachers to examine the fit of a pupil into various aspects of the learning environment. The teacher then tries to make sense of any notable differences by attempting to uncover factors within those settings which appear to contribute to successes and difficulties in learning. The ecological map which was drawn for Gavin is reproduced in Figure 2.1. The solid lines refer to areas of the curriculum within which he enjoys positive learning experiences. The broken lines refer to settings which are problematic.

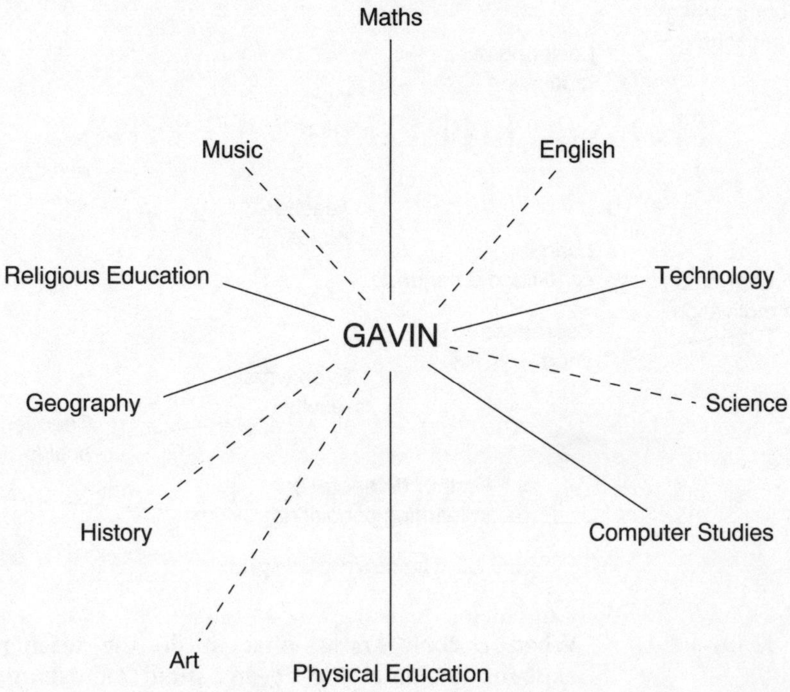

Figure 2.1 Ecological map for Gavin

Despite the fact that Gavin describes schooling as an overwhelmingly distasteful activity, the map (Figure 2.1) confirms that he has a mixture of positive and negative learning experiences. His detailed comments about different settings reveal certain conditions which appear, in his case, to affect learning. He is quite open and truthful about the fact that, in some settings, he does not put as much effort into his work as he should. The resultant interaction between his lack of effort and the conditions for learning which prevail in those settings, produce circumstances which cause him to slip into a downward spiral, as depicted in Figure 2.2. In Gavin's case unsuitable conditions for learning depress motivation, leading to a downturn in effort, resulting in poor academic results. On the next loop of the spiral the teacher's scolding leads to a worsening of learning conditions, against which he privately rebels, resulting in yet further depression of motivation and effort, together with an additional deterioration of academic achievement.

In marked contrast, in other settings, Gavin encounters conditions which contribute towards positive learning outcomes. The following selection of comments reveals the significant impact which good teacher–pupil relationships seem to have upon his learning.

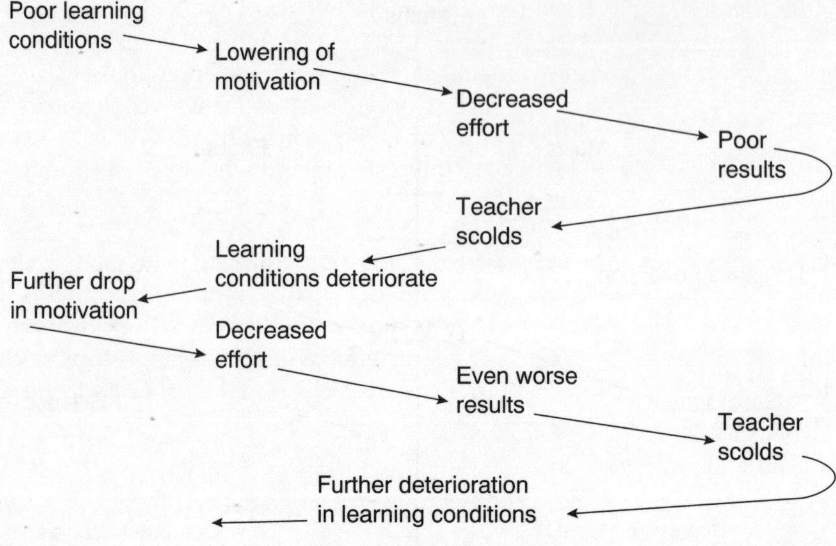

Figure 2.2 The downward spiral

Maths	When I don't know what to do the teacher explains it to me. She doesn't mind me asking. Then I know what to do and it's easy. I can usually do it on my own after that, without any help. The teacher says I try really hard and I am getting good at my work. She makes me work really hard but I never feel stressed out.
Computer Studies	We all get a chance to go on the computer and work at our own speed. If we are stuck the teacher tries to get us to think how to solve the problem for ourselves. If we can, she seems really pleased. She is also really nice to us when we work well together. She is always saying good things about the way we behave, rather than nag, nag, nagging.
Geography	It is really interesting. Sometimes we see videos, sometimes we make models, sometimes we do writing. We never spend 'hours' on the same stuff. Our teacher is sort of strict. He doesn't let anyone mess about, but he never shouts at you. If we do something wrong he tells us why it is wrong. I like that. It's fair. Even when he tells us off he says he likes us. Most of the time we are really good in his lessons.

Religious Education	It's not my best subject. It's sort of OK. The teacher is really nice though. We helped to make little rules. He tells us when we are keeping to them, in a really nice way. He sort of makes you want to work really hard. He comes up to us and asks what we are interested in and what we think about things.

Gavin's teachers and parents were able to confirm that in each of the above settings he achieves good academic results. From his comments it is also quite clear that he feels both comfortable and 'fired up for learning' in those settings. Certain characteristics of his relationships with teachers seem to be particularly important to him. He appears to need conditions in which he:

- feels able to ask for clarification about tasks and activities
- is encouraged to find solutions to his own problems
- is listened to with interest
- is given positive rewards (verbal or non-verbal) for effort, achievement and acceptable behaviour
- is allowed to seek support from other pupils, as well as seeking the advice of the teacher
- receives explanations about undesirable behaviours

Gavin's comments about those settings within which he is on a slippery downward spiral of failure, also emphasise the impact which certain kinds of teacher–pupil relationships have upon his learning.

English	We have to keep our books under the tables on a sort of ledge. Mine were missing. I put them there, but someone took them. I got really shouted at. It has happened three times now. I don't know who takes them but I always get the blame. I've had two detentions already and I didn't even do it. I can't concentrate on the lesson because he keeps staring at me, as if I am going to do something wrong.
Science	When I get work wrong the teacher calls me 'idiot'. He's always calling me idiot. And he calls me Gaz bag, he knows I hate that, I'm sure he does. He always tells me I am doing things wrong.
Art	Someone didn't tidy up and I got the blame. There was some paint on the desk. She just came up to me and made the mess even worse and made me

	tidy up. She is always picking on me. It wasn't even my mess. I know I do things wrong sometimes 'cos I don't know what I'm supposed to do. I don't always 'get it' at first, but some teachers let me ask. I usually understand really well after that. But she goes mad if I don't know what to do.
History	The teacher stands at the front and lectures for 'hours'. It's so boring. When we have to do work he doesn't let us ask questions. He never comes round to our desks to talk to us. We call him 'the Robot'.
Music	During the first lesson we did some singing. He said 'Who's making that silly noise?' We carried on singing. He came round, listening to us all. When he got to me he said 'This silly boy is making the silly noise.' Then he put his hand over my mouth and told me to stop singing. I was trying my best. I like singing on our Karaoke machine, but I hate music lessons.

Certain conditions, in this second group of settings, seem to act as barriers to learning. In particular, and understandably, Gavin does not like to be:

- called names
- scolded for doing things wrong, without being told why
- blamed for things he claims he didn't do
- labelled 'troublemaker' because of a genuine lack of understanding of task requirements
- taught by impersonal and uncaring teachers

The above case shows that pupils, under the right conditions (see Wade and Moore, 1993; Lewis, 1996), can provide useful insights into important matters which affect their learning. By listening to pupils, teachers can gain useful information which will help them to understand some of the factors which influence learning (Cooper, 1993; Cooper and McIntyre, 1993, 1994; Wade and Moore, 1993; Jones *et al.*, 1996).

TEACHER ATTRIBUTES WHICH INFLUENCE LEARNING

Many other children, when asked to discuss conditions which affect their learning, produce comments similar to those voiced by Gavin. Garner (1996) describes the results of a questionnaire survey which elicited comments from over 100 Year 10 pupils. The following excerpt discusses teacher attributes which those pupils considered to have a positive influence upon learning:

> . . . many pupils in the school were conscious of the status of individual teachers and they recognised the professional qualities of those who were well-prepared for lessons. Teachers who 'treated us with respect' and had a sense of humour were more highly regarded by these pupils and firm, but fair, discipline, where sanctions were explained to the recipient, was seen to be an essential teacher quality.

Whittern (see Jones *et al.*, 1996) examined the perceptions of one cohort of Year 5 pupils (N = 85). The teacher quality most favoured by the children was that of 'explaining things clearly'. This attribute was also rated top by pupils in Wragg and Woods's (1984) survey of secondary school pupils. 'Being cheerful' was rated second in importance. Interestingly the third most popular attribute of a 'good teacher', which does not appear in the extant literature, is that of 'forgiveness' if children admit doing wrong. It is clear that children value the sort of respectful and trusting relationships they may have with teachers whereby it is 'safe to tell'. Mutual respect was noted by Kutnick and Jules (1993) as desired more by pupils than an appropriate curriculum. The most disliked teacher behaviour, in Whittern's study, was that of 'punishing the whole class when one person does wrong'. This was closely followed by the personality traits of 'being grumpy' and 'moaning'.

Other studies have elicited comments from children who experience difficulties in learning, or whose behaviours are considered to be problematic. Cooper (1996) argues that such pupils, who are especially vulnerable and sensitive to aversive aspects of their school environments, are often able to graphically describe conditions which have an important influence upon learning. Cooper's (1993) study revealed that a group of pupils who were at risk of being rejected by schools felt alienated from and disregarded by their teachers. In their opinion teachers were:

- too strict
- stuck up
- unfriendly
- intolerant
- humourless
- uninterested in pupils' personal welfare
- not prepared/able to give pupils individual attention
- guilty of labelling some pupils with negative identities
- guilty of treating some pupils unfairly
- guilty of conducting boring lessons
- insufficiently helpful to pupils with learning difficulties

These, and other studies (see Chapter 8) reinforce the fact that certain teacher attributes (e.g. respectfulness, humour, cheerfulness, being firm, trusting, forgiving) create conditions in which children feel well able to learn, whilst other qualities (e.g. being grumpy, moaning, unjust, bossy, unfriendly, intolerant, humourless, uninterested in pupil welfare, unfair) create conditions which could block learning for pupils. It is interesting to note that many of these characteristics are similar to those described by Gavin.

The pupils who were the subjects of the above-mentioned studies were discussing 'learning' as they have experienced it. Any serious discussion of conditions which facilitate or block learning should also look ahead to challenges which children will face in the future. These new challenges might well necessitate a reshaping of the learning processes with which children engage. The 'conditions' which support these new processes of learning might well be different from those which supported more traditional styles.

THE LEARNING CHALLENGE

David (1992, p. 175) draws attention to some of the challenges which children face within a rapidly changing society:

> The changing nature of family life produces children whose lives are more complicated and whose attitudes are more sophisticated and demanding. The modern 'information explosion' is obliging teachers to realise that the knowledge they deal with is more transitory, the demands of learning are more complicated, and the human skills of communication and relationships are becoming more essential, for survival in the future.

Galton (1994, p. 2) draws attention to the fact that, in the name of 'individualised learning' many children are consigned to endless hours of solitary activity, such as the completion of worksheets. He questions the relevance of such activities to the future lives of pupils and recommends that children should be encouraged to develop the skills of co-operative learning:

> Given the rapid changes in the global economy, promoting a need for greater inter-dependence between states, future generations of pupils will need to extend their social and intellectual skills so that they can solve complex problems, often as members of multi-national teams. Children, therefore, from an early age need to learn and value the skills that come from working together in this way.

Others (e.g. Jones, 1992, p. 201) suggest that the skills of thinking and learning might be more important than content knowledge (study skills, for example, are considered in Chapter 14). Ingram and Worrall (1993) are critical of the fact that thinking skills are not promoted in many traditional classrooms, where the teacher does most of the learning, in terms of hunting out information books, preparatory reading, thinking through and reflecting on how to best transmit and organise the children's experiences of knowledge; all skills that children are themselves capable of learning and applying, and which will probably be of vital importance to them in their future lives. These writers draw attention to the importance of participatory, collaborative and enquiry-based teaching and learning strategies which encourage them to take responsibility for their own learning.

Thus new priorities for learning, such as those mentioned above, call for a reappraisal of how children should learn. If the present and future needs of pupils are to be met, some elements of existing practices will have to be reshaped or replaced. New curricular demands are already requiring that teachers reappraise the conditions which support learning. The following example discusses how traditional teacher-dominated practices in mathematics classrooms might have to give way to more pupil–pupil discussion if currently stated aims are to be achieved.

New priorities for learning in mathematics classrooms

Amongst other things, the mathematics curriculum now requires that pupils will:

- use number, algebra and measures in practical tasks, in real-life problems and to investigate within mathematics itself
- estimate and approximate
- look for patterns and relationships
- make generalisations
- select, interpret and use appropriate data
- interpret results

Traditional teaching methods, in which children are required to give set answers to closed questions (see Pimm, 1987) are unlikely to help children to achieve the kinds of learning referred to above. For this and other reasons, teachers have been encouraged to introduce more teacher–pupil and pupil–pupil 'discussion' into mathematics classrooms (Pimm, 1987; Brissenden, 1988). Phillips (1988) elaborates on the kind of talk which might facilitate such learning, suggesting that it will be characterised by exchanges without a clear indication of closure, utterances full of uncertainties, hesitations, substitutions, non-equivalences and sub-topics which are picked up and returned to as the moment demands. The presence of these features (e.g. tentativeness) not only reflects the fact that the speakers are still thinking and coming to terms with what they know, as they interact in the group with each other's ideas, but also that they are collaborating to construct and negotiate knowledge. This type of 'learning' appears to be much more compatible with the achievement of the above-mentioned aims.

Thus, whilst traditional teaching practices might continue to support limited forms of learning, they are unlikely to promote some types of learning which will be required of pupils in the future. Pupils will only be adequately prepared to face new learning challenges if the conditions under which they learn are adjusted appropriately. The above example illustrates the impact which new curricular aims have upon expected learning outcomes, thus necessitating a reappraisal of the effectiveness of existing practices and conditions for learning.

Ong (1988) describes a 'thinking-skills' project which aimed to improve pupils' problem-solving capabilities across a number of content-specific subjects. The children, who were enthusiastic about the project, were able to define, analyse and provide solutions to real-life problems and many of them, on their own initiative, conducted 'research' projects out of school time. Teachers noted that pupils who were involved in the project were more vocal in class and gained in confidence, as their opinions and suggestions were welcomed and respected by their teachers. Similar findings are reported by Yeow (1988), who describes a Higher-order Thinking Skills project which concentrated upon the development of higher-order cognitive skills in reading.

The preceding text has drawn attention to the strong influence which certain forms of teacher–pupil relationship and teaching methods can have upon different types of learning, underlining the need to establish positive 'relationships for learning', alongside a consideration of, and a response to, a whole range of other factors which influence learning.

FACTORS WHICH INFLUENCE LEARNING

Pupil learning will be affected by a whole range of factors which teachers should strive to understand. Factors *within the child*, the *curriculum* and the *learning environment* will influence learning (Jones, 1992, 1994). A failure to adequately consider any one of these groups of factors is to risk overlooking the very heart of what affects learning for a particular child. We have already seen how pupils themselves can throw light on these factors. Teachers should attempt to examine other sources of information which add further to this picture. Each group of factors will be briefly discussed below, before turning attention to some practical ways in which teachers can provide good learning conditions for their pupils.

The child

The most obvious within-child factors which can influence learning outcomes are the level of hearing and vision (see Jones, 1992). If problems are undetected, they are likely to cause considerable difficulties in learning. Research has shown that other less obvious within-child factors (e.g. poor visual or auditory discrimination; sequencing difficulties) can also determine learning outcomes (see for example Tyler, 1990). To give a simple example, a child with specific learning difficulties in the auditory area (e.g. poor level of hearing; difficulties in discriminating between sounds) will experience considerable difficulties in learning when faced with a teacher who relies almost wholly on verbal explanations, without any supportive visual or manipulative resources. Conversely, children are likely to learn much more effectively if their strengths are utilised. For example those with strengths in the visual and kinaesthetic areas, are likely to experience more success in learning to spell if they are given activities which help them to remember the visual characteristics and the feel of words, through the fingertips (Cripps and Cox, 1989). Other research (Thomson, 1991) suggests that approaches to the teaching of spelling which contain a more significant listening element such as 'Simultaneous Oral Spelling' (Bradley, 1985) will lead to better progress with children whose 'auditory' channel is stronger than the visual one.

Whilst it is possible to produce a profile of relative strengths and weaknesses of these within-child factors (see Quah and Jones, 1995), busy class teachers are unlikely to have the time to assess every child's strengths and weaknesses. They should, however, be cognisant of the fact that these 'within-child' factors can influence the ease with which pupils learn. Fortunately, it is not necessary to have an in-depth profile of every child's strengths and weaknesses in order to respond to these factors. The following statement, written by a student teacher who recently undertook a module of study based upon an adaptation of materials from a UNESCO study pack (UNESCO, 1993, pp. 106–109), during initial training, demonstrates the way in which all teachers can respond to the diverse learning needs which emanate from these kinds of 'within-child' factors, by adopting a multi-media approach to teaching and learning:

> . . . the more media available to the teacher the more chances students have to fully comprehend the subject. The teacher employs a variety of media such as verbal symbols (textbooks), visual symbols (charts), photos, recordings, films, exhibits, field trips, demonstrations, drama, contrived and direct purposeful experiences, in order to differentially cater to the stronger senses of the students.

The curriculum

For some children the planned curriculum, without modification, moves too fast and is at too difficult a level. Others become frustrated because they are constantly revising work which is already familiar to them and which moves at too slow a pace. At a general level the match of the curriculum to the needs of a child can be appraised by comparing the child's current levels of attainment (assessed via observation) with the curriculum being offered. If a mismatch occurs adjustments can be made. A more detailed analysis might be required for pupils who encounter considerable difficulties in learning. The 'behavioural objectives' approach is one example of a process which sets out to describe the educational needs of these pupils in precise and observable terms. This approach sets out to provide a detailed description of what the child can do, under what conditions he/she can do it and the level of success achieved. Once a baseline of current performance is established, teachers can then plan an incremental sequence of achievable learning objectives. Activities are then planned to help the child to achieve each of the objectives and thus reach the predetermined goal. This analytical approach has been supported because it can lead to measurable gains in skills development and without it many teachers fail to make necessary adjustment to the curriculum for pupils who encounter difficulties in learning (Gickling and Thompson, 1985).

Whilst it can be claimed that this approach can help to produce conditions under which certain types of learning can occur, it should be used with caution. A number of studies have shown that strict adherence to end-point objectives can lead to the acquisition of skills that can only be performed in limited circumstances and a narrow curriculum where only the measurable is taught. For this reason Thomas and Feiler (1988) recommend that when individual aims and goals are developed the resultant activities should be purposeful and of intrinsic value to pupils, rather than a means to a predetermined end. The following strategies (from UNESCO, 1993) are offered to teachers who strive to make the curriculum more meaningful for their pupils:

1 build new learning from the previous knowledge and experience of students by:
   - brainstorming with the students on a specific topic and letting them relate what they know;
   - giving students a problem and encouraging them to use whatever they already know to 'get into the problem'. The teacher can then introduce new concepts and skills required to solve the problem;
   - allowing pupils to share prior knowledge before tackling a new topic;
2 use a student's daily experience to clarify new concepts;
3 make learning functional by giving the students a chance to apply it to everyday life;
4 use stories to raise interest in lesson content;
5 relate learning to other subjects;

6 plan field trips and projects;
7 introduce games and simulations so that certain aspects of learning can be applied.

Quah (1994) describes how the language curriculum can be made more meaningful for pupils, if teachers use a 'language-experience' approach to the teaching of reading. This approach utilises the child's own interests to generate material for reading and writing, thus ensuring that the teacher works with the child's current level of language competence at all times.

Also consistent with this theme, is a project described by Yap (1989) in which teachers in one primary school in Singapore, made a concerted effort to improve on the low mathematical achievement of Year 5 and Year 6 pupils by organising a Mathematics Camp during the school vacation. An activity-oriented approach was used to provide pupils with meaningful experiences in mathematics. The main objective of the camp was to enable pupils to solve problems or take part in activities based on real-life applications of mathematical concepts such as area, decimals, money, measurement, ratio and proportion. A second objective was to help pupils to solve mathematical problems, either individually, in pairs or in groups, so as to encourage more independent learning and less reliance on the teacher. At the end of the two-day camp pupils completed evaluation sheets. The responses showed that the children had enjoyed themselves and many described it as 'fantastic'. Their teachers reported that the children had performed well on the tasks and were pleased with the levels of understanding which had been achieved.

The most appropriate learning conditions are likely to be created when teachers help children to achieve clearly articulated objectives in meaningful and purposeful contexts, such as those cited above.

The learning environment

The experiences of pupils, referred to earlier in this chapter, drew attention to the considerable impact which certain features of the learning environment can have upon pupil learning outcomes. If the long-term aim is the creation of 'effective schools for all pupils' (Ainscow, 1991), within which all teachers are able to analyse and respond to the teaching needs of all pupils in their regular classrooms, factors within the learning environment (e.g. the way lessons are presented, management of learning, pupil grouping) which affect pupil learning must be 'recognised' and responded to (Jones, 1992; Quah and Jones, 1995). A number of researchers (e.g. Bennett, 1991; Garner, 1996) have drawn attention to key factors which can precipitate and maintain difficulties in learning, some of which are noted below:

- a mismatch between the task and the pupil's current level of performance (one study indicated that 65 per cent of tasks were too difficult for low-attaining pupils)
- poor specification of the learning task
- ineffective time management, thus reducing the amount of time available for teaching
- lack of appropriate pacing
- few opportunities to review, revise and reinforce learning
- the work having an image inappropriate to the pupils' chronological age
- a lack of 'purpose' in learning activities
- inappropriate grouping strategies
- an absence of teaching approaches which encourage independent learning
- poor social skills, thus leading to inappropriate behaviours in certain situations

Conversely, others (e.g. Ainscow and Muncey; 1989; Charlton, 1992) suggest that more appropriate conditions for learning will be created if teachers:

- emphasise the importance of meaning and purpose in learning activities
- set tasks that are both realistic and challenging
- ensure that there is progression in children's work
- provide a variety of learning experiences
- give pupils opportunities to choose
- have high expectations of success and encourage the development of a positive self-concept
- create a positive atmosphere for learning
- provide a consistent approach
- recognise and reward the efforts and achievements of their pupils
- organise resources to facilitate learning
- encourage pupils to work co-operatively
- monitor progress and provide regular feedback
- help pupils to develop negotiating skills such as listening, managing conflict, assertiveness training, taking risks, accepting responsibility and dealing with feelings
- support the development of a positive self-concept, as well as an internal locus of control

A number of the above-mentioned conditions suggest that the most effective relationships for learning might be those in which clear 'support' and 'guidance' are skilfully blended with 'pupil empowerment'. The final sections of this chapter examine ways in which teachers might begin to develop such supportive, yet empowering, conditions for learning.

RELATIONSHIPS WHICH SUPPORT LEARNING

Pupil empowerment

Charlton (1992, p. 35) claims that, although success and failure in learning will be affected by a range of factors, the beliefs which pupils hold regarding the influence of their own behaviour upon academic achievement are crucial:

> Internal locus of control beliefs characterise pupils who believe that academic outcomes are dependent upon their personal behaviour; where they desire success they believe it is attainable through their own efforts. Conversely, those who espouse external locus of control beliefs perceive academic outcomes being independent of their expenditure of time and energy and controlled by extrinsic forces such as fate, luck or chance. On occasions when they desire success they remain unconvinced that they are 'masters' of their own destiny. Beliefs of this type often preclude achievement-striving and serve only to help to guarantee failure.

Charlton (1992) also draws attention to research which supports the reasoning that an internal locus of control belief is a personality characteristic conducive to achievement strivings and high academic grades and test scores, whilst externality has been linked with inferior grades/scores (Bar-Tal *et. al.*, 1980; Walden and Ramey, 1983). Similarly Westwood (1993, p. 21) claims that many children who experience difficulties in learning remain 'external' in their locus of control, feeling that their own efforts have little impact on their progress and that what happens is unrelated to their own actions. Failure is anticipated immediately any new situation occurs and the individual cannot conceive of being able to change this outcome. These students display ineffective self-management skills and need positive help to become independent learners. For this reason, Westwood (1993, p. 17) is critical of teachers who foster dependence, rather than independence. He claims that children who display such 'externality' need help in developing self-management skills, such as knowing:

- how to organise their own materials
- what to do when work is completed
- when to seek help of peer/teacher
- check own work
- maintain attention to task
- observe rules and routines

However, Westwood (1993, p. 22) cautions against attempts to force responsibility on pupils too quickly, suggesting that children who are markedly external respond best, at first, in a highly structured, predictable, teacher-directed setting, particularly for the learning of basic skills. He maintains that suddenly placing children in very open, child-centred teaching environments may only increase the number of occasions when they fail and develop an even greater feeling of helplessness and lack of ability.

Westwood (1993) suggests that the following strategies can be used to help a pupil to gradually move towards internality:

- individual 'contracts' between teacher and child can be introduced in a fairly simple form (child can be allowed to decide on order to tackle the work, how long to spend, when to seek assistance);
- use of self-instructing material – may help child to realise how own efforts result in progress and achievement;
- too much testing without follow-up teaching may increase internality;
- when inappropriate behaviours are displayed, the child should be given the earliest opportunity to act appropriately in a similar situation and should be rewarded and specifically praised for doing so;
- avoid rewarding success if no real effort was required;
- use *wait time*, when orally questioning students. Too frequently the teacher moves on to another student to avoid embarrassment, thus creating a feeling of frustration and uselessness in the students – after a time they don't make any effort to reply.

Charlton (1992, p. 36) suggests that internality will also be encouraged if teachers:

- use positive reinforcement judiciously, making it clear what behaviours are being rewarded;
- encourage pupils to practise analysing problem situations, in order to make them aware of the influence of people's behaviour upon their outcomes and experiences.

Pupils can also be empowered to take more responsibility for their own learning if they are encouraged to work collaboratively with their peers, rather than relying totally upon adult support.

Co-operative learning

Some writers go so far as to suggest that the quality of learning support derived from other pupils can be equally, if not more, effective than that provided by adults. This may be due to their tendency to be more directive; their familiarity with the material being taught; their understandings of the other child's frustrations; or because of their use of more meaningful and age-appropriate vocabulary and examples (UNESCO, 1993).

The development of a collaborative learning environment in which pupils are expected to 'share ideas, help one another and make the most of one another's resources' (Hart, 1992, p. 21) has the potential for pupils to clarify instructions, concepts and thus assimilate new learning into existing frames, as illustrated earlier in the example from the mathematics classroom. It has also been suggested that peer support helps pupils to take risks, a condition which seems to be part and parcel of learning, which requires us to take steps in the dark and try out something when we are unsure about the outcome (UNESCO, 1993). Additionally collaborative work helps pupils to build up social skills which are likely to feature increasingly in their lives.

However, a supportive atmosphere for learning, in which pupils help each other to clarify instructions and concepts, will not simply emerge without careful planning. A suitable, 'sharing' environment will need to be created and opportunities for collaboration sought. Hart (1992) states that teachers will have to reinforce the need for pupils to learn to listen to one another, to show interest in what each other has to say, to respect one another's views. (Listening skills are considered in Chapter 14.) Teachers themselves will have to act as models by demonstrating active listening, responding to new ideas, questioning, exploring, and sharing with their pupils. Two examples of co-operative learning, namely 'peer tutoring' and 'collaborative group work', now follow.

James *et al.* (1991a, 1991b) used *peer tutoring*, in a comprehensive school in the UK, to favourably affect the academic performance of a group of Year 7 pupils who were experiencing learning difficulties. Older pupils, who were selected and trained as 'counsellors', befriended the younger pupils on a one-to-one basis. During weekly periods, spanning some twenty weeks, when each of the counsellor/counsellee pairs met, the aims (on the counsellor's part) were to:

1 listen attentively and sympathetically, and try to understand comments from the younger pupil's perspective;
2 try and build up the younger pupils' self-image by, for example, praising achievements, effort, persistence and appearance; and
3 link outcomes such as academic achievement to effort.

When pupils made comments such as 'I'm no good at reading' the counsellors were asked to emphasise the relationship between personal effort and outcome. For example the 'befriender' might respond, 'I know what you mean. I used to be poor at maths, but I kept trying and I'm quite good at it now.' This peer counselling project achieved very good results, in terms of improved academic achievement, enhanced self-concept and a shift towards internality of the locus of control for learning.

In Singapore, a number of primary schools have instigated a peer buddies approach to help pupils who experience difficulties in reading.

Good readers volunteer to 'adopt' a peer who is experiencing difficulties in reading. The good reader coaches, reads to and reads with their 'buddy' with the aim of helping him/her to improve in reading and other school-related activities. The good reader takes his/her coaching role very seriously as he/she feels somehow 'responsible' for the reading performance of the buddy. These reading sessions are given at different times of the school day, whenever the two buddies have time to spare. This arrangement gives pupils many opportunities to learn to read through the very act of reading itself. The extra time, interest and encouragement which they receive from their peers is invaluable.

At its best *collaborative group work* enables children to share their resources of knowledge, experience, social relationships and their capacity to support and stimulate one another through shared interests. However, this process of collaborative learning does not come about naturally.

Ainscow (1991) suggests that positive interdependence, which is a necessary condition for collaborative learning, may be achieved in different ways depending upon the nature of the set tasks, the content to be covered and the previous experience of the pupils:

- pupils may be required to work in pairs preparing a joint statement about a topic which they will be responsible for giving to a larger group;
- a group may be involved in a task that can only be completed if separate materials that are held by individual members are pooled;
- individual members of a group may be assigned particular roles (e.g. chairperson, recorder, summariser, reporter);
- each member may be asked to complete the first draft of a task, that has to be completed by the whole group;
- grades may be awarded as a result of aggregate performance of work completed by individual members.

Slavin (1990) and Kagan (1990) describe a number of co-operative structures which teachers can use to encourage pupils to develop the skills of collaborative working, some of which are summarised below:

Pairs check

1 Put students into pairs, within sub-groups of four.
2 Give pairs practice sheets.
3 Person number '1' in each pair does the first problem. Person number '2' acts as the coach and offers praise. If the answer is incorrect, the coach will help his/her partner to arrive at the right answer.
4 Partners then exchange roles.
5 When two problems have been completed the pair checks with the other pair in their sub-group.
6 If the two pairs disagree about the answer they can call on the teacher's help.

Numbered heads together

1 Form teams of approximately six pupils.
2 Each team member is given a number (e.g. 1–6).
3 Give teams a short amount of time to study/review material.
4 When study time is up, teacher asks a question and gives teams a few seconds of 'Heads Together' to decide on a response.
5 Teacher then calls a number. Only students of that number can respond, either by writing, by response card, by fingers, or orally.
6 If the answer is correct, the team responds with praise for their rep. If not, they have a short 'Heads Together' time again.
7 If only a few hands are raised to offer a response, allow more 'Heads Together' time.

Team webbing

1 Give each student a different coloured marker.
2 Write the word/topic in the centre of a large piece of paper and enclose the word within a rectangle.
3 Each member (in round-robin fashion) contributes a core concept related to the word/topic.
4 Let the members, in a 'free-for-all', add other core concepts or supporting elements to the word/topic. Do not pass judgement on the quality of responses. Allow only minimal talking.
5 Give them time to discuss what patterns they see or what conclusions can be drawn from the 'webbed data'.
6 Tape the webs to the wall. Facilitate a whole-class discussion about it.

Jigsaw 2

1 The teacher introduces the topic and provides a broad overview of the main facts or concepts.
2 Each team member is assigned one section of the topic to read.
3 Those with the same section of the topics meet in new 'expert' groups to discuss the information which they read.
4 The students return to their 'home teams' and take turns teaching their team-mates about their sections.
5 Students may be given a test, which they take individually.
6 Team scores are added up; awards are given to the teams according to their performance.

Whilst the above mentioned activities have the potential to facilitate learning, they will only be effective if the overall 'atmosphere for learning' is suitable. Appropriate standards of social behaviour must be established and maintained in order to maximise academic progress.

Creating an atmosphere conducive to learning

A number of writers have encouraged teachers to become skilful at preventing, as well as reacting to, problem behaviours. Tattum (1988) indicates that the crisis management approach is predominant in many schools, whereby teachers wait for problems to reveal themselves in personal crises or confrontational outbursts. This approach focuses upon the management of the behaviour of an undisciplined minority, rather than the establishment of an atmosphere conducive to learning for all pupils. Tattum (1988, p. 158) states:

> Too much of our thinking about discipline has started from the wrong end, that is with questions as to how young offenders might be identified, punished and contained rather than how to create learning environments that might encourage productive pupil behaviour.

Increasingly, research suggests that the conditions most conducive to learning will occur when teachers use positive behaviour management strategies (Merrett *et al.*, 1991; Charlton *et al.*, 1995). One such strategy, referred to as 'Rules, Praise and Ignoring (RPI)' has been extensively used with good effect, as a positive classroom management procedure. RPI was originally devised in the United States by Madsen *et al.* (1968). In brief, it requires the teacher to negotiate a set of three to four short, positively phrased rules, covering acceptable classroom behaviours. These often take the form of simple declarations of intent such as 'we try to get on with our work quietly', or 'we put up our hands when we want to ask a question'. Rules act as a kind of prompt and teachers are encouraged to draw attention to them regularly, preferably when pupils are clearly keeping, rather than infringing them. Teachers are required to praise pupils for keeping the rules and to ignore infractions of them. Praise may be addressed to the whole class or to individuals, but should refer specifically to their behaviour in keeping the rules.

Another strategy, recommended by Chisholm *et al.* (1986) involves the adoption of a preventive approach to disruption. The essence of such an approach is based upon the following advice to teachers:

1 *Position* yourself where you have maximal opportunities to oversee and regulate pupils' behaviour. Similarly, when approaching a child to give individual attention there are obvious advantages in assuming a position which requires an upward glance to monitor other pupils' behaviour.
2 Adequately *prepare lesson content*, making sure that materials and equipment needed are available in sufficient quantity and are easily distributed.
3 Use unobtrusive and *subtle management skills* such as proximity control

(standing by, but not looking at, particular pupils) to quell minor disturbances such as talking, unnecessary fidgeting or fiddling and to avoid giving them undue and possible harmful prominence.

4 Develop an effective repertoire of *non-verbal skills*:
- avoid speaking in a monotonous way,
- signal confidence,
- use gestures, eye-to-eye contact, change of voice and posture to discourage certain behaviours.

5 Organise the classrooms in ways which motivate children to work well and so leave little time for misbehaviours. For example:
- apparatus, materials and furniture should preferably be assembled and arranged prior to pupils' arrival,
- prepare activities for those pupils who finish early,
- make work appropriate to pupils' age, ability and cultural background,
- supervise pupils' entrance to the classroom,
- give clear instructions,
- plan smooth lesson changes,
- be vigilant,
- vary teaching techniques so as to maintain interest,
- anticipate the timing of lessons so that the ending can be efficient and orderly.

Positive approaches, such as those mentioned above (Chapter 8 also considers these), can help to produce an atmosphere conducive to learning, within which disturbances are kept to a minimum. However, teachers will also have to respond appropriately to problem behaviours once they have occurred. Charlton and David (1993) offer detailed and practical advice about various methods which can be used in response to such behaviours.

CONCLUSIONS

Pupil learning outcomes will be affected by a whole range of factors, but uppermost in pupils' minds are the powerful influences which personal relationships can have upon their academic achievement. Relationships which are founded upon teacher attributes such as respectfulness, humour, cheerfulness, firmness, trust and forgiveness seem to create conditions in which children are more likely to feel 'fired up' for learning, whilst qualities such as being grumpy, moaning, unjust, bossy, unfriendly, intolerant and humourless can create barriers to learning. These insights underline the need to create *positive learning relationships* which underpin and support academic achievement.

Good educational progress is most likely to be secured if teachers consider and respond to the whole range of factors which influence learning. This will require a three-pronged analysis of factors 'within the child', 'the curriculum' and 'the learning environment' which are referred to in the foregoing text. A failure to adequately consider any of these groups of factors is to risk overlooking the very heart of what might affect learning for a particular child. Additionally, those who plan teaching activities and learning experiences should look towards the challenges which are likely to face children in the future. These challenges might require pupils to engage with new processes of learning. The 'conditions' which support these new processes of learning might well be different from those which supported more traditional styles.

Effective relationships for learning are most likely to be built if teachers skilfully blend clear 'support' and guidance with 'pupil empowerment'. They might begin to develop such supportive, yet empowering, conditions for learning by:

- using multi-media approaches to teaching and learning which differentially cater to pupils' different sensory preferences;
- developing clearly articulated objectives for learning which pupils achieve through purposeful and meaningful activities;
- helping pupils to develop self-management skills;
- encouraging co-operative learning through peer support and collaborative group work;
- creating an atmosphere conducive to learning through the use of positive behaviour management strategies.

In order to maintain and further develop supportive, yet empowering, conditions for learning, teachers will need to continuously reflect upon the circumstances which seem best able to promote good educational achievement. This can be achieved, in part, by observing their pupils at work and listening carefully to their comments about the learning environment.

REFERENCES

Ainscow, M. (ed.) (1991) *Effective Schools for All*, London: David Fulton.

Ainscow, M. and Muncey, J. (1989) *Meeting Individual Needs in the Primary School*, London: David Fulton.

Bar-Tal, D., Kfir, D., Chen, M. and Somerville, D.E. (1980) The relationship between locus of control and academic achievement, anxiety and level of aspiration, *British Journal of Educational Psychology*, 31, 482–90.

Bennett, N. (1991) The quality of classroom learning experiences for children with special educational needs, in M. Ainscow (ed.) *Effective Schools for All*, London: David Fulton.

Bradley, L. (1985) *Poor spellers, poor readers: understanding the problem*, University of Reading, Centre for the Teaching of Reading.

Brissenden, T. (1988) *Talking about Mathematics; Mathematical Discussion in Primary Classrooms*, Oxford: Blackwell.

Charlton, T. (1992) Giving access to the National Curriculum, in K. Jones and

T. Charlton (eds) *Learning Difficulties in Primary Classrooms: Delivering the Whole Curriculum*, London: Routledge.

Charlton, T. and David, K. (1993) *Managing Misbehaviour in Schools* (2nd edn), London: Routledge.

Charlton, T., Essex, C., Lovemore, T. and Crowie, B. (1995) Teachers' approval and disapproval rates and pupils' on-task levels in first and middle school classrooms on St Helena, South Atlantic, *Journal of Social Behaviour and Personality*, 10, 4, 1023–1030.

Chisholm, B., Kearney, D., Knight, H., Little, H., Morris, S. and Tweedle, D. (1986) *Preventive Approaches to Disruption*, Basingstoke: Macmillan.

Cooper, P. (1993) *Effective Schools for Disaffected Pupils: Integration and Segregation*, London: Routledge.

Cooper, P. (1996) Pupils as partners; pupils' contributions to the governance of schools, in K. Jones and T. Charlton (eds) *Overcoming Learning and Behaviour Difficulties (5–16): Partnership with Pupils*, London: Routledge.

Cooper, P. and McIntyre, D. (1993) Commonality in teachers' and pupils' perceptions of effective classroom learning, *British Journal of Educational Psychology*, 63, 381–399.

Cooper, P. and McIntyre, D. (1994) Patterns of interaction between teachers' and students' classroom thinking and their implications for the provision of learning opportunities, *Teaching and Teacher Education*, 10, 6, 633–646.

Cripps, C. and Cox, R. (1989) *Joining the ABC*, Wisbech: Learning Development Aids.

David, K. (1992) A classroom plan for personal and social education in primary schools, in K. Jones and T. Charlton (eds) *Learning Difficulties in Primary Classrooms; Delivering the Whole Curriculum*, London: Routledge.

Galton, M. (1994) Meeting the challenge of diversity through collaborative learning, paper presented at the 8th Annual Conference of the Singapore Educational Research Association, National Institute of Education, Singapore.

Garner, P. (1996) Involving pupils in policy development, in K. Jones and T. Charlton (eds) *Overcoming Learning and Behaviour Difficulties (5–16): Partnership with Pupils*, London: Routledge.

Gickling, E.E. and Thompson, V.P. (1985) A personal view of curriculum-based assessment, *Exceptional Children*, 52, 3, 205–218.

Hart, S. (1992) Collaborative classrooms, in T. Booth, W. Swann, M. Masterton and P. Potts (eds) *Curricula for Diversity in Education*, London: Routledge, in association with the Open University.

Ingram, J. and Worrall, N. (1993) *Teacher–Child Partnership: The Negotiating Classroom*, London: David Fulton.

James, J., Charlton, T., Leo, E. and Indoe, D. (1991a) Using peer counsellors to improve secondary pupils' spelling performance, *Maladjustment and Therapeutic Education*, 9, 1, 33–40.

James, J., Charlton, T., Leo, E. and Indoe D. (1991b) A peer to listen, *Support for Learning*, 6, 4, 165–70.

Jones, K. (1992) Recognising successes and difficulties in learning, in K. Jones and T. Charlton (eds) *Learning Difficulties in Primary Classrooms: Delivering the Whole Curriculum*, London: Routledge.

Jones, K. (1994) Responding to learning difficulties in primary classrooms, *React*, No. 2, Singapore, National Institute of Education.

Jones, K., Charlton, T. and Whittern, R. (1996) Enhancing and auditing partnership with pupils, in K. Jones and T. Charlton (eds) *Overcoming Learning and Behaviour Difficulties (5–16): Partnership with Pupils*, London: Routledge.

Jones, S. (1992) Collaborative enquiry-based learning and training, in K. Jones and T. Charlton (eds) *Learning Difficulties in Primary Classrooms: Delivering the Whole Curriculum*, London: Routledge.

Kagan, S. (1990) The structured approach to co-operative learning, *Educational Leadership*, 47, 4, 12–15.

Kutnik, P. and Jules, V. (1993) Pupils' perspectives of a good teacher; a developmental perspective from Trinidad and Tobago, *British Journal of Educational Psychology*, 64, 400–413.

Laten, S. and Katz, G. (1975) *A Theoretical Model for Assessment of Adolescents: The Ecological/Behavioural Approach*, Madison, WI: Madison Public Schools.

Lewis, J. (1996) Helping children to find a voice, in K. Jones and T. Charlton (eds) *Overcoming Learning and Behaviour Difficulties (5–16): Partnership with Pupils*, London: Routledge.

Madsen, C.H., Becker, W.C. and Thomas, D.R. (1968) Rules, praise and ignoring; elements of elementary classroom control, *Journal of Applied Behaviour Analysis*, 10, 465–478

Merrett, F., Jackson, P. and Fitzpatrick, A. (1991) The effect of changes in teacher response ratios on pupils' behaviour, *Positive Teaching*, 2, 79–91.

Ong, P. (1988) *A Project on Thinking Skills*, Singapore: Curriculum Development Institute of Singapore.

Phillips, T. (1988) Why successful small group talk depends upon not keeping to the point, in M. Maclure, T. Phillips and A. Wilkinson (eds) *Oracy Matters; The Development of Talking and Listening in Education*, Milton Keynes: Open University Press.

Pimm, D. (1987) *Speaking Mathematically: Communication in Mathematics Classrooms*, London: Routledge & Kegan Paul.

Quah, M.L. (1994) A gentle push for reluctant readers, *ASCD Review* (Singapore), 4, 2, 56–58.

Quah, M.L. and Jones, K. (1995) The professional development needs of learning support co-ordinators in Singapore primary schools, *European Journal of Special Needs Education*, 11, 2, 197–206.

Slavin, R.E. (1990) *Co-operative Learning: Theory, Research and Practice*. Englewood Cliffs, NJ; Prentice-Hall.

Tattum, D. (1988) Control and welfare: towards a theory of constructive discipline in schools, in R. Dale, R. Fergusson and A. Robinson (eds) *Frameworks for Teaching*, London: Hodder & Stoughton, in association with the Open University.

Thomas, G. and Feiler, A. (eds) (1988) *Planning for Special Needs: A Whole-school Approach*, Oxford: Blackwell.

Thomson, M. (1991) The teaching of spelling using techniques of simultaneous oral spelling and visual inspection, in M. Snowling and M. Thomson (eds) *Dyslexia; Integrating Theory and Practice*, London: Whurr Publications.

Tyler, S. (1990) Subtypes of specific learning difficulties: a review, in P.D. Pumfrey and C.D. Elliott (eds) *Children's Difficulties in Reading, Spelling and Writing*, London: Falmer Press.

UNESCO (1993) *Special Needs in the Classroom*, Paris: UNESCO.

Wade, B. and Moore, M. (1993) *Experiencing Special Education*, Buckingham: Open University Press.

Walden, T.A. and Ramey, C.T. (1983) Locus of control and academic achievement: results from a pre-school programme, *Journal of Educational Psychology*, 75, 3, 347–358.

Westwood, P. (1993) *Commonsense Methods for Children with Special Needs*, London: Routledge.

Wragg, E.C. and Woods, E.K. (1984) Pupil appraisals of teaching, in E.C. Wragg (ed.) *Classroom Teaching Skills*, London: Croom Helm.
Yap, S.K. (1989) *Its a Maths, Maths World*, Singapore: Curriculum Development Institute of Singapore.
Yeow, S.L. (1988) *A Project on Higher-order Thinking Skills*, Singapore: Curriculum Development Institute of Singapore.

3

DEVELOPING PASTORAL CARE IN THE PRIMARY SCHOOL

A model for growth and development

David Hammond and Jean-Pierre Kirkland

INTRODUCTION

Pastoral care in the primary school may be defined much the same as its counterpart in secondary schools, that is, a system of welfare and guidance for all pupils and staff and other people involved in school life. Such a system helps the growth of a school community where there is a strong emphasis upon caring, nurturing, guiding, counselling and protecting, whilst at the same time promoting qualities more recently defined by the Office for Standards in Education (Ofsted, 1993) as the spiritual, moral, social and cultural development of pupils. However, a good pastoral school would not just restrict this latter part to the children but to all involved in the running and maintenance of the life of the school. Most primary schools tend to be much smaller establishments than the vast majority of their secondary counterparts and therefore have a very much more intimate structure. This structure allows and encourages all the staff to get to know each other well, there is a high degree of co-operation and planning, issues are resolved regularly on a whole-school basis through regular consultation, and all the school staff readily become involved in the lives of the pupils, with concern for their care, welfare and success. If head teachers perceive this as a unique opportunity and act accordingly, then the organisation and management of the primary school can be developed more readily to take account of whole-school approaches to pastoral care. This then will give both shape and form to the school's ethos; the whole school will be concerned with pastoral care as a normal on-going developmental process. It will not be added on, or superimposed, as often has to be the case in larger secondary establishments.

EXPECTATIONS AND NEEDS

One of the fundamental issues underpinning pastoral care in the primary school is that the children have certain expectations both of the school and of its staff, teaching and non-teaching. If the school and its staff fail to meet these expectations, whatever they may be, then it becomes increasingly likely that the school is not providing the service of which it is potentially capable, and thus it is failing to meet the needs of a majority of its pupils. Our combined sixty years of classroom and management experience have confirmed in us that the above expectations from pupils are centred around the school providing for them a healthy learning environment, with skilled, knowledgeable and challenging teachers helping them to achieve high standards, adequate support and guidance, an atmosphere of joy, love, concern and understanding, coupled with a genuine interest in the progress and success for themselves as young people. Taking this on board as a serious issue, pastoral care in the primary school becomes a positive process of continuous whole-school development centred around the needs and expectations of the pupils, but linked to, and coupled with, the ever-increasing needs of staff, their own expectations of themselves as classroom managers and of their expectations of the school itself in supporting, developing and encouraging them. Pastoral care thus helps the school develop an examination of the ways and means of supporting the whole child throughout his or her life in school. It involves everyone in that complex scenario – teaching and non-teaching staff, parents, support agencies, visitors – extending itself quite naturally into the whole school community. It then becomes a major training and development initiative for the whole school, inspired and led initially by management, but gradually devolved in terms of responsibility and ownership to the various factions, outlined above, who make up the whole school community.

THE DEVELOPMENT PROJECT

The origins of this particular method of integrating pastoral care into whole-school training and development, including issues around the National Curriculum and other statutory legislation, had its origins in the appointment of a new head to Gresswell CPS in 1990. The first request for immediate attention to come from staff, as a concern at that time, was behaviour and discipline. The staff up to then had not really been involved in much debate from the whole-school perspective so such a request had to be carefully managed. The head then had to devise a policy of staff training which would allow for the relative immaturity of his staff in this field, whilst recognising the eventuality that national legislation was making fast and furious demands upon staff time and resources. It soon became apparent to the staff that they were in need of quite dramatic training and development. The model upon which most of the internal training and staff development was based was that of John Elliott Kemp (1982) (see Figure 3.1).

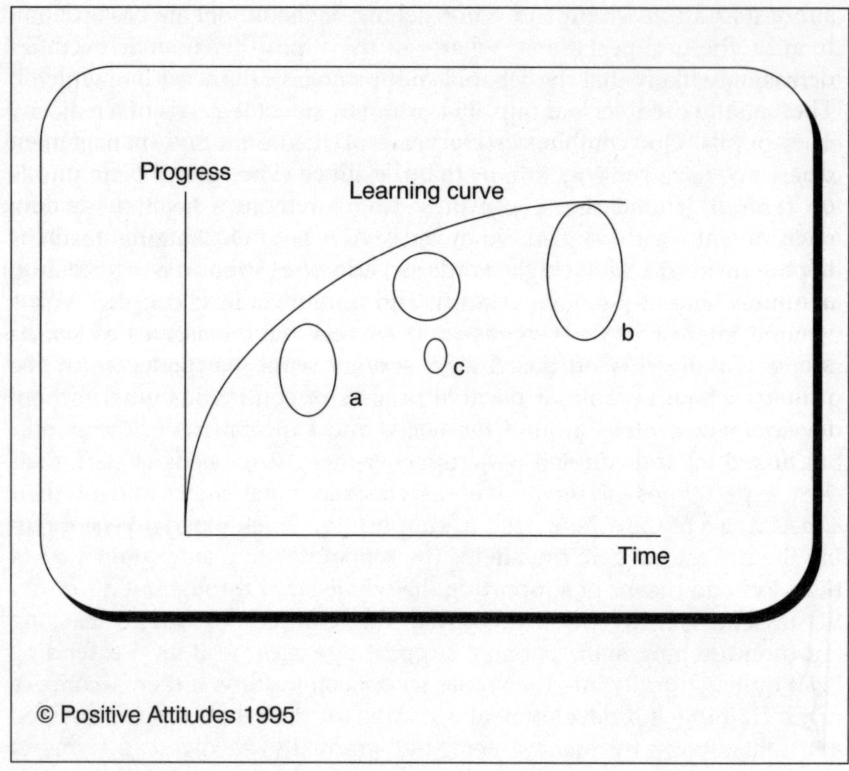

Figure 3.1 Model of staff development

The staff are represented by the ovals on the diagram, initially located a long way down the learning curve at (a). The aim was to move the staff as quickly and comfortably as possibly to position (b) without losing anyone *en route*, as is illustrated at position (c). With a staff of fifteen this became an achievable goal over a period of some eighteen months or so. A tremendous amount of learning took place through meetings, management initiatives, staff initiatives and carefully chosen or planned courses. The result was indeed such a movement from (a) to (b) without any losses. The Local Education Authority (LEA) played an important part here by using some of the staff on its own working parties, the result of which was to help build the self-confidence of the staff so involved, and to introduce them to other staff who were themselves at differing points in their own development and acquisition of skills.

Initially, behaviour and discipline were indeed the agenda items for the staff meetings, which were designed as a series of open forums. To begin with, the head chaired these in order to act as a change agent (Havelock, 1973) but with a staff of fifteen, it was necessary to divide into three sub-groups. This had the effect of delegating some degree of autonomy to each sub-group, with the clearly defined aim of working towards a definition of the nature and causes of the perceived indiscipline problem. The head visited each group, but was not officially a member of any. There was at this point the need for the head to make serious management decisions about the way he was to be involved. The Handy (1978) model of 'Gods of management' proved a useful reference point for making decisions, and the role adopted by the head was a modification of Athene, the task-oriented approach. Jones (1987) examines secondary schools from a modified version of the Handy (1978) model, labelling the Athene version 'Organic' or mature comprehensive. What in fact the head in this school was doing was inventing yet another set of management gods for primary phase. These are very loosely related to the Handy or Jones models, and we present these Hammond–Kirkland cultures in Figure 3.2.

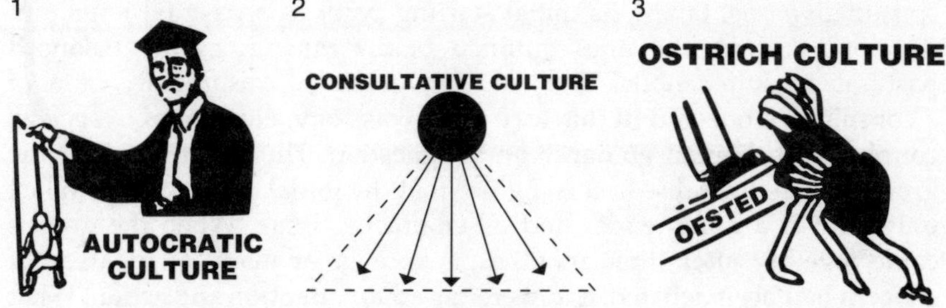

Figure 3.2 Management cultures

The *Autocratic Culture* is the power-based model, with the head at the centre of the spider's web (Handy, 1978) or Catherine Wheel (Jones, 1987). Here, the head holds the reins, rarely delegates, tries to keep tags on everything, and is often fairly remote in terms of human relations and effective communication, but can nevertheless be a powerful or even awesome figure. Some schools and heads survive for quite long periods of time in this mode, but the strain on all can be quite debilitating. Many heads who operate this way cause themselves undue stress and may eventually need to give up by taking early retirement through sheer exhaustion, through breakdown packages, or by moving on and trying again elsewhere. The dangers in this are quite apparent and Hall and Hall (1989) supply useful models for overcoming many of the difficulties that this form of management can involve.

In the *Consultative Culture* the head is in delegation mode, consulting with her or his staff regularly, and attempting to spread the various burdens appropriately throughout the staff. This kind of culture can lean towards the academic or towards the pastoral, but must, if it is to be effective, combine elements of both. The head here still needs to keep fairly central to the Catherine Wheel or spider's web, but will, in a successful model, develop lines of communication which are delegated channels of trust. Other staff, too, must be able to trust each other to complete their section of task and be working towards the same goal. The *Ostrich Culture* is the 'bury my head in the sand' model, where the culture can be either evasive: 'If we ignore it, it might go away', or protectionist: 'It is my duty as head to protect my staff from all this unnecessary legislation etc.' The chances of this model surviving long, particularly with Ofsted breathing ever closer down necks (buried or otherwise!), are fairly remote. What often happens here is the collapse of the system with dire consequences for the children who do not receive their entitlement, and heads and other staff disappearing at an alarming rate on breakdown pensions or early retirements.

The pastoral model which was developed in the school was the consultative one, taking its initial starting point as a pastoral issue, but developing along the lines outlined below into an evenly balanced pastoral/academic model. The head's involvement was initially, more of a consultative one and in this way there was some element of overview, coupled with limited guidance and suggestion. The result was that the groups began to realise and recognise that the initial problem was in fact only part of a much wider and all-embracing issue. When the groups came together after three months or so, a great many other areas of concern had been debated, and were raised for attention and action. What subsequently emerged was a policy that not only embraced the discipline issues, but took on a much wider brief and began to explore the whole area of pastoral care. With subsequent whole-school debate, a policy for personal and social education was devised which incorporated the behaviour and discipline, but which went much further. It began to examine needs, not just of the children, but of the staff as well. And as the process itself developed, so did the need for placing a safety net around it. In order for the staff to feel that they could raise points and issues, and express attitudes and opinions without fear of reprisal or hostile criticism, the ethos of meetings needed to become safe and comfortable. To do this, the principles of person-centred counselling, emanating from Carl Rogers (1961) were adopted. This meant having an approach of unconditional positive regard for each member of staff, granting them due respect in terms of where in the debate they were starting from, treating them with genuineness, being able to empathise with them in times of difficulty, and providing them with adequate periods of reflection during which they were able to take on board and assimilate new ideas, principles and concepts.

STAFF DEVELOPMENT STAGES

During these relatively early stages of the developmental process, it became necessary to prompt, listen and give limited advice. What began to happen was the natural development and operation of the Kolb (1984) learning cycle (Figure 3.3).

The first stage was the initial clarification of what the staff really wanted when they asked for a behaviour and discipline policy. The underlying need which subsequently emerged was much wider in its scope and far more detailed. This became the main aim of the exercise and eventually appeared as the school's mission statement, 'Starting with a quality education' (a). The second stage was when the staff moved on into their own sub-groups, following the initial model, but this time

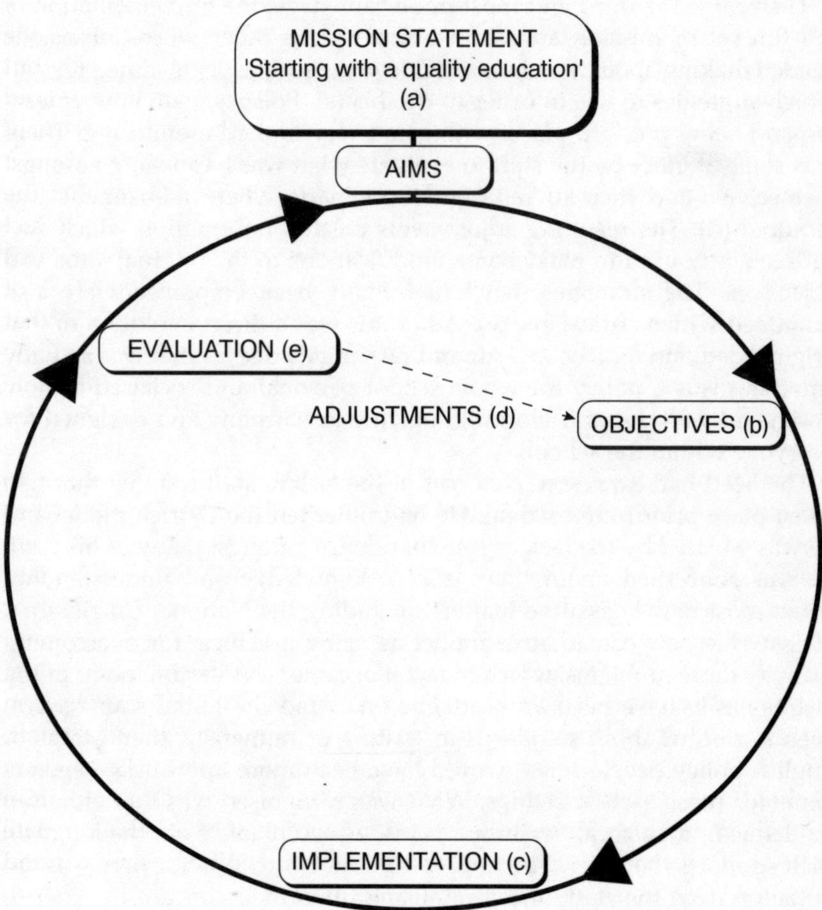

Figure 3.3 The learning cycle (according to Kolb, 1984)

grouping themselves on an interest basis, each group in essence opening up a new area of thought based upon the mission statement and thus developing a series of objectives for the whole school (b). It was at this stage that the staff began to empower themselves as a body, gaining in both expertise and confidence. They read through in-service literature avidly, and asked to go on various courses directly related to the main thrust of the process, and they used the meetings to feed back information, ideas and new concepts so that the process might be moved on. As yet, their self-confidence was still relatively low, and their skills, although present, were not being adequately exploited, so that the pupils were not yet gaining the full potential of what the staff might be able to offer them. The process needed time and it took just over two years for these initial stages to be accomplished.

Then came the third and most important stage, the implementation of the full set of mission aims and objectives. In other words, decisions needed making about how best to achieve the results being aimed for and which strategies to use in order to do this (c). Policies were now emerging and being put into place, with some very limited monitoring. There was some attempt by the staff to evaluate what was happening amongst themselves, and then to redesign those parts where adjustment was required (d). The resulting adjustments created information which was subsequently used to make some modifications to the original aims and objectives. The strategies that had initially been employed were also examined with a critical eye (e). All of this was a direct evolution of that original demand for a behaviour and discipline policy. What was actually emerging was a policy for whole-school personal and social education, designed by all the staff working together in harmony and designed for everyone within the school.

The head had expressed concerns at the lack of staff training that had taken place prior to his arrival. He had inherited the Ostrich model and he was worried by the lack of self-confidence amongst many of his staff; he was concerned about their lack of knowledge and understanding about most new legislative matters, including the National Curriculum. He saw his new consultative model as being a vehicle for overcoming many of these problems, which in fact it became. The starting point might just as easily have been an academic one. Had the initial staff request been a concern about standards in writing or numeracy, then Maths or English policy development would have been more appropriate agenda items for those early meetings. What was recognised was that either an academic or a pastoral beginning is just as acceptable as in the long run each supports the other. The important, if not crucial factor here was the initiation from the staff, and capitalising upon their concern in order to use their energy and enthusiasms to stimulate the debate and to motivate each other. Common ownership was thus established at the initial stage, and was absolutely fundamental for the future development and success of the management initiative.

Equally important and striking was the development within the school of extremely good interpersonal relationships, the raising of self-esteem amongst many staff, the development of the individual into a person in his or her own right, and the continual development of higher-order skills. All these attributes were indirect offshoots of that original request so that, in effect, the standards of achievement rose by having better informed and more knowledgeable teachers in front of classes, the quality of learning improved as teachers began to recognise issues such as pacing lessons appropriately, encouraging pupils to learn in a collaborative way and beginning to understand how to help pupils to begin to evaluate their own work. The quality of teaching also improved, with teachers setting clear targets and setting high yet attainable challenges, whilst developing the confidence to try out new methodology, using assessment and feedback as motivating forces.

The next stages in the development of the process were to lift this initial micro-model and to transform it into a macro-scale operation. This was done by the head moving temporarily into Autocratic mode and sharing his vision of the school with his staff. Once again, a person-centred approach was taken, using phraseology such as 'I believe we are at a point . . . what do you think?' or 'I feel we have reached . . . where do you think we are at?' This resulted in a series of hares being released and set running. The Kolb (1984) learning cycle was in motion again, but this time the initiatives were coming not just from a group of staff, but from the head and individual members of staff who now believed that they could cope with developing their own areas of responsibility adequately. Staff had become confident. The original discipline/behaviour demand had been rooted firmly in the concept of the staff owning the request, but, at that time, they had no means of knowing what to do with that request nor how to develop it into anything meaningful. By now they had acquired sufficient skills to take the development process by the horns and set off in small sub-groups with enthusiasm, motivation, interest, determination and a self-perpetuating vigour of their own. Managerial skills in chairing small groups, delegating certain routine tasks, and setting realistic deadlines and targets were now becoming commonplace features. Higher-order skills such as the selection of realistic strategies for managing processes were also being acquired by the staff, which resulted in the formation of teams headed and led by subject or aspect co-ordinators. Staff were now becoming increasingly aware of themselves as professionals through using applied experiential models which in turn began to lead them into a recognition of what the pupils might be expecting of them as well.

THE LINK WITH PUPIL DEVELOPMENT

By realising that they had expectations of each other as staff, it soon became apparent to them that young people would have similar expectations of them as teachers, even though such expectations were less well articulated. Coghill and Goodwin (1991) make the point that teaching and learning may change significantly if attention is switched from the needs of teachers, syllabus or institution, and focused upon the learning needs of pupils in relation to statutory requirements. They go on to claim that there are striking parallels to be drawn between pupil developments often outlined in pupil reports to parents, and the personal and professional development of the staff associated with them. Certainly the evidence here is that this is readily borne out as and when the teachers began to implement their newly defined strategies with their classes, in their relationships with parents and in relationships with outside agencies. Kirk (1987) makes a similar point when describing the way in which the acquisition of staff management skills learned through such exercises as simulations and experiences in areas of delegation, communication, use of time, decision making and team building soon begin to have effects within the classroom. The changes which begin to occur, if professionally evaluated, should lead to even greater motivation and achievement all round.

EVALUATION

This notion of professional evaluation can come from within or externally. From within, staff need to become aware of the sort of criteria that they need to be looking for in order to take measurements of progress. Such measurements, or performance indicators, can all too frequently become wholly quantitative, and although it is recognised that there will always remain a place for this kind of measure, the qualitative side must never be ignored. Many of the benefits and gains from developmental models have to be expressed qualitatively. Examples would include the building of staff or pupil self-esteem and self-confidence, the quality of display work in corridors or classrooms, the relationships with parents, and indeed the quality of learning of both staff and pupils (see Appendix: Performance Indicators). It is often very difficult for a school to be really objective about qualitative issues. Comparison models do not always work, particularly as individual schools need to develop their own ethos and characteristics. Outside objectivity can come from an Ofsted inspection, an LEA-led evaluation or from a consultant who has knowledge of various schools in many different environments and across a variety of LEAs. Whatever objective information is available, it can readily be fused with any internal subjective material available, so that the school benefits from the matching and comparison of the two, and can thus plan accordingly for the next stages in its development. The school needs as an essential prerequisite before moving on, to have had a period of reflection or 'fallow' time, whereby everyone can come up for air, relax a little and do some gentler assimilation. Equally important at this stage is the need for double-checking: is everyone still together? Do all the staff and non-teaching staff share the same vision? Is there a communality of both understanding and approach? Do pupils, outside agencies, all governors and most parents share this vision? If such questions are not asked, results checked out and any faults remedied at this stage, then there will be an ever-present danger of a dual system developing. In fact the system could be in danger of splitting, with teachers going one way, pupils believing they are going another, parents floundering in the middle, and the governing body not terribly sure of what is happening. The key to prevent this from occurring is the dimension of self-support through self-reliance. Employing strategies that interlink and involve all people in the life of the school, and depend for their success on the outcomes of other strategies and which tend to coincide chronologically along a school development plan, are likely to prevent sub-cultures, cliques or divisions from forming or developing.

PARENTS

Following on from this comes the very real need for parents to understand the concept of a pastoral school. Parents have been encouraged by successive waves of legislation to become more involved in the education of their children. Primary schools have always led the field in this by encouraging parental participation in the whole education process much more than was the case with their secondary counterparts, but if the term pastoral school is to be properly interpreted, then there is an element of parental education involved also. This can occur in a number of ways. Parents who come into the classroom as support for say reading, often pick up many messages relating to the ethos and atmosphere of the school as do those who regularly attend open assemblies. Similarly, parents who accompany teachers on school outings, or those who regularly attend school plays and fund-raising events also pick up important messages. But in a truly pastoral school, more is needed. Parents themselves have got to become part of the process so that they are leading their children in the same direction and using the same kind of approach.

The initiative for extending the pastoral care network into the parental field came from the staff who themselves were developing professionally and personally, and recognised that, in many parents, a similar need existed but was rarely articulated, as many of the parents themselves had not reached a stage of recognising that need in themselves. The school was in regular contact with parents through the more normal channels of structured reporting evenings for parents and through a regular and chatty newsletter. What the head and staff began to recognise was the need to develop workshops for parents which could help educate them in the learning processes their children were experiencing, and also give them a more experiential approach to the learning of factual information. Getting the language right for all was quite a problem as teachers generally do tend to use a lot of jargon. So it became vital to address the issue of equal access to the learning process in a well thought-out and appropriate manner.

Following on from this came a further initiative that the school undertook which was a weekend residential for parents at a residential centre some few miles from the school. This was structured in such a way as to raise for parents questions on a series of educational matters, yet allow for a very carefully balanced programme of personal growth and development using a model similar to the one developed by Kirkland and Beresford (1991). Although only a relatively small proportion of the total parent population attended, those who did attend found it to be a most worthwhile experience, enlightening them to a series of issues which ranged from classroom methodologies and learning styles through to coping with stress. More such ventures are planned, but the process has to be undertaken slowly, and each stage monitored and evaluated carefully.

FURTHER PUPIL GROWTH

Having parents, or at least a significant number of parents, committed and involved helps the school to move on into another important area of growth, namely that of promoting the spiritual, moral, social and cultural development of pupils. There are many and varied ways in which these four aspects of a child's development may be promoted, through the various areas of the formal curriculum and through careful consideration of the informal curriculum. But we do not believe for one moment that the promotion of these aspects by the school alone is going to have any real meaningful long-term beneficial effects unless the parents are fully involved, supportive and understanding of what is happening or of what is planned to happen. If standards are to be raised and quality is to be a keynote feature of a child's education, then the school has a duty to ensure wherever possible that the parents have also been educated to the degree that they at least recognise and understand what is occurring, and a majority openly echo their support for it. If not, the child will receive one set of messages at school, and may well receive a different and often contradictory set of messages at home. Such disparity is only likely to lead to a series of tensions and problems which confuse, disorient and upset the child. Very few, if any, children of primary age are likely to be able to understand and appreciate two differing culture systems being applied at the same time. Adolescents have more of a chance of weighing up the odds, but the potential disservice to our young people that could be caused by not attempting to reach parents is a dangerous one.

Imagine what goes on in the mind of the child who is taught not to lie at school, but is then allowed to get away with that at home. Imagine what happens to a child who is encouraged to show respect for people of differing cultures whilst at school, but is then fed racist messages at home. We appreciate that our prime job is to be involved in the children's education, but elements of parental education must of necessity be present. Whether we will ever change some of those deeper-rooted mistrusts or prejudices remains to be seen, but at least if we try to help parents understand and appreciate what we are saying and teaching in the school, then a contradictory message may not be given, even if there is a lot of tongue biting taking place. Monitoring of this process in terms of pupil response is also a vital ingredient, and the staff undertook their own assessment of how children were responding. The result was a very positive one indeed. A large number of children have great expectations of the staff, they are generally happy and feel well supported throughout their school life. They know and understand the main methods of communication and readily discuss their problems or other issues with the staff.

The obvious effects of the importance of parental support in the promotion of the spiritual, moral, social and cultural aspects comes when such things as bullying, stealing, vandalism and racism occur. Without complete parental support, they become issues almost impossible to deal with. The effects upon standards and quality can be disastrous. Schools also expect good attendance from children, and parents who do not themselves appreciate that need certainly require some form of education rather than pure threats. And of course, as was highlighted at the outset, there are large numbers of children who have very definite expectations of staff; they will have similar expectations of their parents, and how vital it then becomes to try to unite the parents and staff in order to meet these expectations.

Having reached a point in the school's development where many of these issues had been to a large extent resolved, the staff began to dwell more on the notion of co-operation in its widest sense. In the junior section of the school, a monthly forum is held in the form of a non-religious assembly. Full debates have been initiated by the children on issues such as bullying and vandalism, and the children have defined and elicited strategies for dealing with the problems. A second initiative arising out of the process has been the establishment of a system of prefects whose job is to help with the work of younger pupils on wet days when in the classrooms. As a third initiative, a school council has been formed with form representatives elected to serve on the body which takes charge of planning the pupil forums, organising the debate and for preparing the inputs on the day. All this is being carried out with both confidence and a real sense of responsibility. In fact, what the children are now doing is following the staff through the same process of self-esteem, self-confidence and team building along the lines of the learning cycle explained earlier.

COUNSELLING

Last, but by no means least, the school has made available to staff the services of a fully qualified and trained counsellor. Staff are able by arrangement with the head, to access this service when problems of a professional or personal nature occur. The head is kept informed of general progress only, and of the number of appointments attended. Issues of confidentiality are clearly laid out and barriers are respected and maintained. Counselling is off-site, and usually in the teacher's own spare time, unless it takes place during a prolonged illness. The service is there if staff feel the need to talk in confidence to someone who is distanced from the problem and has no personal or professional investment with the school. The service is used as and when the need arises, and it has helped several members of staff successfully to work through problems affecting their professional performance by putting them in touch with their feelings. This has helped them to become 'more responsible for their own survival and unique fulfilment' (Nelson-Jones, 1986), thereby helping them to continue to provide a quality education for the children whilst continuing to help to raise standards.

CONCLUSION

Pastoral care in a primary school is thus very much a whole-school affair. As HMI (1989) point out in their paper on personal and social education:

> If children's personal and social development is to progress satisfactorily, it needs to be well supported. Parents have the major part to play, but the role of all teachers is vital. . . . It is something from which no teacher can opt out.

We believe that for pastoral care to be effective across the whole school it has to be thought through very carefully, planned into the developmental process, monitored and evaluated very painstakingly, but, more important than anything else, it needs to become part of the school culture, stemming from within. Simply writing policies or planning a few odd pieces of in-service training are not going to provide the results or realise the potential that a good school may well achieve. The model offered here is one that has worked well and is continuing to work well by having developed a logic and momentum of its own. It still needs attention and still needs careful overseeing. But once in motion, it can and will bring a lot of joy and happiness into the educative process for all involved, making the profession far more rewarding than many teachers may think possible.

APPENDIX: PERFORMANCE INDICATORS

Listed below is a series of Performance Indicators which the school arrived at through debate in order to have some benchmarks for monitoring and evaluating the whole process. These are still in their infancy and are thus in a state of flux. Also they have been evolved out of the process rather than being picked in a random fashion. They are presented here as a guide for schools to help develop their own.

1 Commitment of staff: this includes the numbers on in-service courses, the number of courses taking place, the quality of display work and the quality of learning in the classroom.
2 Degree of staff teamwork: this includes meeting goals for the completion of tasks and the degree of harmony with which jobs are undertaken.
3 Job satisfaction: includes feedback from teachers, from parents and from children.
4 Levels of staff expertise: including expertise in practice, variety of in-service training and gains in skills and knowledge.
5 Staff attendance: including not just raw numbers, but the underlying reasons for absence and our receptiveness to the problem.
6 Standards of achievement: including raw numbers but in comparison to past and national norms, to children's capabilities, and across the whole curriculum, formal and informal.
7 Curriculum targets: including the appropriateness of linking planning to assessment, monitoring and evaluation techniques and comparisons with other similar schools locally and wider afield.
8 Resource care and usage: including general tidiness, frequency of damage to equipment, equitable distribution of resources and accessibility.
9 Systems management: including the ability to retrieve information stored, finding the correct personnel, and the smooth running of the school office.
10 Financial targets: including successful budgeting and resource implications.
11 Feedback from parents and children: including children's and parent's attitudes when approached, ability to converse and work, and pupils' response to visitors.

12 Relationships with parents including complaints/praise: including the level of either, attendance at parents' meetings and assemblies, and their willingness to participate as partners.
13 Governor involvement: knowledge of their roles, of school policies, how many become involved in the life of the school and whether or not they know the staff and vice versa.
14 Quality of displays: state of corridors, classrooms, entrance hall, etc.
15 Levels of pupil attendance: including raw numbers but a more in-depth analysis also.
16 Wider community: including general relationships, use of community by the school and the community's view of the school.
17 Exclusions/punishments: raw numbers and reasons.
18 Accidents: including raw numbers, whether policies are effective and degree of severity.

There will inevitably be more added to the list, and there will be alterations to some of the criteria within categories. But without such a list it becomes almost impossible to reach an objective overview of the whole process and situation.

REFERENCES

Coghill, J. and Goodwin, A. (1991) Teachers learning, in D. Hustler, E. Milroy and M. Cockett (eds) *Learning Environments for the Whole Curriculum*, London: Unwin Hyman.

Hall, C. and Hall, E. (1989) *Human Relations in Education*, London: Routledge.

Handy, C. (1978) *The Gods of Management*, London and Sydney: Pan Books.

Havelock, R. (1973) *The Change Agent's Guide to Innovation in Education*, Englewood Cliffs, NJ: Prentice Hall.

Her Majesty's Inspectorate (1989) *Curriculum Matters 14: Personal and Social Education 5–18*, London: HMSO.

Jones, A. (1987) *Leadership for Tomorrow's Schools*, Oxford: Blackwell.

Kemp, J.E. (1982) *Managing Organisational Change: A Practitioner's Guide*, Sheffield: Hallam University.

Kirk, R. (1987) *Learning in Action*, Oxford: Blackwell.

Kirkland, J.-P. and Beresford, E. (1991) Parents' residentials, *Home and School*, 18, (Winter).

Kolb, D. (1984) *Organisational Psychology*, Englewood Cliffs, NJ: Prentice Hall.

Nelson-Jones, R. (1986) *Human Relationship Skills*, East Sussex: Cassell.

Office for Standards in Education (1993) *Handbook for the Inspection of Schools*, London: HMSO.

Rogers, C. (1961) *On Becoming a Person*, London: Constable.

4

CO-ORDINATION IN PERSONAL AND SOCIAL EDUCATION

Anita Ryall, Gillian Goddard and Irene Travis

INTRODUCTION

This chapter examines the need for co-ordination of personal and social education (PSE) in nursery and primary education. It will identify the role of the co-ordinator as seen by those presently undertaking that responsibility. It will present research carried out on the co-ordination of PSE in nursery and primary schools and consider the constraints on effective co-ordination, including the impact of the National Curriculum and other government-led policy initiatives. Case studies of good practice will be described and ways forward presented.

Home is the setting for initial and on-going personal and social learning but realistically this provides a limited environment for the full development of 'persons'. In some homes the setting is actually inappropriate for positive and productive learning. A broad range of opportunities for all pupils is needed in order to begin to enhance the skills, attitudes, knowledge and understanding necessary to live fully and effectively with self and others.

Although traditionally schools have emphasised academic learning, most primary teachers would consider that the personal and social development of children is their concern and that much of what they do on a day-to-day basis contributes to this development. Personal education is often seen by primary teachers as arising naturally through the relationships between teachers and pupils with social education being achieved through the experience of schooling itself (Brown, 1990).

There is a danger inherent in this way of perceiving PSE for it can suggest that children develop personally and socially as an incidental by-product of their total schooling experience. If education is about helping young people to 'develop those powers of reasoning, feeling and acting responsibly which distinguish someone as a person' (Pring, 1984, p. 14) then it is too important to be left to chance encounters, experiences and relationships. There is a need therefore for specific planning and co-ordination in PSE as in any other aspect of the curriculum.

It is generally acknowledged that the school's hidden curriculum has a powerful effect on the transmission of its own cultural norms and values. Schools, however, are often unable to be precise about what those values are. In order to begin to consider what is desirable for the sound personal and social development of pupils they may need to be more explicit about exactly what values are deemed to be of importance, how they can be justified and how they relate to the needs of the children in the school. This requires commitment and honesty from each member of the staff and a climate of mutual trust.

Primary schools will need to look more critically at their current practice – relationships, organisation, management, curriculum, and to consider whether, in fact, that practice does indeed foster positive personal and social development. As Pring (1984, p. 110) maintained, 'there is clearly a need to examine the values which are often hidden in the unexamined methods of teaching, structures of authority and modes of control and yet which correlate so strongly with educational behavioural outcomes'. It is only from this critical evaluation of current practice that primary schools can begin to plan for and co-ordinate a more coherent and structured form of PSE. This co-ordinated approach in the primary school is important if young people are to be presented with a planned range of opportunities and experiences which build on and extend their existing personal and social competences.

SURVEY

Lang (1988) suggests that a successful PSE programme requires strong leadership from the head teacher or a designated co-ordinator as well as staff involvement and ownership. A survey was conducted to look at how PSE is co-ordinated in some nursery and primary schools. Questionnaires were distributed to 320 primary and nursery schools from nine LEAs in the North West of England used for teaching practice by Liverpool Institute of Higher Education; 199 were returned and from this a statistical analysis was undertaken. The results are tabulated in Figures 4.1 and 4.2.

Results from the questionnaire in Figure 4.1 show that 98 out of 199 schools had nominated PSE co-ordinators and in 90 out of 199 schools there was no PSE co-ordinator. Governor involvement was also evident with 27 out of 199 nominated governors designated for PSE and 28 out of 199 for pastoral care. There was significantly more governor involvement in sex education, which reflects the current legal requirements.

From the survey it was apparent that the responsibilities of the PSE co-ordinator have much in common with those of curriculum leaders.

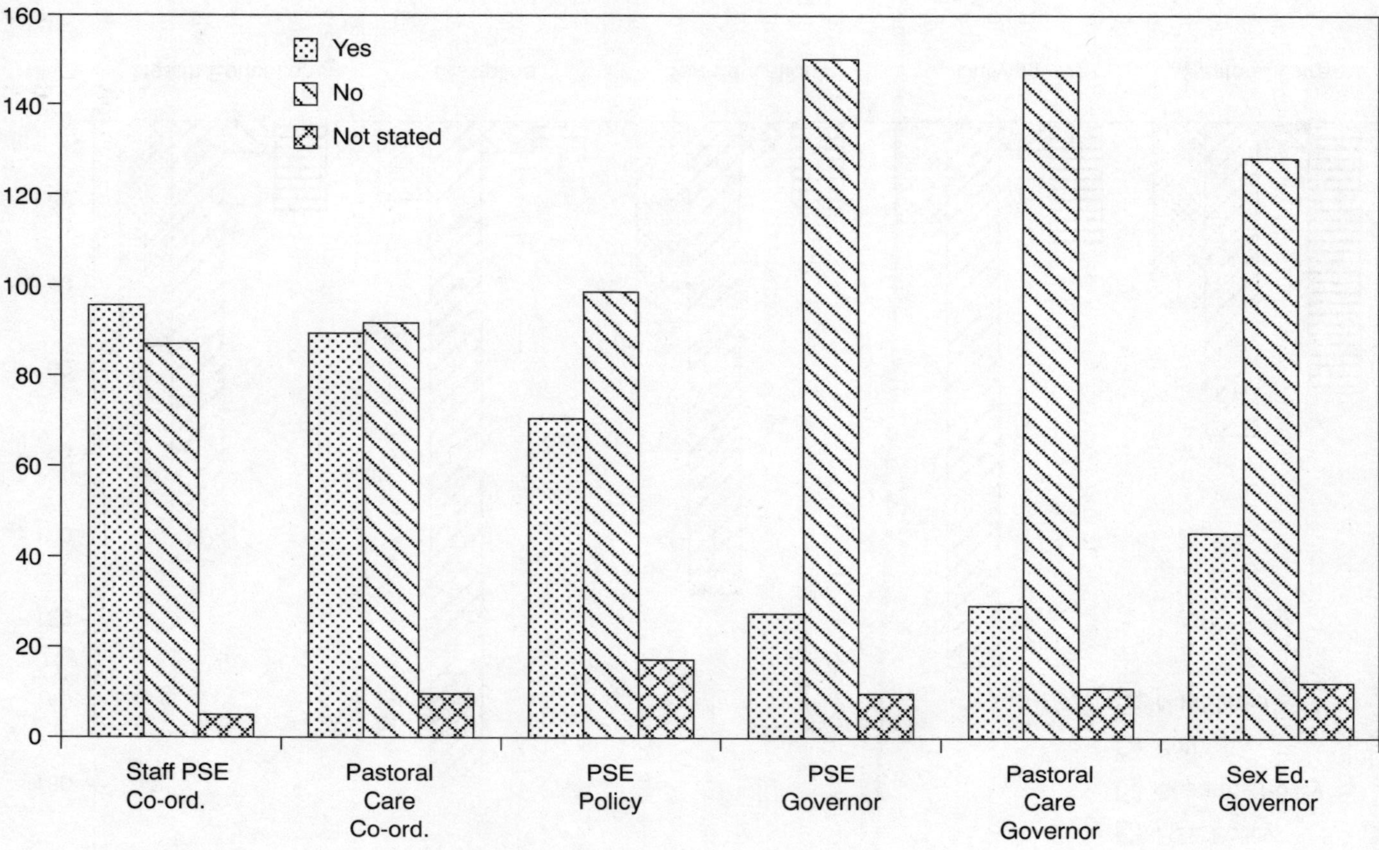

Figure 4.1 Responses to the questionnaire

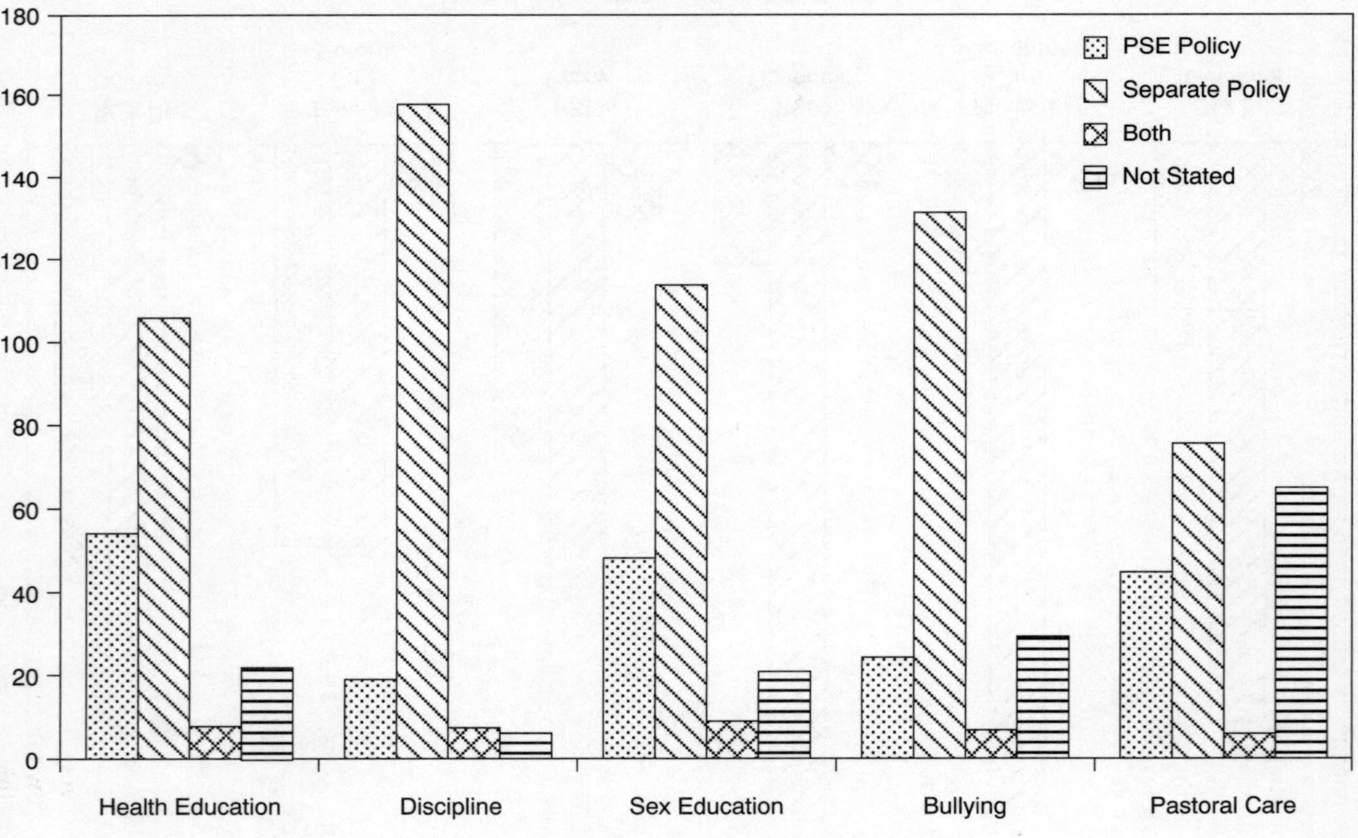

Figure 4.2 Number of schools with a PSE or Separate Policy

Respondents identified monitoring and reviewing practice, facilitating Inset, attending courses, liaising with parents and outside agencies, managing resources, disseminating information, reporting to governors and raising awareness as key aspects of their role.

Revising and writing policies was highlighted as a main feature of the co-ordinator's role. There were 68 policies for PSE. A number of schools incorporated specific elements, such as health education or discipline into their PSE policy (see Figure 4.2). It is significant that a far greater proportion of schools separated elements such as these into individual policies.

Fragmentation of PSE in this way undermines its essentially holistic nature. If it is seen as a series of separate issues it will be monitored in this way. It ignores the totality of the whole-school experience for individual children and will affect the coherent co-ordination of PSE.

Based on the results of the survey it would seem that schools are attending to the legal requirements, that is, formulating policies required for inspection (sex education, discipline, bullying). The pressure of inspections is implicit and the impact of legal requirements is leading to fragmentation. The need to produce a comprehensive PSE policy is less pressing. Therefore a whole-school approach to policy and practice is difficult to achieve in view of this fragmentation. Effective co-ordination of PSE is almost impossible to achieve if there is no agreed whole-school policy.

School governors are beginning to become involved in PSE and pastoral care. Their increased awareness and involvement could help raise the status and importance of PSE throughout the school.

CASE STUDIES – GOOD PRACTICE IN CO-ORDINATION

Case study 1: Initiating an audit

This case study focuses on a large junior school with links to a separate feeder infants' school. Following a governors' curriculum sub-committee meeting to consider the creation of a Sex Education Policy, it was considered inappropriate for sex education to stand alone. From that understanding it was recognised that there was a need for this issue to be incorporated within a general PSE policy. Consequently the PSE co-ordinator, together with the infant school head teacher and the shared named governor formed a sub-committee to initiate the PSE policy. Following preliminary discussions the two schools set about developing their own individual policies.

At this stage the PSE co-ordinator in the junior school was freed to seek out further information and expertise in this area. This included consultation with Higher Education Staff and the LEA Health Education Office. A meeting was arranged for the Health Education Officer to talk to the staff in order to raise awareness and develop their knowledge of health education and PSE. Following this, it was decided that an audit of existing PSE work should be undertaken in order to identify and clarify current practice in the classroom.

A sub-group from the junior staff was then formed, consisting of the PSE co-ordinator, who was also a year head, the three other year heads and the named governor. This group was given one week of non-contact time to conduct the audit. Initially the headings from the HEA Primary School Health Survey were adapted into monitoring sheets on which each class teacher recorded where they delivered their current PSE curriculum. The sub-group year heads then completed more detailed planning and monitoring sheets designed by the co-ordinator in order to identify the content and coverage in more detail.

Three strands were identified and each was further broken down into sub-headings. Strand one, Looking After Myself, included aspects such as personal hygiene, safety and sex education. Strand two, Relationships, included aspects such as friendship, responsible attitudes and social skills. Strand three, Community and Environment, included community service and care of the environment. Appropriate subject areas and National Curriculum links were then identified for each sub-heading as were links between the strands. The co-ordinator and year heads were then able to match work already covered for each sub-heading.

The involvement of the teachers at this initial stage was crucial for raising awareness of the extent to which PSE work was already being undertaken and to reinforce a positive belief in the teachers' own PSE delivery. It also provided opportunities for participation and informal discussion amongst the staff.

From this audit gaps were identified and recommendations made for future PSE provision. These recommendations were circulated and discussed with the staff and governors and from them a policy and programme are currently in preparation.

It is significant that the recommendations included a separate timetabled slot which would be used to focus specifically on PSE in areas such as 'equal opportunities, safety issues and personal awareness which need a more sensitive and pastoral approach' (School Working Group Recommendations, 1994, unpub.). This suggests that in practice PSE cannot be entirely provided for through the National Curriculum core and foundation subjects.

Throughout, the head teacher supported the work of the co-ordinator by giving her realistic levels of non-contact time, funding to attend courses and access to teacher and pupil resources. The time period for preparation was also realistic and limited to one year in total to ensure its completion. The head signalled clearly that the issue had priority and status within the school.

The strengths of this approach are:

1 The long-term commitment of the head teacher to PSE.
2 The investment of time and expertise in the PSE co-ordinator, creating a stable and knowledgeable base.
3 The starting point of an identified and recognised need and therefore a clear purpose to the audit.
4 The precision of the audit.
5 The potential of the audit for future planning, co-ordination and monitoring of PSE.
6 The audit was linked to National Curriculum subjects to ensure that PSE is embedded within the taught curriculum.
7 Staff involvement was incorporated into specific stages in the audit and formulation of the policy.
8 There was involvement of a named governor in detailed initiation of policy and practice.
9 There was cross-phase consultation.

The constraints:

1 PSE was identified in the audit as predominantly content-based with less emphasis on the process of teaching and learning strategies. These processes are necessary to develop skills and attitudes which will support the actual on-going personal and social development of the children (e.g. co-operative group work, problem solving, experimental work and role play).
2 In the audit, there was a class focus which may disregard the impact of the whole-school context on personal and social development, such as assemblies, the playground environment, whole-school rewards and sanctions policy.

The audit is a useful device whereby a PSE co-ordinator can critically evaluate the school's current practice and begin to move towards a comprehensive planned approach. The constraints identified in this case study are not insurmountable. The next stage of the process might be to identify explicitly the values and attitudes that the staff as a group consider to be the most important for PSE. Only when discussion has resulted in an agreed consensus, the most difficult part of the process, can appropriate teaching and learning strategies necessary for underpinning the PSE programme be specified and put into practice in all classes.

The staff discussion on values and attitudes would also enable the school to move towards further critical examination of the whole-school context. Management strategies, hierarchy, rituals, rules, routines, rewards, sanctions, supervision and arrangements for children with special needs, can be reviewed in terms of how they currently support the values and attitudes identified by the staff and, more importantly, how they might be adapted or changed in order to add further support to PSE (see Figure 4.3).

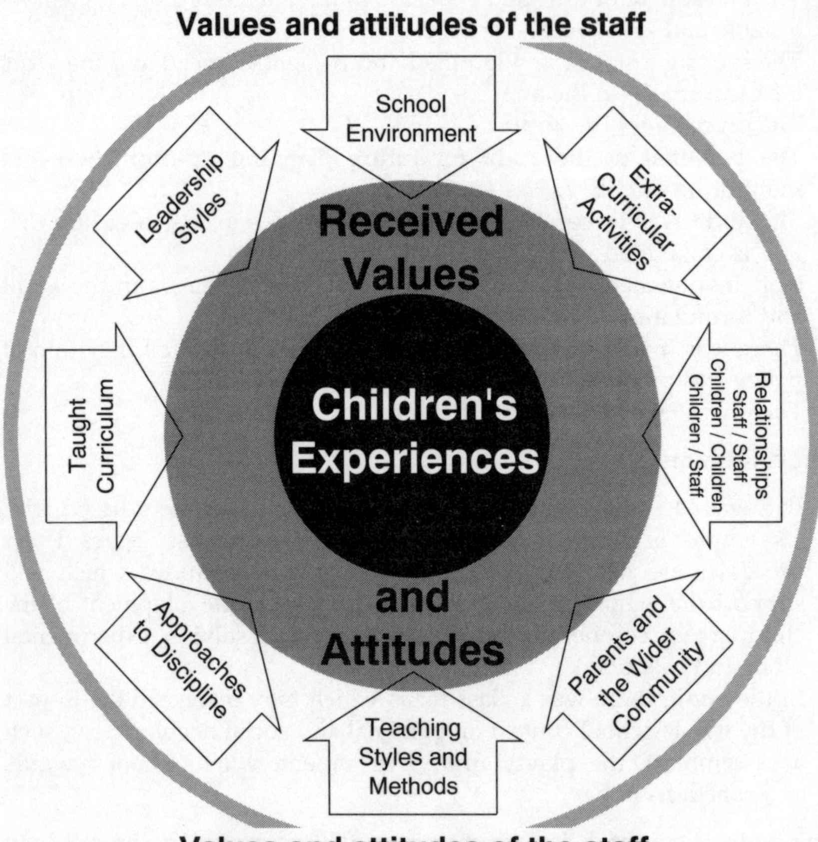

Figure 4.3 Values and attitudes of the staff

Thus the implicit is made explicit. The PSE co-ordinator is therefore better able to ensure a co-ordinated approach whereby there is a closer match between the school's aims for personal and social development and whole-school practice.

Herbert (1993) confirms the importance of staff clarifying for themselves and opening up to public scrutiny the values, attitudes and personal qualities which the school views as significant. In this way relevant classroom teaching strategies and methodologies which actively encourage, support and further develop the skills and attitudes required for personal and social competence can be identified and incorporated within the school's curriculum planning framework.

The matrix (Table 4.1) has been constructed using key issues which Pring (1984) suggests classroom teachers need to consider in order to translate values and attitudes into supportive practice. The values and attitudes presented in the matrix can be used as a starting point for schools who wish to undertake an audit of the affective curriculum. It can also be used for subsequent planning, monitoring and evaluation by class teachers and the co-ordinator (see Table 4.2).

Case study 2: The structured pastoral care model

This study focuses on a large primary school with 410 pupils, 14 teachers, one full-time nursery nurse and two part-time nursery nurses with two deputies, one in each key stage. The head, two deputies and two class teachers form the senior management team. Responsibility for pastoral care rests with three designated team leaders representing infants, lower juniors and upper juniors. The upper junior team leader is one of the deputies and so provides the link between management and pastoral teams. There is no PSE co-ordinator because PSE is seen as a function of pastoral care.

The head teacher is a powerful direct communicator with very clear requirements and a tangible rationale. He establishes a clear and resilient structure to his organisation. This structure aims to maximise the achievement of personal and social development of the children as well as supporting an efficient delivery of the National Curriculum. Within this organisational structure there are clear, designated responsibilities.

Pastoral responsibilities extend at Year 6 to embrace strong links with the secondary school. Pastoral care includes discipline, with the resolution of disciplinary issues being the responsibility of the team leaders. Mid Day Assistants (MDA) are given training and support and meet with the head on a regular basis where the agenda is set at every other meeting by the MDAs.

In the head teacher's view pastoral care is a vital precursor to effective learning and this is reflected in the explicit provision for personal and social development. Children are involved in setting their own targets for development and reviewing them termly. The priorities of the school are seen as the twin goals of pastoral care and National Curriculum management.

Empowerment represents the key word for the school, for children, parents and staff. There is a determined commitment to the involvement of parents in a variety of ways in their child's education and the running of the school. There is a categoric affirmation of the vital importance of partnership with parents. Parental involvement begins with a pre-school

Table 4.1 Planning matrix for PSE (adapted from Pring, 1984, p. 110)

Values/ attitudes	Teaching methods	Classroom procedures/ routines	School procedures/ routines	Curriculum subjects	Extra-curricular activities
1 Mutual respect					
2 Caring and fairness					
3 Sense of achievement/ personal worth					
4 Deliberation and reflective learning					
5 Discussion of social/moral issues					
6 Co-operative learning					
7 Care for group and wider community					
8 Group responsibilities /decision making					

programme that has established strong links between the nursery feeder school, play groups and the primary school. There is a book loan service for pre-school children, home visits by the reception teacher to all starters before they come, meetings for parents, workshops and booklets. There are parent representatives for each class on the PTA.

Pastoral care for staff is evident in a strong commitment to their well-being and career development. There is open access to courses and to the head teacher.

Strengths of this approach:

1 Clarity of purpose, responsibilities and methods.
2 A rationale which is explicit and comprehensive.
3 The structure of delegation allows for ownership and a resilient system which survives staff absence or departure.
4 There are clear links between staff as post holders, clear lines of communication and awareness of dovetailing of roles. It is a co-ordinated management structure.
5 Respect and involvement of all staff, children and parents is based on a genuine belief in their value and self-worth. The system has integrity.
6 The system has its own in-built monitoring capability. It is self-regulating.

Constraints:

1 The system demands personal commitment from every member of the staff to the high profile and involvement of the parents. Not all staff may be able to do this.
2 The presence of formal structures for pastoral care could lead to individual class teachers abdicating their responsibility to the children in their class.

This approach and organisation requires strong leadership and a determination to translate a philosophy and belief into external structures and tangible responsibilities. The governors would need to be, not only taken along with the ideology, but also become fundamentally committed to the approach so that change of headship would not disrupt the continuity of belief.

Case study 3: The climate approach

This school is a 5–11 age range mainstream primary school. The school is designated by the LEA as supportive and appropriate for statemented children with physical disability. In addition they have a number of children previously excluded from other schools for behavioural difficulties. The opening up of the school to children with specific learning difficulties has radically changed the staff's and children's perceptions and awareness of disability and challenged hidden stereotypes.

Table 4.2 Audit/planning for PSE

Values/attitudes NB These are examples; schools will need to devise their own.	Teaching methods	Classroom procedure/routines	School procedure/routine	Curriculum subjects	Extra-curricular activities
1. Mutual respect	Problem-solving. Co-op group work. Paired work. Discussion. Visits and visitors. Teachers and children - negotiating. Teaching using democratic processes (when appropriate).	Rota of classroom helpers – *all* children involved. Parent helpers. Equal opportunities *practice*. Circle time. Newstime 'show and tell'. Displays.	Assembly, e.g. good work assembly. Themes, e.g. 'We are all special'. Class assemblies. Parental involvement. Projects. Programmes. Links with local SEN units/schools.	RE English Drama	Sport. Visitors. Parental involvement. Educational visits. Residential visits.
2. Sense of personal worth/achievement	Range of opportunities for *all* children to succeed (not just in core subjects). Teacher focuses on children's strengths. Drafting work. Practising skills. Partner work. Opportunities for reflection.	Specific self-esteem work (see Resources). Rewards system. Class assemblies. Display: range of curriculum areas/children. Sharing personal successes (in and out of school) with own class and others.	Reward system. Good work/behaviour assembly. Letters home regarding achievements. Praise cards. Badges. School helpers, e.g. greeting and escorting visitors to school.	All subjects (opportunities for and recognition of achievement for all levels)	Clubs, e.g. IT Gymnastics Dance Chemistry Art Sport

3. Care for group and wider community	Local environment and community used as a learning resource in a variety of curriculum subjects. Visits/visitors. Group work. Problem-solving activities. Teacher and children share ideas/feelings/experiences. Teacher develops links with parents and local community.	Class rules. Class helpers. Circle time. Problem-solving and mediation techniques used to resolve conflict.	School discipline policy - rules, rewards, sanctions. Anti-bullying strategies. Training and support for MDAS. Parental links, e.g. home visiting. Local community links. Development of school yard/gardens/field.	History Geography RE Health education	Local community links. Home/school links. Sport.
4.					
5.					
6.					
7.					

The head teacher is the co-ordinator for PSE. He identifies PSE as being subsumed within the climate of the school. He takes a central leadership role in determining the interpersonal climate and sees this as focusing strongly on the relationship between the teacher and the child. His rationale is that policy should arise from practice not vice versa and that the climate of the school should create a supportive atmosphere which includes a 'sensitive understanding of the child's life beyond the classroom' (interview notes).

He stresses that the key to establishing an effective climate is communication and that this is critical. He notes that communication between children, parents and colleagues is significant. The climate should be wholly positive and enable growth. This is achieved by maintaining an open-door policy, by seeing and being seen around the school and by taking the first part of the Inset day in September to reiterate the school's philosophy of a child-centred focus to the work of the school.

The approach with staff is indistinguishable from the climate overall. There is a caring, positive, developmental approach to all employees, with individual access to the head teacher, an avoidance of hierarchy from the lunch time assistants to the teachers and an avoidance of labelling (for example there are no curriculum co-ordinators). Instead, there is team-work, consultation with teachers with special interests, school-based Inset for all in preference to named individuals attending courses and good communication networks.

Within the general climate for personal and social development there are specific elements which have been adopted by interested teachers. These include equal opportunities provision, the child's environment at work and play and health education.

The focus on successful academic achievement is centred on two mutually dependent components. The first is the teachers' ability to plan and deliver the curriculum to match the children's needs, a curriculum which is predominantly based on the child's previous experience, which is structured and delivered in a supportive way, and one in which the child can succeed.

The second component is the enhancing of the child's own sense of self-worth, confidence and security, so that the child can tackle the unfamiliar and challenging without fear of failure. The head teacher expressed concern about the development of a society that values material and academic success and encourages ruthlessness in obtaining it.

The head teacher sees residential experiences for the staff and children as an essential part of the children's PSE. The children learn to live with their peer group, develop survival skills in terms of self-care and organisation and it gives them an opportunity to see their teachers in a less formal setting. Knowledge of the children and the opportunity to see the children exhibit aspects of their personality not shown normally in school gives the teachers the chance to enhance their own understanding of the children.

Pastoral care is a term not used within the school but when pressed the head teacher defined it as creating an environment that enables 'children to be sufficiently at ease to talk with you [the staff] as they would to their parents'. Pastoral care is not just about 'patching up' hurt, but should be positive and encourage personal growth.

Discipline issues are dealt with on a personal and negotiated basis. The emphasis is on positive praise. The school has recently adopted a reward system involving 'good work' badges handed out at a 'good work' assembly, three badges lead to a permanent badge with age-related logos. The system is at present well received by the children.

Strengths of this approach:

1 The approach is one with strong leadership and personal responsibility.
2 The head teacher leads by example and enthuses rather than commands.
3 The formal structures are kept to the minimum, instead the emphasis is on daily practice, efficiency achieved by communication and openness.
4 Instead of sub-dividing the specific components thereby fragmenting the PSE, it unites them under one approach, one individual, the whole-school ethos.

Constraints:

1 The model can only be effective if initiated and run by the head. It requires power, influence and opportunity.
2 If the head teacher leaves the system could fall.
3 The present educational and social climate militates against a child-centred approach. There may be criticism.

Case study 4: The nursery school

This study is of a 120 place part-time nursery school with a head teacher, three nursery teachers, three nursery nurses and a classroom assistant. The school is set in an established council estate with high levels of unemployment. Children from the nursery feed into infant schools in close proximity to the nursery.

The head teacher is, in effect, the co-ordinator of PSE in the nursery. Her dual role as leader and member of the nursery team enables her to be particularly effective in this capacity. She sees PSE as empowering children and parents. The process of empowering children can only be achieved if each child is seen within the context of his or her family and the wider community as well as the school.

Many parents come to the school with a view that the nursery staff have 'the answers' and so they can 'hand over' their children confident in the staff's ability and expertise to begin the process of formal education. The school's philosophy, however, is based on the notion of partnership with parents in the educative process.

The school feels it is important to enable parents to appreciate the crucial role that they have already played in their children's education. The head teacher makes it explicit that parental contribution is valued and respected and needs to continue through partnership with the school for the benefit of child, parent and staff. This partnership is achieved through carefully considered strategies which begin by introducing new parents and children to the school through home visits, pre-entry visits and facilities such as a loan resource for books and toys. This will set the climate for a parent–school partnership which the head sees as a central focus for PSE within the school.

A major feature of this school's approach to PSE is Records of Achievement (ROA). The involvement of children and parents in the process of constructing ROAs ensures their use as a vehicle to form and develop relationships, to generate an exchange of information and to give tangible evidence of the children's achievement and parents' contribution. They underpin the school's approach to PSE and pastoral care.

The strengths of this approach are:

1 The head teacher assumes a central role and is involved 'day to day' with the nursery team, children and their families. She is therefore able to co-ordinate effectively.
2 The active involvement of the parents, especially their role in compiling ROAs, facilitates the co-ordinating role of the head teacher.
3 This nursery supports a holistic approach to working with young children encompassing the child and his/her family.
4 The involvement of parents ensures recognition of their worth. It raises the profile of their involvement in the education of the child and the part they play in PSE.
5 The parents' view of what constitutes education is broadened.

Constraints:

1 Effective co-ordination of PSE could stop at the conclusion of the nursery stage.
2 The nursery is not in control of how or if ROAs are used at the next stage of education. Does their effectiveness end after nursery?
3 The level of partnership established in the nursery may not automatically continue in the next stage of the child's education.
4 It may be difficult to convince parents of the value of their role as co-educators without affecting their confidence in the professionalism of the nursery staff.

Case study 5: A nursery school for children with special educational needs

The nursery school is an assessment centre for children with a wide range of special educational needs. Where possible it also takes siblings and other children who 'don't have difficulties' (interview notes). There is a head teacher, three full-time teachers, one being the deputy head, and one part-time teacher. The teaching staff are supported by ten special schools assistants and two special needs assistants working full time plus an occupational therapist, physiotherapist and a language therapist who work at the centre on a part-time basis.

There is a clear management structure which consists of the head teacher and four teams. These are led by teachers one of whom is the deputy head. The deputy head teacher co-ordinates and supports the work of these teams ensuring that the centre's aims of valuing individuals, developing independence and involving parents are achieved.

Her responsibilities include co-ordinating issues which stem from her role in senior management, the implementation of a High/Scope (see Hohman and Weikhart, 1995) approach throughout the centre, the weekly in-house staff training and the Inset development programmes.

The school has adopted the High/Scope approach because it can provide a flexible framework for its curriculum. The key principle of High/Scope is the empowering of children through choice and decision-making. The school has adapted the plan–do–review cycle which is central to this principle, in order to 'meet the individual needs of children functioning at very different levels' (Watson, 1994, p. 1). Some of the underlying principles of High/Scope can be identified with PSE. These include:

1 Developing a positive sense of self and value for children.
2 Promoting shared power between adults and children.
3 Encouraging children to make decisions.
4 Encouraging children to develop a sense of responsibility.
5 Developing children's confidence.

The school's PSE is not a single identifiable element of the curriculum but is an integral part of all the work undertaken with children and parents. The staff aim to develop children's confidence and ability to participate socially and cope outside the security of the home environment.

As in the previous case study the high profile of parents stems from the belief that parents are primary educators of their children. Parents of children with special educational needs have a particular role to play in their child's personal and social development. The school, where necessary, helps parents to see their child as an individual who has value. It enables the parents to develop their child's physical, social, emotional and intellectual abilities through their involvement in the school and through support groups, home visiting and a Portage service. The school develops parents' decision-making skills which in turn supports the development of their role as advocates for their child.

The strengths of this approach are:

1 The management structure enables the co-ordinator to work effectively with all strands of the team.
2 The co-ordinator's role as a team leader and deputy head enables her to monitor the planning and implementation of PSE.
3 The High/Scope approach necessitates team-work which in turn promotes a whole-school approach to PSE.
4 High/Scope requires a whole-school approach, and this in turn ensures that PSE is implemented within a coherent framework.
5 The philosophy underpinning High/Scope supports many of the principles of PSE.
6 The parents are actively involved in their child's PSE.

Constraints:

1 School staff need to have a clear understanding of High/Scope in order to adapt it and use it effectively for children with special educational needs. This requires a commitment to on-going training.
2 Parents also need to have some knowledge of High/Scope and PSE which requires additional staff time and commitment.

FEATURES OF THE CASE STUDIES

Some features of good practice evident from the case studies are:

- A clear view of PSE throughout the school.
- PSE being recognised as having value in its own right.
- Explicit values and attitudes being nurtured in the school.
- PSE incorporated, in real terms, in the daily life of the school.
- Tangible evidence of structures being used to promote effective PSE.
- The development of the whole child being central to PSE.
- An inherent link between PSE and the process of pupil empowerment and achievement.

Co-ordination

- Strong, clearly defined leadership central to the co-ordinator's role.
- Clear management structures which support PSE.
- Clear lines of communication.
- Staff involvement and ownership.
- The importance of the parents' role and the need for partnership.

CONCLUSIONS: WAYS FORWARD

1 The head teacher to lead and co-ordinate PSE wherever possible in order to develop the philosophy, ethos and structures needed to promote PSE and to avoid its fragmentation. This is supported by Tattum and Tattum (1992) who identify the need for someone with 'status and authority' in order to avoid the haphazard presentation of PSE (p. 169).
2 If the co-ordinator is a member of staff s/he will need designated status, explicit support from the head teacher, clear definition of role and responsibilities, and training for the role of co-ordinator. Harwood (1992) warns of low-key approaches to curriculum innovation which lead to low status and teacher uncertainty. He advocates the enhanced status of the co-ordinator role and the need to communicate clearly the definition of the role to both co-ordinator and staff.
3 The potential for whole-school and staff development can be exploited through the co-ordination of PSE. If the co-ordinator's role is viewed as that of a potential agent of change rather than merely a subject consultant then staff and school development can go hand in hand (Edwards, 1993).
4 There is a need to review existing relevant school policies (for example, sex education and discipline and consider how they might be encompassed in a broader more coherent PSE policy).
5 Raise awareness of the importance of PSE with governors and parents.
6 Develop and extend partnerships with parents.

ACKNOWLEDGEMENTS

All schools who returned the questionnaire and the co-ordinators who contributed to the discussion group. Particular thanks to: Sycamore Lane C.P. School, Warrington; Woolston C.P. School, Warrington; Woolton Junior School, Liverpool; Stalisfield Nursery School, Liverpool; Medecroft Opportunity Centre, Winchester.

REFERENCES

Brown, C. (1990) Personal and social education: timetable ghetto or whole school practice? in B. Dufour (ed.) *The New Social Curriculum – A Guide to Cross-curricular Issues*, Cambridge: Cambridge University Press.

Edwards, A. (1993) Curriculum co-ordinator: a lost opportunity for primary school development? *School Organisation*, 13, 1, 51–59.

Harwood, D. (1992) In at the deep end: a case study of the co-ordinator in a 'low key' innovation, *School Organisation*, 12, 1, 17–25.

Herbert, G. (1993) Changing children's attitudes through the curriculum, in D. Tattum (ed.) *Understanding and Managing Bullying*, Oxford: Heinemann.

Hohman, M. and Weikhart, D. (1995) *Educating Young Children*, Michigan: High/Scope Press.

Lang, P. (ed.) (1988) *Thinking About . . . Personal and Social Education in the Primary School*, Oxford: Blackwell.
Pring, R. (1984) *Personal and Social Education in the Primary School*, Oxford: Blackwell.
Tattum, D. and Tattum, E. (1992) *Social Education and Personal Development*, London: David Fulton.
Watson, J. (1994) *High/Scope for Children with Special Educational Needs*, A Training Document, Medecroft Opportunity Centre, Winchester.

Part II

ASPECTS OF PASTORAL CARE

5

WELFARE AND LIAISON

Kate Wall

INTRODUCTION

Welfare and liaison are just two pieces of the pastoral care jigsaw which cover a wide range of educational issues. For a school to provide appropriately for the individual needs of the pupils, pastoral care issues must be dealt with within a planned pastoral care programme to ensure the children's personal and social skills are assessed and developed. In addition, procedures to deal with welfare issues that affect the children should be known to all staff members.

When children are experiencing difficulties, teachers need to observe, examine and assess the whole child, looking at all the influencing and contributing factors involved before planning an intervention programme. It should also be remembered that all children have personal and social needs throughout childhood and adolescence and therefore all children should be supported throughout their educational life. Pastoral care programmes are relevant to all children at all times.

Through consideration of the teacher's role in observation and appropriate intervention, the types of welfare issues involved, relevant legislation, the range of support services available and school/parent liaison, the importance of these issues will be highlighted and ways forward suggested.

THE ROLE OF THE TEACHER

Even in the 1960s both the Newsom Report (Central Advisory Council for Education, 1963) and the Plowden Report (CACE, 1967) referred to the importance of welfare issues within the school, the former suggesting the introduction of teacher/social workers to deal with the social problems that children experience and the latter suggesting planned support programmes, co-ordinated throughout the welfare network. The pastoral care issue had been raised, and in many schools has developed in subsequent years. Teachers are now required to be more accountable to the public, and society expects that they are able to deal effectively with the many social and welfare difficulties that can arise. Teachers, perhaps more now than ever before, have to deal with a range of children's needs, and academic achievement will partly depend on the individual child's social well-being to cope with the education offered. The underlying premise is that a child needs to be functioning emotionally and physically to achieve maximum benefit from formal education. If, through any circumstance, a child is experiencing emotional difficulties then cognitive learning may be impeded. Bloom (1976) suggested three factors which directly relate to pupil achievement, clearly demonstrating the importance of emotional stability:

- cognitive entry behaviour (thinking)
- affective entry characteristics (feelings and attitudes)
- quality of instruction (teaching)

The teacher, therefore, must consider the whole child and his/her individual needs to maximise the child's learning potential, and consequently the school must deal with the pastoral as well as the curriculum needs of the children. Hamblin (1978, p. xv) emphasises the place of pastoral care:

> Pastoral care is not something set apart from the daily work of the teacher. It is that element of the teaching process which centres around the personality of the pupil and the forces in his environment which either facilitate or impede the development of intellectual and social skills, and foster or retard emotional stability.

The need for primary school teachers to cope with welfare issues within the school situation has, therefore, become more accepted and these front-line educators are in an influential position as they see the children on a daily basis and, because of their training and expertise, are able to assess any changes in the child's academic progress or behaviour. The open door policy within many primary schools will facilitate the pastoral role of the teachers. An effective pastoral care programme combined with a working knowledge of the range of support services available will place the school in a position to help the child experiencing difficulties at any time. It may be suggested, however, that some primary schools do not have such programmes to cater for the welfare needs of the children. Crises are dealt with by teachers as they arise but a failure to know the families and understand the roles of all the supporting agencies, combined with the lack of clear procedural guidelines, may hamper appropriate intervention. Marland (1989, p. 19), discussing the relationship between parents and tutors, comments:

> the tutor should know better than anyone (other than sometimes the middle-management pastoral-team leader) the pupil's home and

family. Despite the shortage of time for tutoring, she or he should have studied the file and know the family composition, home circumstances, and attitudes. The tutor is likely to have met more often the adults caring for the pupil, and to have spoken on the phone and exchanged letters. It is to the tutor that parents or guardians should turn first for information, worries, or to make suggestions. Families should trust a tutor to speak for them and respect them.

Within the current educational climate, schools and classroom teaching have undergone considerable change over the past decade. The introduction of the National Curriculum, local management of schools and opting out to grant maintained status are just three factors that have placed considerable additional pressures on the teacher. If a school is to embark on an evaluation and update of the pastoral programme then factors such as staffing, training, resources, financial implications and good leadership skills will be crucial factors in the outcome. It should also be remembered that the school can utilise the expertise of the support network of which they are an integral part, providing advice and support throughout the evaluation process.

WELFARE ISSUES IN THE PRIMARY SCHOOL

As previously mentioned, class teachers are in the front line to observe and monitor any changes in their pupils' behaviour. Any such changes may well indicate problems, created by factors inside or outside of the school. Possible factors could include:

- Exclusion
- Non-attendance/truancy
- Bereavement
- Family breakdown
- Unemployment/low income
- Social deprivation
- Low self-esteem of the child
- Physical, sexual or emotional abuse and/or neglect
- Bullying
- Friendship problems
- Problems with academic work
- Emotional difficulties of the child
- Unrealistic expectations of parents and/or teachers
- Peer pressure

Though obviously not exhaustive this list suggests a broad range of welfare problems that might need to be covered in any primary school, and would be recognised by the majority of class teachers.

In such cases the underlying causal factor must be determined before appropriate intervention can commence. Within the primary school the class teacher, who spends the greater part of the school week with her/his own class, will have considerable knowledge of each child, their family background and their academic achievements. If the causal factor can be identified and appropriately dealt with within the school then intervention can be set in motion. If, however, the cause is from outside the school, most likely within the home, then the school may need to draw upon the resources of an outside agency.

In the primary school non-attendance/truancy can be caused by a variety of factors from embarrassment created by poor clothing, free school meals, lack of cleanliness and lack of possessions (toys), any of which can lower self-esteem, through recurrent illnesses to a genuine dislike of the teacher and/or school. The daily register monitors attendance and would highlight those children whose absences appear excessive, regular or form a recurrent pattern.

When children are known to have been abused, either through disclosure or information passed by the parents or an outside agency, the school should follow the procedures and advice laid down in the local authority guidelines. Current estimates indicate that there are at least several abused children in every primary school (Creighton, 1987, suggests 10 per cent of the child population), but sadly the school will be unaware of or have insufficient grounds to take action in many cases. The editors consider abuse further in Chapter 14.

Such difficulties as bereavement, deprivation, family breakdown and unemployment/low income may appear to be outside the teacher's role but there are instances in which the teacher can be instrumental in helping the family. The teacher may be the first professional to be approached by the family and whilst the teacher may not be able to resolve the difficulties, an introduction to the relevant outside agency may be appropriate. In other instances the family may approach the school requesting help with a problem outside the school's range, and for a variety of reasons the family may be unable to contact the relevant agency direct. Simple difficulties such as no access to a telephone and poor telephone skills can prevent some people from seeking help. Again, the school's assistance can be crucial. There are many people who simply do not have the confidence to approach some of the 'helping' agencies and therefore approach the trusted teacher/school instead, using the school as a mediator to enable an introduction.

A child's self-concept is crucial to a positive outlook and progress towards his/her full potential and a range of factors can create a positive or negative self-concept. Research, (e.g. Charlton and David, 1993) has shown a strong link between poor self-concept and low achievement and/or unacceptable behaviour, whilst the work of Charlton and David

(1989, p. 73) demonstrates the link between children's expectations of their future performances with their self-concept:

> Expectations reflect the ways in which pupils predict their own performance level. This in turn depends on previous experience. *Self-expectation* is therefore learned. It is influenced by parents, teachers, and others, who signal their expectations through their interaction with individuals.

They continue to suggest how teachers can help to improve the self-esteem of their pupils:

> Teacher characteristics such as *empathy, unconditional positive regard for pupils* and *genuineness* seem likely to encourage the growth of positive self-esteem in pupils.
>
> (Charlton and David, 1989, p. 215)

Teachers and schools are in a position to work on enhancing the self-esteem of all the children, but particularly those experiencing difficulties. Burns (cited in Charlton and David, 1990) offers six factors to enhance self-esteem:

- Making the child feel supported
- Making the child feel a responsible being
- Helping each pupil to feel competent
- Teaching the pupils to set realistic goals
- Helping the pupils to evaluate themselves realistically
- Encouraging realistic self-praise

Within the classroom situation Canfield and Wells (1976) and Lawrence (1987) both offer suggestions for enhancement work.

Friendship problems, peer pressure and bullying can be devastating to the school age child and the primary school topic-based curriculum lends itself to approach these problems. Through carefully planned topic work the issues can be raised with all the children, in a group, a single class or throughout the whole school. The involvement of the non-teaching staff is also required to ensure their general awareness of the potential problems and ability to cope with specific problems. Additional training for the mid-day supervisors, and in some instances the staff, may be appropriate.

Where children's problems arise through the development of learning difficulties then the school's special educational needs policy should clearly identify the processes of assessment, intervention and evaluation. As Jones and Charlton (1990, p. 5) suggest:

> In our attempts to provide for children with special educational needs, we are likely to encounter a variety of obstacles (e.g. lack of time, resources, knowledge) which may impede our efforts to help

> the children concerned. Those obstacles must not be brushed aside. Like all other factors which help or hinder access to learning, they must be assessed and responded to. If we are serious in our attempts to open up the breadth and depth of the curriculum for all children, we must attempt to recognise and attend to all factors which facilitate or hinder such access.

It is therefore clear that every factor impeding a child's education should be examined before effective intervention can take place, embodied within a whole-school policy.

SUPPORTING AGENCIES WITHIN THE WELFARE NETWORK

If teachers accept their changing role to encompass the welfare needs of the child as a person rather than considering only the academic child then they must also accept the need to be a working member of the welfare network. Whilst some welfare problems can be effectively dealt with within the school there are many that require the specialist skills and expertise of outside agencies. The range of agencies will include both statutory and voluntary services. Welton (1985, p. 64) recognises the important role that teachers have to play:

> The alert, concerned and well trained classroom teacher backed up by experienced senior colleagues and in some cases by counsellors, can identify children who are at risk in various ways and draw them to the attention of the appropriate profession or agency.

The range of welfare agencies has consistently increased over the years, starting with the education and health services, then the social services and now a vast range of voluntary groups and societies responding to an increasing variety of needs. If each aims to help the child and/or family then clearly effective co-operation and collaboration must exist to provide a clearly defined response to identified needs. For this to be achieved all personnel involved must understand and respect each other's role. While this may seem a tremendous task it must be remembered that teachers have a knowledge of the workings of most of the outside agencies they are likely to deal with, but perhaps a deeper understanding combined with local policies for working together would benefit all. Hamblin (1978, p. 274) suggests regular meetings to improve working relationships. He claims that:

> Both teachers and social workers would benefit from regular meetings where each discusses the viewpoint of the other profession and develops mutual respect. In some schools the social services and interested members of the staff meet on a monthly basis to discuss

topics of interest. This is a device for extending understanding and developing the links essential for effective action.

In addition to the growth of statutory and voluntary welfare agencies we have also seen a growth in school-based specialists. Many teachers have undergone additional training to enhance their expertise and broaden the scope of the school. Such specialists could include trained counsellors, home–school liaison teachers, and special educational needs teachers. Thus a picture emerges of a wider skill range within the school combined with a greater range of outside agencies. All of these agencies need to work together, with respect, commitment and understanding, to provide appropriately for all children and their families. The network of welfare support available to primary schools can be divided into three categories:

Within-school support:
- Class teacher
- Head teacher
- Curriculum co-ordinators
- Home–school liaison teacher
- Special educational needs co-ordinator/department

Area-based education department support:
- Education welfare officers
- Educational psychologists
- Special educational needs support service
- School nurse

Other area-based support services:
- Social services department
- Department of social security
- Health department
- Probation service
- Voluntary groups (e.g. NSPCC, Citizens' Advice Bureau)

Whilst all the groups involved will have their own clearly defined roles there will be, in some circumstances, occasions where the work will overlap. This is when co-operation and collaboration are crucial to ensure that the best provision is made available and to avoid the duplication of effort. However, each agency will have its own policies and framework within which to work and these may not be conducive to effective multi-disciplinary liaison. It is clear that schools, along with the other agencies, need to develop ways in which to improve the standard of multi-disciplinary work and to increase awareness and understanding. Welton (1985, p. 75) suggests three ways forward:

Firstly, by raising the general professional sensitivity to the need for collaboration and joint action to meet children's needs. Demonstrating how by working with other professions, a social worker, medical doctor, or teacher can provide much more effectively for their clients' needs. Secondly, through the development of informal contacts between members of each profession and service. Thirdly, through the development of formal systems of welfare coordination at policy making, administrative and professional levels.

As the school has the most regular contact with the child and the family it could be said that the school can be the focal point for all inter-agency work, and that inter-agency work should exist as part of an established working network rather than the result of a crisis forcing fragmented provision.

To ensure effective inter-agency liaison each agency must understand the workings of the others involved in the network. This requires an awareness of their individual roles within the network and knowledge of how and where to make contact when the need arises, ensuring prompt action is taken at relevant times. A summary of the roles of the main agencies involved within such a network follows.

Education welfare service

The education welfare service is responsible for ensuring all children in the area receive full-time education and supporting those children experiencing welfare problems.

1 Through regular visits into school officers can check the registers and discuss particular children of concern with the staff. As a result they may arrange a home visit to discuss the problems with the family, trying to identify the causal factor(s), with suggestions for action from within their own resources or from other agencies following. If after a period, non-attendance at school still remains a problem, and the parents are deemed responsible, then court action can be instigated. By developing contact with the home, the needs, stresses and concerns of the family can be understood and the school can be better placed to understand the problem the child is experiencing. This in turn should hopefully lead to appropriate help and advice being given, taken and acted upon.

2 Those schools fortunate enough to have home–school liaison teachers, who regularly undertake home visits, will already have extensive knowledge of their pupils' home and family backgrounds, but for the many schools that do not have a liaison teacher the information gathered by the education welfare officer could be critical for the pupils concerned.

3 For children with identified special educational needs, where formal statementing is required, then the education welfare officer can support the school and the parents throughout the process.
4 In cases of child abuse the education welfare officer will follow county procedures and guidance to ensure that any necessary action is taken. The officer, if having worked with the child and his/her family previously, may have important information to share and the school and parents can also be supported throughout an investigation and subsequent court action.
5 The service also provides a wealth of information to parents regarding their legal rights and responsibilities along with information on grants/funds available for children and their families.
6 Training for teachers and other professional groups can be arranged through the education welfare service on all issues related to the work of the service.

As a close link between the home, the child, the school and other agencies, the education welfare officers play an important supportive role, bringing them into regular contact with most of the supporting agencies.

Educational psychology service

Educational psychologists are qualified and experienced teachers who have undergone additional psychology training and are available to help children with problems they may be experiencing within or outside of the school setting.

When a school needs additional professional help to assess the difficulties of pupils and either advise them of appropriate intervention strategies, or counsel the child to enable them to cope themselves, then the educational psychology service can be called in. Through careful assessment and observation the psychologist can advise the school on ways forward, submitting verbal or written reports as appropriate. Typically, the educational psychologist would be called in to help with specific emotional and behavioural difficulties, physical difficulties, sensory impairment and/or learning difficulties, and, in cases where formal assessment is instigated, written reports by the psychologist will be required by the local education authority. The assessments undertaken may take place over a period of time and could include observation, developmental assessment, psychometric assessment, attainment testing and interviewing. Throughout the assessment process the psychologist will be in close contact with the parents with whom a close working partnership is crucial.

The educational psychology service is also available to parents, either through the school or directly, to seek help and information. In addition they can advise the local authority on all issues related to the special educational needs of children and are often instrumental at senior management level in local authority policy making. Collaboration with other services is a vital part of the work.

Training can be arranged by the psychology service for parents, school staff members and other professional groups in such areas as; assessment, current and/or new legislation, special needs, roles of special needs co-ordinators, roles of mid-day supervisors, parental liaison, behaviour difficulties and curriculum management.

Social Services Department

Within the local social services, which provides for all people experiencing social difficulties, will be a department catering for the needs of the children and their families within the area. In times of difficulty or crisis the social services will work with the family, suggesting help and strategies to alleviate the difficulties being experienced and attempting to keep the family together throughout. Unless the children are deemed to be at risk then the social services will work, sometimes over considerable periods of time, to alleviate the problems. By helping the family identify the causal factors and offering support and help to reduce the difficulties it is hoped that the family will progress, and become more able to cope and care for their children as a functioning unit.

Within the service a wide range of support and advice can be offered:

- Children's homes for those children either unable to remain at home or with no home
- Day care services, including local family centres for parents with children under school age, plus after-school clubs in some cases
- Provision for children who want to be fostered or adopted, plus advice for prospective foster and adoptive parents
- Registration and inspection service for all care providers
- Advice and counselling for parents experiencing difficulties
- Specialist provision and support for children with disabilities
- Protection of children at risk emotionally, physically, sexually or through neglect
- Advice on support, benefits and practical help families can receive
- Assessing the short- and long-term needs of families and children

The nature of the work gives social workers, like teachers, considerable knowledge about the families with which they work, and it is clear that liaison is essential. The professionals complement each other well and in many instances the gathering of information will be in the best interests of the family and child, so clear procedures for the regular sharing of information should be established, bearing in mind the code of confidentiality. Marland (1974, p. 177) suggests:

The generic social worker has much important and confidential information about the child which will be of great value to the teacher. Likewise, the teacher will have much valuable information which will greatly assist the generic social worker in his or her work. Although the school will be asked to supply periodic reports about children in care, there is a need for teachers and generic social workers to be in personal contact so that meaningful and helpful information can be passed from one to the other. (People are usually prepared to be far more frank in their speech than in their writing.) Confidential information will only be shared if there is mutual trust and professional regard.

Health Service

The physical state of health of a child is crucial to ensure overall development and the health service (considered also in Chapter 6), with its wide range of specialists, promotes the well-being of all school-aged children in the locality. From birth, the health visitor attached to the local GP practice will monitor the child's development, assessing progress at regular intervals. If at any time the health visitor is concerned, the child can be referred on to a specialist for further and more detailed assessment. From an educational standpoint the health visitors are crucial in the early identification of the full range of special educational needs, ensuring referral and assessment leading to appropriate pre-school placement. The health visitor also monitors the immunisation programme for all pre-school children and on school entry the programme is transferred to the school medical service.

The school medical service, as part of the local health service, monitors pupils' progress throughout the school years. In the primary phase regular medicals, including immunisations and dental checks, are held as a matter of routine. Parental permission is sought for these medicals and it would be quite rare that a parent would refuse unless there were problems they wished not to disclose. Schools and parents can also request medicals for specific reasons at any time. When specific problems are highlighted then the school doctor and/or school nurse can refer the child on to the appropriate medical specialist or clinic for further investigations.

Department of Social Security

The Department of Social Security is responsible for providing financial support, and in some cases material help, to people and families who are unemployed, disabled, homeless and/or sick. Schools will not usually become directly involved with the department but may have families who are in receipt of state benefits. School clothing grants, milk subsidies and free school meals are funded by the department and there may be occasions when parents approach the school for advice on benefits they are entitled to. Familiarity with the benefit system and a source of contact within the department would be helpful, as would the availability of information leaflets within the school.

Probation Service

The role of the probation service is to monitor, advise and support offenders on probation and thus will not come into contact with the primary school unless exceptional circumstances exist. However their role with juvenile offenders will often involve close liaison work with the family which may include younger siblings attending primary school. As probation officers are trained in family counselling they may well need to share certain information with the school, to the benefit of the younger siblings. Stresses and tensions created at home by the offender will often have an effect on the other family members.

Voluntary groups and organisations

As previously mentioned the range of voluntary groups aiming to help children and families has grown considerably and includes:

- Catholic Marriage Guidance Council
- Childminders' Association
- Citizens' Advice Bureau
- Contact-a-Family
- Dr Barnardo's
- Gingerbread
- National Children's Bureau
- National Children's Homes
- National Council for One-parent Families
- NSPCC (National Society for the Prevention of Cruelty to Children)
- Playgroups Association
- RELATE (Marriage guidance)
- Samaritans
- Victim Support Group

The NSPCC is probably the most well-known of the above agencies and as a charity of long-standing provides a wide range of services to the public. Perhaps best known for their work in child abuse cases the NSPCC has its own telephone helpline where advice and support can be found for children and adults alike. If appropriate the social services department, local NSPCC branch and the police will work together. In addition, information and training are offered on a range of child welfare issues.

Whilst it is not practicable for schools to be familiar with the workings of every agency it is valuable to be aware of their existence to pass on information to families experiencing difficulties or in crisis. In most areas the local Citizens' Advice Bureau would be a good source of contact for finding out the availability and aims of local welfare groups.

EFFECTS AND RELEVANCE OF RECENT LEGISLATION

Education is constantly undergoing legislative change and perhaps never more so than during the past ten to fifteen years. An examination of the most far-reaching legislation, highlighting the main areas to affect schools will be discussed.

Today's education practice and law stems from the Education Act of 1944 (DES, 1944) making education compulsory for all children from the age of 5 years. In addition school sessions were governed and registration was introduced to monitor attendance.

The Warnock Report (DES, 1978) examined the needs of children with special educational needs, suggesting that 20 per cent of the child population would experience special educational needs at some point during their education. At that time 2 per cent were receiving their education within special schools. The issue of integrated provision was highlighted, Warnock recommending full integration where possible, and the importance of effective multi-disciplinary work was emphasised. The Education Act of 1981, which followed the publication of the Warnock Report, legislated for children with special educational needs, giving new terminology and making it the responsibility of the local education authority to identify and provide effectively for children aged 2 years and over. Formal assessments were introduced leading to a statement of need for the individual child laying down the provision required by the local authority to address those needs.

The 1986 Education Act stipulated the policy documents to be produced by each school and changed the format of the governing body. However the Education Reform Act of 1988 overtook the previous Act changing the legislation again, whilst the 1988 Act brought radical changes to the education system effecting considerable change. The key changes were:

- The introduction of the National Curriculum, dividing the curriculum into four key stages.
- The introduction of statutory assessment and testing at the ages of 7, 11, 14 and 16 years.

- Parental choice of open enrolment to schools, with the Secretary of State setting the admission levels.
- Local Management of Schools (LMS) giving the control of finances to the individual school via the general schools budget received from central government plus additional monies for individual schools calculated through formula funding.
- The option for schools to apply for grant-maintained status (opting out) whereby the school is released from local authority direction and the governing body has greater control over all aspects of the running of the school.
- The option to create City Technical Colleges.

The main effect this legislation has on the pastoral care of the school is through the increased power given to governors, the national curriculum and LMS leaving the priority of pastoral care programmes very much to the discretion of staff and governors. In addition, staff training opportunities in pastoral work now depend on the agreement of the school for funding, whereas previously the local education authority would provide the funding and/or the courses available to staff. As Charlton and David (1989, p. 149) suggest:

> Local management of schools is likely to reduce the advisory and supportive roles of local education authorities, of which an increasingly centralised government is so sadly dismissive and apparently ill-informed. With in-service work being financed from school budgets there may be less support for teachers' development in pastoral as well as academic work.

The change of emphasis forcing testing and examination results to the fore when competing, in market fashion, with other schools, may well deflect curriculum planning from the pastoral field, which is not tested or judged in any way. It may be suggested, however, that without effective pastoral care programmes the children as people may well be overlooked, their academic achievements being the only concern. Without that pastoral care many children will not be achieving the academic results that the school is working towards.

The Children Act of 1989 brought together all the previous private and public law regarding children and whilst it may be seen as legislation affecting, for the most part, the social services departments, there are implications for schools. The key points within the Act are:

- A new term of 'parental responsibility' for all people who have rights and responsibilities to an individual child.
- The welfare principle is introduced stating that the welfare of the child is paramount in all cases and that the wishes and feelings of the child should be taken into account.

- Court proceedings should only be instigated as a last resort and delay should always be kept to a minimum.
- New court orders appear, namely Section 8 orders and care and supervision orders to replace all existing orders, offering unity in all family courts.
- The duties of the local authority regarding the provision of services for children and families are laid down, including the registration and inspection of all providers, the provision of accommodation for those in need, investigative responsibilities, duties regarding children in local authority care and complaints procedures.
- Introduction of new laws regarding child protection cases, combined with clearly defined procedures, all stressing the importance of effective multi-disciplinary child protection work.

The Children Act has implications for all welfare agencies, including schools, as familiarity with the workings of the Act and close liaison with other welfare agencies are seen as crucial. Hodgson and Whalley (1992, p. 21) reinforce the need for co-operation:

> The 1989 Children Act, particularly through its recognition of children in need, could have important, valuable implications for the work of pastoral care in schools. These implications, and the advantages that should come with them, will only be realised if there are discussions, based on the Act's requirements, between Education and Social Services at one level or another.

Following the Children Act a joint document entitled *Working Together Under the Children Act, 1989* was produced by the Home Office, Department of Health, Department of Education and Science and Welsh Office to highlight the need for multi-disciplinary co-operation with regard to the protection of children in need. *Working Together* outlines the roles of all agencies that may be involved in such cases and suggests planned approaches to co-operation and collaboration. The document suggests that:

> There are a number of essential concepts which need to be accepted by all those who provide services under the inter-agency arrangements described in this Guide. The basis of an effective child protection service must be that professionals and individual agencies work together on a multi-disciplinary basis, with a shared mutual understanding of aims, of objectives and of what is good practice. This should take into account the sensitive issues associated with gender, race, culture and disability.
>
> (1989, p. 25)

In 1993, the Education Act and code of practice were brought into force, changing again the field of special educational needs. The new legislation brought the 1981 Education Act up to date and laid out clear principles and procedures for local education authorities and schools. In the process it also took on board the relevant changes from the acts of 1986 and 1988. The 1993 Act introduced the following:

- Five-stage model for intervention and assessment
- Responsibilities and duties of governing bodies
- School special educational needs policies and annual report
- Role of the school's special educational needs co-ordinator
- Record keeping

LIAISON WITH PARENTS

When children begin their education the school does not take over responsibility of that education but rather becomes partners with the parents. Until school age is attained the parents are the educators, using their skills and expertise to enable the child to learn to walk, talk, eat and so on. The school will add specialist expertise to enable the child to work towards achieving his/her full potential, but this learning will take place alongside the continuing education at home. To achieve maximum benefit the parents and the school should become active partners.

In the majority of primary schools the open door policy welcomes parents at any time and works towards a real interactive partnership with the parents and families of the pupils, as well as the local community. In the primary phase there are many initiatives to involve parents, friends and the local community in the day-to-day life of the school, to the benefit of all concerned, not least the children.

Recent legislation encourages the role of parents and has greatly increased parental power and choice. Within the school welfare system an open, active partnership with parents should help lead to the resolution of difficulties being experienced by the parents, the children and/or the school.

Many schools will have social and fund-raising events and parents' evenings, each of which will bring parents into the school. Much greater effort is needed, however, through a planned programme to ensure full, effective parental involvement within school life. With effective working relationships comes the acceptance and respect of the roles of all parties involved. It is often the case that the parents teachers really need to see at parents' evenings are invariably the ones that do not attend, but little effort is made to find out why they did not attend or to remedy the situation.

If parents are simply to be used in schools to perform menial tasks then the effect on the children will be negligible, but if the skills of parents are respected and utilised the benefits could be tremendous. Bell and Best (1986, p. 126) encourage the recognition of parental skills:

> Despite a long series of prestigious and official reports (Newsom, 1963; Plowden, 1966; Court, 1976) the majority of schools underestimate, undervalue and underuse the contributions parents make in the education of their children. As an educational resource, the parents must be the most neglected items of teacher support, and the influence they have on their children is either barely grasped or else crudely cited as a factor in explaining poor performance.

Social deprivation and poor parenting are often cited by teachers as causal factors for a range of difficulties experienced by their pupils, combined with the view that parental apathy exacerbates the situation. However parental views have rarely been sought so these opinions may be presumptuous. Some parents only encounter schools when they are summoned to attend to discuss their child's behaviour and/or performance or to support the school's events. If they felt they were a part of their child's learning process then successful interaction could result. In some instances circumstances exist outside the school situation and school control that will, nevertheless, have an effect on the emotional well-being of the child. Whilst the schools cannot change those circumstances they can support the child and his/her needs involving other welfare agencies as appropriate, taking into account the dynamics within the family structure.

Home visits by teachers, before and after school entry, are time-consuming, but can help to create strong relationships between home and school. Within the family home, barriers are lifted and parents feel more confident in their familiar setting without 'professionals' seated behind desks to confront.

Investment in a planned programme to encourage and promote good relationships will pay many dividends to the school, to the pupils and to the parents. In this era of accountability and open enrolment offering parental choice it is crucial that schools take on board the issues to help promote their schools within the locality. In addition all pupils will benefit either directly or indirectly.

Conclusion

Welfare and liaison are crucial aspects of school life that need addressing in a planned and co-ordinated way to ensure welfare support is available to all who need it. It is not sufficient to respond only to crises. Schools need to improve liaison with parents and the extended welfare network to utilise all the expertise and skills available whenever they are needed. Familiarity with the workings of other agencies is essential for all members of staff, not just the teaching staff, and systems should be established to ensure regular contact and liaison. Teachers are not social workers and cannot solve problems outside of their training and skills, so need to be aware of this network to support children and families. Combine the knowledge of and respect for other agencies with good working relationships and this should lead to a more enabling education which regards all the needs of the children. The school needs to have a support programme in force to deal with these needs.

CASE STUDY

Stephen attended the local opportunity centre providing for pre-school children with special educational needs. He had been attending for 11 months and was originally referred with global developmental delay. The home–school liaison teacher of the local infant school was invited to attend his progress review prior to school entry, where transfer to mainstream school was recommended and agreed upon. Prior to school entry the home–school liaison teacher needed to complete a pre-school record sheet for Stephen and an appointment was made for Stephen and his mum to combine this with a school visit. It took three subsequent appointments before they appeared in school. Mum seemed supportive of all the help Stephen had already received and was quite adamant that he was now ready for school entry.

Mum did not attend any of the pre-school introductory meetings and Stephen did not attend any of his pre-school visits so the home–school liaison teacher undertook several home visits. The home situation was quite disturbing, with very poor standards of care and hygiene and only basic furnishings.

In September Stephen did not appear at school and another home visit was made. Mum had forgotten his start date. He did, however, start the following week, being quite reasonably presented.

Over the next few months many worrying signs were noted within the school:

- Mum's new co-habitee arrived in school to inform us that dad had left and he was assuming the role of step-father. Three days later he returned to make unfounded complaints against the school, being verbally abusive to the head teacher and home–school liaison teacher. Within an hour he telephoned the school to apologise and inform them that as Stephen's behaviour was unmanageable he was to live with his father.
- Stephen's progress in school had been negligible in the first 2 months and he had been observed as being disruptive and unco-operative in class. He had very poor attention and concentration skills and had been observed scavenging for food although he brought crisps for break and had a free school meal.
- Stephen now presented as a dirty, unkempt child with inadequate clothing.

At the beginning of his second term in school the home–school liaison teacher became involved in the preparation of his younger brother David for school the following September. He currently attended the local opportunity centre. At this stage the social services department had become involved as the opportunity centre staff were becoming increasingly concerned about David's apparent neglect. The mother and her partner had been visited by the social worker and been advised that improved conditions were essential for the future health and safety of the children.

The school was invited to participate in a case conference which was called to examine recommendations to help both the children and the whole family (who now had four children under 4 years of age). Parental support at this point declined drastically and the school became the target of much abuse as they were the first daily contact point. The case conference recommended that all four children be placed on the 'at risk' register for neglect. Sadly, the family continued to resent and oppose any intervention, support or advice from the agencies involved and a further catalogue of difficulties presented over subsequent months. A core group, comprising the social worker, head of the opportunity centre, home–school liaison teacher and health visitor met on a regular basis to co-ordinate the support that was being given, but, without the parental involvement, it was a very difficult and distressing situation. All the professionals were in agreement that the family should be kept together if at all possible, to minimise the disruption for the children which would just exacerbate their current social and emotional difficulties, which in turn affected their learning abilities. However, following evidence of physical abuse on two of the children, constant verbal and threatened physical abuse on the professionals, combined with a blanket avoidance of advice rendered, court action became the only option to protect the children. After many court attendances, initially offering assessment and intensive help which was not subsequently taken up, the courts decided that Stephen and David should be taken into care and the younger siblings (by now there were six children) were all placed on the 'at risk' register. As soon as the two eldest were removed into foster care the family moved out of county and no contact was made with the children despite appointments being made at their request for supervised access-appointments they failed to attend.

Although the outcome was far from ideal the welfare network had worked closely throughout, each agency offering their specific skills for the benefit of the children. There were obviously occasions when disagreements arose but through regular meetings the multi-disciplinary co-operation worked well, with each agency respecting the roles of each other. Whilst several agencies were involved the school was the focal point of all interaction, due to the daily contact with the family. The final outcome was, for the children, the only satisfactory option, and it is known that despite all the emotional difficulties they experienced they have since settled well and are progressing well at their new school. The original school addressed the needs of the children through a combination of play therapy work, establishing a close relationship between the children and the home–school liaison teacher and working with the special needs teacher. Through effective multi-disciplinary collaboration and co-operation these children had been supported through a tremendously difficult and traumatic period of their young lives.

POSSIBLE INSET AGENDA

Suggestions for discussion leading to increased awareness of relevant issues and preparation of whole-school policy on welfare and liaison.

1 Brainstorm: what problems now arise in school that would, in the past, be viewed as outside of the teachers domain?
Are these dealt with effectively?
How could improvements be made?

2 What resources are available for the staff to draw upon?
- Within the school
- Within the local community
- Within other professional agencies
- Within the network of voluntary organisations/agencies

Are all staff aware of these resources?
Are these resources sufficient?

3 How aware are the staff of the roles and responsibilities of other agencies?
If they are not aware how can this be encouraged?
How can effective multi-disciplinary co-operation and collaboration be brought about?

4 Is there a local multi-disciplinary forum to discuss the issues and any problems being experienced?
If not, is one needed?

5 Are effective working relationships in existence with the other relevant agencies?
If not, should they be established?
How could this be achieved?

6 Are all staff members familiar with the county guidelines on specific issues, for example child protection?
If not, how could this be addressed?

7 How effective is the home–school liaison system?
How could improvements be made?

8 Do parents and local community members play an interactive role in school life?
If not, should this be brought about, and how?

REFERENCES

Bell, P. and Best, R. (1986) *Supportive Education*, Oxford: Blackwell.

Bloom, B.S. (1976) *Human Characteristics and School Learning*, Maidenhead: McGraw-Hill.

Canfield, J. and Wells, H.C. (1976) *100 Ways to Enhance the Self-Concept in the Classroom*, Englewood Cliffs, NJ: Prentice Hall.

Central Advisory Council for Education (CACE) (1963) *Half Our Future* (Newsom Report), London: HMSO.

Central Advisory Council for Education (CACE) (1967) *Children and their Primary Schools* (Plowden Report), London: HMSO.

Charlton, T. and David, K. (1989) *Managing Misbehaviour*, Basingstoke: Macmillan.

Charlton, T. and David, K. (1990) *Supportive Schools*, Basingstoke: Macmillan.

Charlton, T. and David, K. (1993) *Managing Misbehaviour* (2nd edn), London: Routledge.

Coppersmith, S. (1967) *The Antecedents of Self-Esteem*, London: Freeman.

Creighton, S. J. (1987) Quantitative assessment of child abuse, in P. Maher (ed.) *Child Abuse: The Educational Perspective*, Oxford: Blackwell.

Department for Education (1993) *Education Act*, London: HMSO.

Department of Education and Science (1944) *Education Act*, London: HMSO.

Department of Education and Science (1978) *Report of the Committee of Enquiry into the Education of Handicapped Children and Young People* (Warnock Report), London: HMSO.

Department of Education and Science (1981) *Education Act*, London: HMSO.

Department of Education and Science (1986) *Education Act*, London: HMSO.

Department of Education and Science (1988) *Education Act*, London: HMSO.

Department of Health (1989) *An Introduction to the Children Act*, London: HMSO.

Hamblin, D.H. (1978) *The Teacher and Pastoral Care*, Oxford: Blackwell.

Hodgson, K. and Whalley, G. (1992) The 1989 Children Act: some implications for pastoral care, *Pastoral Care*, 10, 3, 20–21.

Home Office, Department of Health, Department of Education and Science and Welsh Office (1989) *Working Together Under the Children Act*, London: HMSO.

Jones, K. and Charlton, T. (eds) (1992) *Learning Difficulties in Primary Classrooms: Delivering the Whole Curriculum*, London: Routledge.

Lawrence, D. (1987) *Enhancing Self-esteem in the Classroom*, London: PCP Education Series.

Marland, M. (1974) *Pastoral Care*, London: Heinemann.

Marland, M. (1989) Shaping and delivering pastoral care: the new opportunities, *Pastoral Care*, 7, 4, 14–21.

Welton, J. (1985) Schools and a multi-professional approach to welfare, in P. Ribbins (ed.) *Schooling and Welfare*, Lewes: Falmer.

6

THE CHANGING SCHOOL HEALTH SERVICE

Health services for school-aged children

Jean Price

INTRODUCTION

It is an interesting idea and possibly a salutary lesson, that current thinking regarding child health has been influenced by events as long ago as the Boer War. At this time recruits were found to be extremely unhealthy, many aspects of which could have been averted by earlier attention to health problems. This was probably the first time that it was recognised that healthy children were more likely to become healthy adults and that this could have an implication for the health and wealth of the nation.

In 1904 in the UK there was a report published by the Interdepartmental Committee on Physical Deterioration. Amongst its fifty-three recommendations were several that were specific to children, including areas such as juvenile smoking, alcoholism, food and cooking, adulteration of foods, physical exercise and medical inspection of school children. Following this, school nurses and doctors were appointed. There was little extension of this until 1948, when the National Health Service was developed after the Second World War and there was a reconfirmation of the need for a strong school health service. It is fascinating that here we are in the 1990s and the document *Health of the Nation* (Department of Health, 1992) is stating very similar objectives to that of 1904.

CHANGES

Unfortunately, as with all other public services, the Community Child Health Services have to be cost efficient and have finite resources to meet ever-increasing and expensive demands. There have been many changes over the last ten to fifteen years which have had their impact on this service, not least: social and cultural changes; lifestyle changes; and managerial and medical manpower structural changes. These will be described in greater detail, followed by an overview of current expectations of such health services for children, as recommended by the British Paediatric Association. Suggestions as to how we can better work together to be as effective and efficient as possible will be made.

Social and cultural changes

Our social structure is changing. We have the highest rate of divorce in Europe and 30 per cent of children are born outside marriage, many to teenage mothers (De'ath, 1988). Hence there is an increasing number of single parents with little or no support, many being on state benefit, nor do they have good social and extended family support because of mobility of our population in search of work.

Unemployment is high and many employees are female part-time workers. Child care arrangements are costly, difficult to come by or are unsatisfactory. Psychiatric literature states that parents' stress reduces their ability to provide adequate support and parenting of young children. Aggressive and delinquent behaviour are linked to family discord and disharmony (Rickman, 1977). Our current social structure would imply that there is an increased likelihood of children behaving in this way when stress becomes so great that children develop poor social attachments, controls, and boundaries, and ultimately their school work suffers. This leads to poorly adjusted young adults who parent badly and produce a second generation of problem children.

There is growing evidence of an inequality of wealth with the rich getting richer and the poor poorer. Homelessness and families in temporary accommodation are also on the increase. These families are mobile, vulnerable and prone to illness and infection: for example, there is a high rate of tuberculosis among the homeless in London.

Children can no longer gear themselves to a career that will provide life-long security. They will increasingly need to acquire different skills in order to open up alternative employment. As a consequence they may experience emotional and financial insecurity.

Ethnic minority groups struggle with the difficulties of children growing up in a very different cultural society from the one that they knew, thus experiencing considerable stress and anxiety.

Case study 1

A second-generation Asian girl was repeatedly seen in school with bruises. She would never open up and complain, or inform the teaching staff as to how these were caused, although they were occasionally quite worried about them. She would miss a lot of school and complain repeatedly to the school nurse of headaches and stomach aches.

Eventually, as she got to know the school nurse more she confided in her that she was repeatedly beaten, by her father, because she continually wanted to lead a Western lifestyle. She wanted to wear Western clothes and go out to discos and meet boys. She also wanted to wear make-up. Her father could not cope with this and was in the process of planning an arranged marriage for her. This had resulted in a major row within the family and as a consequence the girl took an overdose. She was admitted to hospital and prior to discharge the community paediatrician was notified because of the excessive bruising on her body. The whole story came out and a series of counselling and support sessions were set up for both the girl and her family.

Lifestyles

Whilst there is more than enough food available we have become a fast food nation and we are far less active, leading to problems of obesity, increased blood pressure and cardiac disease. Despite increasing costs and much health advice there is still a high incidence of smoking. Young teenagers are still attracted to this abuse and appear to be blind to its association with lung cancer. Advertisements for designer drinks encourage ever younger children to try them. We now have a very worrying increase in the use and abuse of drugs across our country. Many users end up involved in criminal activities to fund their habit and require considerable support from health services, family and friends, if they are to give the habit up.

Between 5 and 20 per cent of school aged children have tried a drug and 2–5 per cent use drugs weekly, or more often. There is a peak prevalence between 14 and 16 years of age but the age at which adolescents start is getting lower (British Paediatric Association, 1995). The recent recorded deaths of adolescents from single tablets of ecstasy are very worrying. This is not to mention the emotional, social and behavioural problems these children may exhibit.

Fortunately, there are an increasing number of Parents' Groups who are working with statutory agencies to help them stem this tide. We must all work together to this end and health promotion within schools, with the support and advice of school nurses, community paediatricians and health promotion groups, can and does have a vital role to play as do innovative schemes for teenagers – run along lines acceptable to themselves.

General health of the population

We are generally thought of as a much healthier nation, with increased awareness amongst adults of what is required to maintain health. We have a recorded decrease in infant and childhood mortality and an improved survival rate for low birth-weight babies. We have better treatments for epilepsy but against this we have an increase in the reported rate of asthma and allergic conditions. We still have a proportion of low birth-weight babies who survive with significant disabilities and an OPCS study (Bone, 1989) indicated that there were 3.5 per cent of children aged between 10 and 15 years, who had conditions that would significantly affect their everyday activities. Amongst these were those with significant behaviour and communication difficulties, continence, locomotion, intellectual functioning, personal care and hearing problems.

With the transfer of pre-school child health surveillance to the primary health care teams (GPs and Health Visitors), the NHS Report (Department of Health, 1990) and immunisation targets being set by the government, there has been an increased immunisation uptake rate, i.e. approximately 90–95 per cent across the country. This has obviously resulted in a reduction in deaths, disabilities and morbidity due to infectious diseases. We may, however, still be subject to epidemics of familiar diseases, for example, the predicted measles epidemic of 1994, which led to mass immunisation against measles and rubella. This occupied community nurses and paediatricians for several weeks.

Managerial and medical manpower structural changes

We are now in the purchaser/provider arena, which means we must work to contracts and justify the need for services for school-aged children. The services for chronic illness, disability and emotional and social problems are often difficult to justify against the services for premature babies, or renal and cardiac transplants. We all have a vital role to play in speaking forcefully for the needs of the children of today as being the health and wealth of our nation of tomorrow. We must be the advocates for children.

It is recognised that child health services should be a combined seamless service, involving primary health care (i.e. GPs), community paediatricians and secondary acute paediatric services. GPs have a specific responsibility to provide child health surveillance up to school age and they receive payments for this, as well as for immunisations. GPs remain the prime carers whenever a school child has an acute illness.

At the opposite end of the spectrum, the acute paediatric services deal with all major emergencies that involve admission to hospital. Community paediatrics spans primary to secondary health care services but, more importantly, brings acute paediatric care into the community and nearer to the environment in which the child lives. This provides a highly specialised service which is available to schools, children themselves and their parents. It is vitally important that we further develop good ways of communication with schools and this needs to be based on the old-style school health system whereby each school has a named nurse and doctor to whom they can refer.

The old style school health service no longer exists and the school nurses are now the key profession for the whole school population, with school doctors having been superseded by more specialised community paediatricians and paramedical teams of physiotherapists, occupational and speech therapists, as well as clinical psychologists. There are considerable variations in staffing levels across the country, as stated in *Seen but not Heard* (Audit Commission, 1994).

COMMUNITY HEALTH SERVICE PERSONNEL

The school nurse

The school nurse has a vital role to play and is the prime and key worker within the schools where the health needs of children are concerned. She still carries out some child health surveillance. More importantly, she liaises carefully between the child, parent and school. She identifies problems and refers them on to the appropriate agency, with the more common minor ailments going to the GP. Those problems which may impact on the education of the child will be referred to the community paediatrician, where a more involved and detailed assessment can be made. Such illnesses are more likely to be developmental, emotional and behavioural, or may be to do with hyperactivity or with social problems such as child abuse.

Many of the early emotional behavioural problems can be nipped in the bud by the school nurse and community paediatrician but the more long-standing ones may need a more involved assessment, leading on to therapy which may involve child psychologists or psychiatrists and their teams.

Many have specialised in paediatrics and some have trained specifically for school nursing. Their roles, however, have expanded and they need additional training in certain aspects of emotional and behavioural disorders, in order that they can support and advise teachers and possibly counsel children within the school setting. They need additional skills in health promotion and health education. This may take the form of providing support and advice to schools or of the nurses being more actively involved. They need to link carefully with health promotion services who may have additional ideas, teaching aids and contacts.

School nurses must have adequate knowledge in order to recognise children with difficulties and the importance of these problems as they present. Some nurses will develop special skills in the areas of hearing, enuresis, behavioural modification, parenting skills and counselling.

School nurses must closely liaise with schools and their staff. Teachers must ensure that they know who their school nurse is and how to access her quickly. The school nurse will not, however, be freely available to carry out first aid. This is the role of the nominated first aiders within the school. There will never be a problem if the nurses are within the school and are asked to provide first aid as morally in such circumstances she would find it very difficult to refuse. She cannot, however, be on the premises for the whole school day and it is therefore essential that others are trained to manage minor accidents and ailments. The school nurse may be involved in part of this training, for example – management of anaphylaxis and administration of medicines. The school nurse will not be available to act as the old style 'Nitty Nora'. She will, of course, offer support, advice, health promotion and education with regard to head lice but we can no longer use this expensive resource in this way. We must help parents to appreciate that head lice are national pests primarily controlled through good grooming and communication between parents when there is an outbreak.

The community paediatrician

I have already discussed the management structure outlining the need for a unified structure for child health services in general. Strong professional leadership for this service was recommended in the Court Report (DHSS, 1976) and now, some twenty years later, we are beginning to see some of the recommendations implemented, although there is still a need in certain parts of the country for their further development.

The implementation has taken the form of community paediatricians, i.e. paediatricians with expert knowledge of chronic handicap and disability, educational medicine, social and emotional problems and, more specifically, child abuse. This breed of doctors is very suitably trained and experienced to bridge the gap between primary health care and secondary acute paediatrics. It is an appropriate profession to lead such a complex and diverse service for a population of children.

The disability team

A second recommendation of the Court Report that has been implemented is the development of a multi-disciplinary team consisting of a Community Paediatrician, Clinical Psychologist, Social Worker, Physiotherapist, Occupational and Speech and Language Therapist. Such a service has been developed in most parts of the country and is proving invaluable in terms of identification, assessment and treatment of children with disabilities. Some of these children are placed on a disability register, which is shared with Social Services as recommended in the Children's Act 1989. This allows such children to be monitored in terms of their needs, up to and at

the point of leaving school. It helps with ensuring that they receive ongoing services after they have left school.

Psychiatrists and psychologists

Educational psychologists are now more often than not fully occupied with carrying out assessment for Educational Statements. This has seriously eroded the amount of time they have available for advice to parents and schools on the management of disturbed behaviour and conditions such as dyslexia. As a consequence many more children end up being referred to clinical psychologists, child psychiatrists and community paediatricians. The psychiatric and psychology services available for children are, however, very patchy across the country and in some areas are woefully wanting. It is for these reasons that the school nurse and community paediatrician need to develop their expertise in emotional and behavioural disorders.

Wherever there are child psychiatric and psychological services they are usually very stretched. Such services offer very valuable advice and support to schools and therapy to children and their families on psychiatric conditions such as psychosis, depression, suicide and eating disorders. Clinical psychologists tend to work more with the less severe emotional and behavioural disorders. There is considerable overlap in the treatment of conditions such as enuresis, encopresis, hyperactivity, attention deficit disorder, autism and sexual abuse with psychiatrists, psychologists and community paediatricians all playing a part and often jointly developing services.

Multi-disciplinary work

It is important that we all understand and respect each other's roles and specialisms but it is equally important to the child, family and school that there is not conflicting advice from the different professionals. Our roles need to be clearly identified and understood. Multi-disciplinary training, where we can inform others of our expertise, limitations and constraints, goes a long way to helping this and certainly dispels many myths and preconceived ideas that we have about each other's roles.

LEGISLATION

During the last fifteen years there have been two important pieces of legislation which have had a major impact on working with children. The first was The Children Act (DHSS, 1989). This laid broad duties on Social Services with regard to 'Children in Need'. This Act brought together many pieces of legislation pertaining to children and one of its key themes was collaboration between agencies, i.e. Health, Education and Social Services to provide better services for such children in need. This means that we are obliged to share information, provided it is in the children's interests. It also states quite clearly that 'the children's interests are paramount' and lays particular responsibility on all agencies to work with parents and help them, wherever possible, to meet the needs of children.

Second were the Education Acts of 1981 and 1993. These have primarily led to children with special needs being educated and integrated into mainstream schools, as opposed to being concentrated in special schools, although there is still a place for some special schools and special units within mainstream schools. This has obviously led to increased complexity for the organisation, management and provision of health services to such children.

Alongside this there has been a change in the management of schools, in terms of schools being individually and locally managed by a board of governors. This provides them with greater autonomy and gives them some freedom to decide priorities but it will be important for the Health Services along with teachers to convince the boards of the various schools that the health aspects of children's school experience are as important as the teaching aspects. This has also brought about a change in the terms of education advisers to schools as this service has been lost to schools, meaning that again Health will need to work more closely with Education in terms of planning and providing health education.

PRIVATE SCHOOLS

Whilst there is a relatively good system for providing some form of health assessment and medical service to most local authority schools, this is not so for independent schools and all children should be offered the same services. Much work still needs to be done in looking at how this can be achieved.

VOLUNTARY SERVICES

We all recognise that the development of our services is constrained by finance and we are now being encouraged to work much more closely with voluntary services. Some are long established and will be known. The NSPCC have moved from a detection of cruelty to a more preventive and therapeutic approach. There are many occasions when we as statutory agencies are rejected by families whereas the NSPCC is still acceptable.

Case study 2

Joanne made an allegation of sexual abuse against her stepfather. Her mother had great difficulty in accepting this and immediately lost her status as a foster mother as well as the financial and emotional support of her husband. Her dependence on these became very apparent at an early stage. Stepfather denied all the allegations and called Joanne a liar. It wasn't long before Joanne retracted her statement despite there being supportive clinical evidence. All members of this family withdrew and it became impossible for statutory agencies to work with them. They did, however, agree to work with the NSPCC and after a prolonged and difficult piece of work, stepfather was allowed back into the house.

Other voluntary agencies such as National Children's Homes and Barnardos have developed Family Centres and do valuable work alongside us in helping parents develop their parenting skills and deal with anger control. As a consequence we can expand the services offered to neglected and abused children and those who fail to thrive or who have parents who abuse drink or drugs.

Nor must we forget the very valuable support work that patients who have had unfortunate life experiences offer to others in similar circumstances, for example, parents of children with disabilities such as Down's Syndrome or Tay Sachs disease. Others with children with learning difficulties or hyperactivity attention deficit disorder join forces and gain, as well as give, considerable support. This relieves pressure on Health Services and probably offers better and more realistic support to families.

Case study 3

Gemma, a very much wanted baby, was the second child of a nursery nurse. Initially, she was a bright cheerful baby and developed normally until the age of 1 year when mother noted she appeared to be losing skills. Unfortunately, she was diagnosed quite quickly as having Tay Sachs disease, a deteriorating neurological disorder. She became blind and lost all muscle tone, developed epilepsy and required frequent admissions to hospital for infections and respite care. Gemma died 18 months later. Shortly after her parents got over their grief they set about getting help for a voluntary support nursing service to provide appropriate respite care for children in similar positions to be nursed and cared for at home. This service is now up and running and proving an invaluable support to our overstretched community nursing service.

THE FUNCTION OF SERVICES TO SCHOOL-AGED CHILDREN

This can be divided into four areas which are developed in the following sections: first, services to the total population, including the surveillance programme and health promotion; second, services to groups of children, parents or teachers; third, services to individual children; and fourth, liaison and planning of services and training requirements.

Surveillance of the total population

This is a service that should be applied to every child within a population whatever the school or nursery they attend. The number of contacts that are made with each individual child throughout their school life has been considerably reduced over the last five to ten years. In some areas this may be in the form of medical examinations by a doctor but in other areas the school nurse will use parent questionnaires, summaries of the pre-school surveillance, and information from school staff to select out children for medical examination. Those children who are selected for medicals are usually those who have received incomplete child health surveillance prior to entry to school or have some chronic illness or developmental problem, or where the parent and/or teacher are expressing concerns about the child's behaviour, level of functioning or general health. Parents will be invited to all appointments that are set up with the doctor. Some clinics are still held in school but increasingly are more likely to be held in the nearest health clinic to the school.

The other points of contact which the school nurse has with all children are usually at 7–8 years and 11–12 years. These are further opportunities for children to have their visual acuity, height and weight checked. On each occasion and as with any contact the school nurse will opportunistically enquire about general health and offer health promotion and accident prevention advice. A final general check is usually offered at 14 years. This is a general health check together with a questionnaire to parents and pupils. These latter questionnaires may still be in the process of being developed in certain areas of the country.

Whole-population immunisations are also checked at age 5 years. It is now expected that all children, by the time they enter school, should have had a full course of immunisations against diphtheria, tetanus, whooping cough, polio, haemophilius influenzae B (meningitis), measles, mumps and rubella (German measles). Those who are not complete in their immunisations have the opportunity of catching up at the point of entry into school where the school nurse, in most cases, will refer them back to their primary health care team (GP). There may be some areas where these immunisations are carried out opportunistically at school but this is not the norm. Because of the national measles and rubella campaign in 1995 there is now no longer a need to have a rubella immunisation offered to all children aged 12–13 years but in the majority of areas in the country most children are Heaf tested and a proportion will be followed with BCG against tuberculosis. This is becoming increasingly important as there is a higher incidence of tuberculosis in those that are homeless and those ethnic groups that originate from high-risk areas of the world, particularly if they still have visiting contact with relatives. Tuberculosis has also been found in HIV sufferers in America. This may be something we need to be aware of in Britain. Finally, at the age of between 14–15 years parents are advised to take children to their GP for diphtheria, tetanus and polio immunisations. In this way we can continue to keep at bay some serious infections that would affect children, their education and their general health.

Some children are offered an audiological screen during their first year in school. This is carried out either by school nurses or audiometricians.

You will also note that all of the whole-population surveillance is carried out by the school nurse and it is only at the point where a 'problem' is identified, which is serious enough to warrant much fuller assessment and investigation, greater than that which would normally be provided within the primary health care team, that the community paediatrician becomes involved. These would be more specifically with individual children and will be dealt with later under that heading.

Case study 4

Anna is an 11-year-old child identified through child health surveillance. She is of mixed parentage, mother being English and father Greek. Anna was a high achiever both academically and musically. She was noticed by school staff to be exercising excessively much more than her peers. She was wearing more clothes and was thought to be losing weight.

School expressed their concerns to both mother and the school nurse. The school nurse saw Anna, together with her mum and found that she had lost weight dramatically. The previous two heights and weights at the 5 and 7–8-year-old child surveillance had shown Anna's height to be on the 90th centile and her weight on the 75th centile. At the point of referral her height was still on the 90th centile but her weight had fallen through three centiles. Initially the school nurse offered support, advice and counselling to the mother and Anna on appropriate diet and decreased exercise, and asked Anna to return in two weeks. At this time her weight was continuing to fall and the school nurse quite rightly referred her urgently to the community paediatrician. During the doctor's interview both Anna and her mother admitted that Anna had stopped eating with the family some time previously. As the interview continued it became apparent that Anna had a very distorted body image and was feeling herself to be quite fat, particularly her ears and toes. She was a tall, dark, attractive girl and was obviously following her father's Greek origins but she wished to be small and blonde. Further enquiry during the interview revealed that the parents were no longer living together. They had had an acrimonious divorce earlier in the year and Anna had spent some of the summer months with her father in Greece. She had returned in a very distressed state. Initially the paediatrician attempted to offer support, advice and counselling but it very quickly became apparent that Anna required more involved therapy as she was very dissatisfied with herself, her current lifestyle and her family circumstances. She was referred to the child psychiatrist who confirmed the anorexia and commenced therapy. Anna continued to have psychiatric input on a regular basis, needing only a very brief period of admission, in order to stabilise and then reverse her weight loss. Once she was back at school, the school nurse continued to work closely with the psychiatrist, in terms of support and regular weighing of Anna. Over a period of time Anna began to make slow progress. Now, five years on, Anna is a stable, happy teenager who is popular with her peers and is making good progress academically and musically. It took all the professionals, including school, a considerable amount of time and energy to help Anna make the necessary adjustments.

Group interventions

This may involve the school nurse and the community paediatrician in offering support and advice to the teachers around health education and accident prevention. School nurses may be directly involved in some of the health education programmes, if they have particular expertise in teaching. They can, with or without this qualification, offer support and advice to teachers about specific health topics that are dealt with in the National Curriculum. Most of this centres around self-esteem, the impact of life events on individuals, sex education, contraceptive advice, accident prevention and such things as healthy eating. If the school nurse feels she does not have appropriate expertise she has enough contacts to find alternative sources of advice from experts. She will also closely liaise with the health promotion groups that are set up across the country.

We still have the occasional outburst of infectious disease that requires sudden and immediate intervention. It is usually the school nurses and community paediatricians that are called upon to meet these needs. Meningitis is the one that immediately springs to mind and, particularly where one or more children may have contracted this within a school setting they become seriously ill and occasionally one dies. Normally, with only one child infected, their immediate contacts, such as family and close friends, would receive prophylactic treatment and immunisation. However, if two or more children become infected within a school, and particularly if they are not within the same immediate peer group, then the whole school population may be offered prophylactic treatment and immunisation. In order to mobilise adequate resources very quickly those services available to school age children are the obvious choice.

Services to individual children

Most children in this category are seen by a community paediatrician and come under the heading of 'Children in Need'. Such children are defined in the Children Act as being:

- unlikely to achieve or maintain, or to have the opportunity of achieving or maintaining a reasonable standard of health or development without the provision of services by the local authority; or,
- their health or development is likely to be significantly impaired or further impaired without the provision; or,
- they are disabled.

Those with disability

Such children may have a medical or a behavioural problem and, as well as falling under the definition of 'Children in Need' within the Children Act, they may also require assessment under the 1993 Education Act, leading to a 'Statement of Special Educational Needs'. Examples of such children are presented in case studies 5–7.

Case study 5

James is an 11-year-old boy with cystic fibrosis who requires frequent hospital admissions and is cared for by a well-established team at a children's hospital. There are no educational concerns and an educational psychologist felt that he did not need a statement of special educational needs for transfer between primary and secondary school.

The local comprehensive schools, however, were not suitable because of their geographical layout and a place was offered, on medical grounds, at a secondary school with a special unit with facilities for medical conditions. This school, unfortunately, was 10 miles away from the child's home and the staff there also felt they were unable to provide suitable facilities for James because they did not have appropriate physiotherapy and could not supervise him taking his medication, nor his rest periods, without him being the subject of an educational statement, i.e. they needed additional manpower.

It became obvious to the community paediatrician covering the primary school that the mother and the child were caught up in a very distressing situation between the various schools, the educational psychologist and the education department. The children's hospital team recognised all of the child's needs but were not able to find their way through the maze of bureaucracy within the educational system.

The community paediatrician was able to act as an advocate on the child's behalf and after numerous phone calls and letters provided a satisfactory solution. This situation could have been avoided by good liaison between the initial primary school, community paediatrician and the educational psychologist who may then have agreed to carry out a statement of educational needs in the first place.

Case study 6

Brian had developed diabetes and was insulin-dependent at the age of 4 years. His mother also had diabetes and there were many social problems within the family. During primary school Brian's behaviour became very difficult indeed. He became stubborn and disruptive within the classroom and would frequently not take his medication putting himself in considerable danger and having repeated hypoglycemic episodes (low blood sugar) where he would become close to and sometimes comatose. This was extremely frightening for both the children and teaching staff. On one occasion an ambulance needed to be called and Brian was taken to the paediatric ward in the local hospital.

The consultant paediatrician overseeing Brian's care and the community paediatrician worked jointly with Brian and his mother, counselling them to alleviate some of their stress and educating them in how to support each other and the school staff. Following a professional meeting with school, with the medical staff, mother and social services the family were provided with additional support and some respite care, thus relieving many of the social concerns. Brian slowly became more compliant, both at home and at school and was more prepared to care for himself as far as his diabetes was concerned.

Case study 7

Joanne was an adopted child whose behaviour presented as very bizarre within school. She was referred by the school nurse to the local disability consultant, who was also a community paediatrician. He diagnosed 'dyspraxia' and offered global assessment of Joanne, in conjunction with her home environment. Support and advice was offered to Joanne and her family through occupational therapy. At the same time an educational psychologist became involved because of Joanne's difficult behaviour within school. Quite separately she assessed Joanne and suggested that she had 'Asperger's Syndrome' and discussed this with her mother. Quite obviously the adoptive mother was given conflicting advice from two different sources and this led to considerable confusion and difficulties with the management of Joanne. This came to the notice of the community paediatrician covering the school and these difficulties were resolved by the paediatrician arranging a meeting between the parents and all the relevant professionals involved with Joanne. The diagnosis became less relevant but it was obvious that Joanne needed a statement for special educational needs in order that her individual needs within school could be met appropriately. In a small unit that could accommodate Joanne's odd behaviour and with some more individual teaching she made good and steady progress and could cope better with everyday life events.

Children with developmental problems

The majority of these are usually identified prior to entering school through the excellent child health surveillance programme provided by GPs and health visitors. These disabilities not only include physical problems but also difficulties of hearing, vision, and speech and language. Many of them may well overlap with children later having learning difficulties and behavioural problems.

Obviously the assessment of such children is a multi-disciplinary task and requires a well-organised and co-ordinated approach. Such services are usually based within child development centres, following the recommendations of the Court Report (DHSS, 1976). Most of these development centres are run by community paediatricians with a special interest and expertise in children with disability, but other community paediatricians have very easy access and referral routes into such services. Other paramedical services such as physiotherapy, speech and language and occupational therapists and psychologists are all part of the team making a global assessment of a child and his/her family.

Once children reach school age it is less likely that they will be identified *de novo* as having a developmental problem and most of those so identified prior to entry to school should be made the subject of an educational statement during their pre-school years so that they are initially steered into the right and most appropriate form of education for their needs. Just occasionally, however, children may not be adequately assessed at the pre-school level because of a family's mobility or poor compliance with services offered.

Case study 8

One such child, Richard, aged 2 years, had initially been referred to the developmental centre by the primary health care team because the health visitor felt he was not reaching his milestones. He was slow to walk and talk and, once he became mobile, appeared quite poorly co-ordinated, disruptive, hyperactive and had an extremely poor attention span.

Richard's mother had moderate to severe learning difficulties and her parenting skills were poor. She herself needed considerable attention and behaved in a very immature fashion. She had recently left a violent relationship with Richard's natural father. She and Richard moved in with another man, who also had mild learning difficulties and a verbally aggressive approach to professionals.

Many appointments were not kept. Very shortly after school entry it became obvious that Richard was not going to cope and the parents eventually allowed a full assessment when a diagnosis of global developmental delay was made. Richard was made the subject of an educational statement and offered a place within a school for moderate learning difficulties. The full assessment also allowed the professionals to support step father in his application for a Disability Living Allowance to help with Richard's care. This certainly improved relationships between step father and the professionals. He now keeps most appointments with his three subsequent children, all of whom have similar problems.

Child protection

The Children Act and recommendations from *Working Together* (DOH and DES, 1989) require that children who are at risk of abuse should be identified and provided with services. The total number of abused children is never accurately known but in 1992, 38,600 children were placed on child protection registers and 59 per cent of these were between 5 and 15 years. This works out at 3.7 per thousand children and the numbers of children placed on registers is rising, probably because of better identification. All local authorities across the country have child abuse/protection procedures and these procedures are recommended by the DHSS and are developed locally by multi-disciplinary child protection committees. Education, Police, Social Services, Health, voluntary bodies, Housing and Legal Departments are all represented on these committees and all staff are expected to adhere to the procedures. It is extremely important that all field workers are aware of these procedures and are able to work within them. They will require training in order to understand and help them to gain knowledge in identification of abused children. Much is gained if this training is multi-disciplinary as it helps us all to understand each other's backgrounds, strengths, weaknesses and circumstances under which we work. Many children are referred on a daily basis to community paediatric services by teachers who identify unusual bruising or injuries and where there is no satisfactory explanation for these injuries.

Case study 9

Jack was an 11-year-old boy with spastic diplegia. He was already the subject of an educational statement and attended a school for moderate learning difficulties. He was the eldest of two children, of mixed parentage, mother being English and father West Indian. Mother was known to suffer from severe depression and was repeatedly admitted to hospital. She had always had a difficult relationship with Jack and tended to use respite care inappropriately, as a form of rejection. One day during the summer Jack was noticed in school with bruising to his neck. He informed the teachers that his mother had tried to strangle him. He was referred to the community paediatrician, who also found that he had signs of hyperpigmentation in the shape of belt marks across his back, indicative of physical abuse. On questioning, his mother and grandmother admitted that both his father and grandfather had hit him with a belt. Jack and his sister were placed in foster care, whilst work could be done with both parents and an assessment of him could be carried out.

Other vulnerable groups

We must not forget children who fall into other very vulnerable categories for example, travellers' children, children who are in temporary accommodation and who are homeless. The various agencies find these groups are very difficult to follow up because of their frequent moves and frequently the medical and social issues and needs are not addressed.

Children with life-limiting/life-threatening illness, whose families and schools need considerable support by all agencies, are also vulnerable. They may, at some stage, require home tuition, home nursing and respite care. Ultimately all involved may need supportive counselling in order to come to terms with the inevitable death of such a child. These services can be co-ordinated by school nurses and community paediatricians.

Case study 10

Matthew was a 5-year-old who had a very complex congenital heart condition, with a very poor prognosis. He was treated at the local children's hospital but also had to make frequent visits to a more specialist hospital in London. Initially illness prevented him from attending school, therefore it was extremely difficult to assess his special educational needs within a school setting.

He was referred by the primary health care team to the local community paediatrician to explore issues of education. It was felt that he needed a package of home tuition, with a gradual and slow introduction into the local primary school. This was agreed between the mother, community paediatrician, educational psychologist and the educational welfare officer. Whilst Matthew was able to be integrated for several half days per week with transport to and from school he was unable to take part in the full curriculum but did get much from his involvement with children of his own age and was able to make friends. Three years later, however, he deteriorated markedly and could only cope initially with home tuition. Ultimately the family needed considerable support from nurses and other volunteers going into the home. Eventually he died and this allowed the school to explore the concepts of disability, chronic illness and death with the children in his class and the rest of the school. The community medical team of nurse and doctor were an invaluable asset to the school at this time, as well as being able to ensure the family received appropriate support. Very good guidelines for dealing with such tragedies are dealt with in *Wise Before the Event* (Tulle and Gold, 1993).

Gradually, across the country, voluntary nursing services are being developed to support families with children with life-limiting illnesses. Most families that have experienced such services cannot sing their praises highly enough.

Hepatitis B, HIV and AIDS

Hepatitis B is often a concern for children, particularly those with special needs, i.e. those with physical disabilities or moderate to severe learning difficulties. There is *no* need for concern or panic with such children. Transfer of this infection, as with HIV and AIDS, is only via body-to-body fluids. It follows therefore that, provided good hygiene measures are followed, no one should be at risk.

Those responsible for clearing up should wear gloves, mop up the spillage with disposable cloths and wipe down the surface with Chlorhexidine. All materials and gloves should then be placed in a special plastic bag marked 'infected material'. These are usually a distinctive colour and are collected for incineration. All staff in schools must be aware of their local guidelines and strictly adhere to them. It is also advisable for such staff to be immunised against Hepatitis B.

Children with paediatric conditions

Just occasionally children with unusual paediatric conditions come to the notice of community paediatricians, either via the primary health care team or the school.

Case study 11

Matthew was 7½ years old. School was reporting that he was avoiding PE and would not get changed and the school nurse reported that he was above the 97th centile (i.e. only 3 per cent of children his age would be taller). Neither of the parents was particularly tall and nor were any of his siblings. At interview with a community paediatrician mother reported that Matthew was now quite embarrassed by pubic hair, particularly when changing for PE. The community paediatrician became quite concerned that this young child appeared to have precocious sexual development. The mother needed to be seen on more than one occasion as she was finding it very difficult to come to terms with the fact that there could be something wrong with the child. Eventually she agreed to a referral to an endocrinologist who made a diagnosis of congenital adrenal hyperplasia and appropriate treatment and counselling was initiated.

Allergies and administration of medicines in schools

Children with allergic conditions appear to be on the increase. The mechanisms for this are not fully understood but if a child has a severe allergic reaction (anaphylactic reaction) it is very frightening for all concerned, the child and any adults and other children around at the time. Allergies may be caused by many things but the most common severe reactions are to fish or nuts. Once identified the obvious management of allergies is to avoid the stimulus. Nuts can be a problem, however, as they may be in biscuits and pastry, and children with such allergies need to be very aware of such possibilities. All such children are provided with tablets, and severe cases will have a self administration syringe (epipen) and should be wearing a Medi Alert Bracelet.

Other medications also occasionally pose problems within schools. By and large most children can cope with their own medication, for example, asthmatics and diabetics. Whatever the problem the school nurse is available to offer help, advice and training to school staff (particularly the nominated first aider) on such issues.

Those children with epilepsy are usually well controlled but occasionally they may have a severe and continuous fit (*status epilepticus*) when they may require rectal medication. This may be life saving and the controversial issues of who should be responsible for such administration should not be an issue. Training in such procedures is always available and often the responsibility for this rests with school nurses.

Liaison, planning and prevention, and development of services and training

Senior Community Paediatricians act as a point of contact for other professions such as Education and Social Services, where joint planning of services becomes increasingly important. With the ever-increasing demands to have cost-effective ways of working, all statutory bodies are now looking closely at voluntary agencies to help develop and support their services. One such would be a multi-disciplinary group working with a voluntary group known as 'The Pyramid Trust'. At the time of writing this has only been used as an experiment in certain areas around London and has more recently extended to Bristol. It is still in its infancy. The idea is that children are identified within school as being vulnerable but not yet requiring full intervention or educational statements. They may be very withdrawn, insecure and/or teetering on the brink of a behaviour disorder. Most have very low self-esteem. They are put into a small group which is run by volunteers who have some knowledge of child development (for example, student social workers, psychologists or teachers). This volunteer group is given training and can then run the children's group as a club over a period of 10 weeks, concentrating primarily on raising self-awareness and self-esteem. To date these appear to be proving very successful and many parents and schools are pleased with the outcome. This experiment is proving its worth and secondary schools are beginning to support such groups within their feeder primary schools, as they appreciate that such ventures may reduce some of the problems that they will inevitably inherit.

Other areas that multi-disciplinary administrative services can and do usefully look at, in order to find better ways of meeting the needs of children, are on alcohol and drug abuse, sex education and services for adolescents. In such cases they may well look to what the children themselves identify as being what they need and how they would like to have it delivered. Several such ventures, in terms of adolescent services, have been developed and tried, not least the Nottingham Venture, 'A positive alternative for Nottingham youth. A teenage health care project' (Daniel, 1989).

Multi-disciplinary groups could also look to how they can help schools generally promote a healthier environment, even to the point of the schools themselves becoming good healthy environments. For example, *Health-promoting Schools* (Cambridge Health Authority and TACADE, 1990) or *The Health-promoting Primary School* (Moston and Lloyd, 1994). Similar ventures can also work in accident prevention, which inevitably requires a whole environmental approach, including housing and environmental health and traffic departments. Such groups can plan safer playgrounds and traffic calming schemes.

At the same time multi-disciplinary groups require to collect good and appropriate information, data and statistics on the incidence of accidents or unhealthy living, teenage pregnancies, alcohol or drug abuse, in order that the whole oversight of such unhealthy lifestyles can be viewed and jointly worked on to find alternative ways of helping the young population. It is imperative that we all work together on such major issues.

There is also value in organising multi-disciplinary training in a number of areas. This not only breaks down barriers between different professional groupings but leads to a far better understanding of the specific skills we all bring to our work and also prevents duplication. One such particular area where multi-disciplinary *training* pays off, time and time again, is in the child abuse and prevention arena, as indicated in the following case study.

Case study 12

Marianne and Madaleine are aged 14 years. Marianne had been known to the Education Service for a number of years. During the previous years Marianne was the subject of an educational statement and had been attending a special school for moderate learning difficulties for two years. Most children in this school had been suspended and expelled from a number of schools prior to being ultimately referred to this particular school. All had quite severe behavioural problems. Many took drugs and committed regular offences. Marianne was known to be taking drugs and to be sexually active. She was making very little headway at school and her attendance was appalling.

It was during an appointment with the community paediatrician that had been arranged by the educational welfare officer, because of her and the school's concerns around the possibility of sexually transmitted diseases for Marianne, that it became apparent that Marianne and her twin sister Madaleine were both very interdependent. It also became apparent that Madaleine was not getting to school and that she appeared to be spending much of her life under the influence of drugs, thus putting her at considerable risk. The community paediatrician arranged to see and examine both girls and found them to be slightly underweight but not particularly unhealthy. She felt that the girls, who were quite willing to talk, were finding life quite difficult at home as they frequently witnessed their mother being physically assaulted by her then co-habitee. As a consequence of this mother would drink excessively and would then spend long periods of time totally inebriated. There was little or no control exerted by mother and it was as if she didn't care. Together the educational welfare officer, school and community paediatrician requested a case conference, as they felt these two girls were being neglected and emotionally abused.

At the case conference mother's probation officer also attended and it became apparent that mother required considerable support and help, in order to get back on her feet. There was obvious care and affection between mother and the girls but they needed some guidance and support in order to resolve their difficulties. A year later, mother, with support from probation, had been able to end her relationship with the violent co-habitee. She had attended an alcoholic detoxification group and 9 months later was free of alcohol. She had managed to get herself a small part-time job and was feeling much better about herself. She had quite recently developed a new relationship with a very supportive man, with whom the girls got on well. Also during this period of time Madaleine too had been made the subject of an educational statement and it was agreed that both girls should attend the same school for moderate learning difficulties. At the time of review they were attending regularly and making good progress. Although we were still not clear that they were not abusing drugs the evidence appeared that this was much less. Their self-esteem was improved and they were beginning to develop some career plans.

CONCLUSIONS

As you can see the Health Services for children within school are very different to those we knew, even ten to fifteen years ago. Hopefully now they go a long way to meeting children with special needs and I am sure everyone would agree that as we all have limited resources we need to focus our energies much more on those children that have specific and special needs. We can only do this by working together and by supporting each other, whatever our discipline, in our identification, diagnosis, treatment and support of these children and their families. This multidisciplinary approach needs to span the whole of our profession, from top to bottom, from those working in the field to the managers who develop policies. It is becoming increasingly important that we look to joint commissioning of services in order to meet the needs of those children that we have greatest difficulty in getting services to, specifically those children that belong to travellers' families or who come from families in temporary accommodation and also those who come from very disrupted families where there is poor understanding of children's needs and development. It may be that we should be looking very much more imaginatively at how we develop services in future. Education with help from other agencies should not only look to meet the needs of disabled children but also try to extend its services, through a multidisciplinary approach, to meet the needs of the parents of some of these children, by providing reading schemes, health education and projects to improve self-esteem.

BIBLIOGRAPHY

Audit Commission (1994) *Seen but not Heard: Coordinating Community Child Health and Social Services for Children in Need: Detailed Evidence*, London: HMSO.

Bone, M. (1989) *The Prevalence of Disability among Children in Great Britain* (Office of Population Censuses and Surveys Report 3), London: HMSO.

British Paediatric Association (1995) *The Health Needs of School-aged Children*, London: HMSO.

Cambridge Health Authority and Teachers' Advisory Council on Alcohol and

Drugs Education (1990) *Health-promoting Schools – A Training Manual*, Salford: TACADE.
Daniel, S. (1989) *A Positive Alternative for Nottingham Youth. A Teenage Healthcare Project*, Nottingham: Memorial House.
De'ath, E. (1988) *Focus on Families: Divorce and its Effects on Children*, A Briefing Paper, London: Children's Society.
Department for Education (1993) *The Education Act. A Code of Practice*, London: HMSO.
Department of Education and Science (1981) *An Act to make Provision with Respect to Children with Special Educational Needs*, London: HMSO.
Department of Health (1990) *General Practice in the NHS – the 1990 Contract* (the NHS Report), London: DOH.
Department of Health (1992) *Health of the Nation. A Strategy for Health in England*, London: HMSO.
Department of Health and Department of Education and Science (1989) *Working Together under the Children Act*, London: HMSO.
Department of Health and Social Security (1976) *Fit for the Future. Report of the Committee on Child Health Services* (the Court Report), London: HMSO.
Department of Health and Social Security (1989) *The Children Act*, London: HMSO.
Earls, F. and Jung, K.G. (1987) Temperament and home environment as causal factors in early development of childhood psychopathology, *Journal of American Academy of Child and Adolescent Psychiatry*, 26, 491–498.
Elliot, B.J. and Richards, M.P.M. (1991) Effects of parental divorce on children, *Archives of Disease in Childhood*, 66, 915–916.
Fitzherbert, K. (1982) Communication with teachers in the health surveillance of school children. *Maternal and Child Health*, 7, 3, 100–103.
Health Education Authority (1992) *Tomorrow's Young Adults. 9–15-year-olds Look at Alcohol, Drugs, Exercise and Smoking*, London: HEA.
Lambert, L. and Streather, J. (1980) *Children in Changing Families*, London: Macmillan.
Moston, R. and Lloyd, J. (1994) *The Health-promoting Primary School*, London: David Fulton.
Rickman, N. (1977) Behaviour problems in pre-school children: family and social factors, *British Journal of Psychiatry*, B1, 5, 23–27.
Tulle, W. and Gold, A. (1993) *Wise before the Event. Coping with Crises in Schools*, London: Gulbenkian Foundation.
Wicks, M. (1989) Family funds: insecurities and social policy, *Children and Society*, 3, 67–80.

7

PUPILS' LIFE CRISES

Philip Carey

INTRODUCTION

Increasingly, teachers are expected to attend to pupils' psychosocial as well as academic needs (London, 1987). In line with this role, teachers have to deal with the wide variety of possible stressors (stress-causing events) that young people may face. Pupils' reactions to these can manifest themselves in a variety of ways. Behavioural problems, for example, or lower academic achievement may be a form of stress reaction (Southern and Smith, 1980). Therefore, dealing effectively with pupil stress will benefit the individual as well as the whole school. It is the author's belief that every teacher will have some responsibility for this, as they all effectively have a pastoral care role. Despite this, initial teacher training appears to include little on pastoral care. As a result, a gap has developed between what teachers are expected to do and the training that they receive (Grant, 1992). The view of the author is that the development of counselling skills will benefit teachers in fulfilling their pastoral role.

The chapter places the need for counselling skills within the context of stress in young people and the school's reactions to it. It does not examine discrete incidents and responses. Rather, the chapter explores the effects of a personal crisis within a general framework of young people's stress. This involves a consideration of the coping strategies that young people may adopt. Following from this there is an exploration of the personal and societal influences that may affect how a young person copes with stress. The chapter then goes on to explore what the school can do to help the young people involved. This includes a description of counselling skills and consideration of some of the strategies the school can employ to help pupils.

WHY COUNSELLING SKILLS?

In 1991, a small-scale qualitative research project explored the question of how school teachers deal with pupils' life crises (Carey, 1992). Primary school, secondary school and student teachers were involved in the research. These teachers identified an enormous range of potential life crises, including various health-related problems, bereavement, parental separation or bullying. However, a major finding of this study was that the significant issue for teachers was not the actual cause of the problem. Instead, they were more interested in the pupils' reactions. How the individual teacher, or indeed the whole school, could act to help the pupil deal with a personal crisis was a particularly pertinent issue to these teachers.

Exploration of this matter identified a major gap in teacher training. This related to the development of a skills repertoire that teachers might employ when they are dealing with a pupil's crisis. The study found that appropriate skills should be generic, not problem-specific. Given the wide variety of potential life crises, it would be absurd to expect teachers to develop specialised skills to help them cope with distinct problems. What they appeared to require were transferable skills for use in all sorts of crisis situations. The consensus view of the teachers in this study was that counselling skills would be appropriate for this role. However, they drew a clear distinction between the use of these skills and the actual process of counselling. This concurs with the view of the British Association of Counselling that the use of counselling skills is only a part of being a counsellor (BAC, 1992). In line with this, it is appropriate for a teacher to use counselling skills in dealing with a pupil's reaction to their life crisis. Yet, it is inappropriate for that teacher to act as the pupil's counsellor. This is because the role of a counsellor in helping young people deal with life crises is necessarily different to that of a teacher. The counsellor will work by a set of professional procedures and boundaries that may be inconsistent with a teacher's role.

WHAT IS A LIFE CRISIS?

In effect the answer to this question is simple – a life crisis is a stressful life event. Of course, this begs a further question – what is a stressful life event? There are many life events that may be considered potentially stressful to young people. A survey of self-defined stress in young people identified nearly 3,000 major stress events (Compas *et al.*, 1987). This figure excludes the day-to-day hassles that can trouble young people's lives.

A 'stressful' life event does not necessarily translate into stress. Some individuals can experience potentially stressful situations without becoming stressed. Indeed it has been suggested that no event is stressful unless the individual involved defines it as such (Lazarus and Folkman, 1984). According to this view, people appraise how stressful an event is by considering how relevant it is to them. This involves self-assessment of whether the particular event constitutes a threat. If so, they decide whether it may be harmful, threatening or challenging. Following this, people then consider whether their coping resources are adequate for dealing with that particular stressor.

There are many definitions of coping, but a common theme is that coping is the process of dealing with stress. Five common coping strategies used by young people have been identified (Dise-Lewis, 1988). These are:

1 *Aggression,* a classic negative response to stress. It occurs when the young person's reaction to stress is violently directed at another person. One example of this is involvement in fights or bullying.
2 *Stress-recognition,* an acknowledgement by the young person of their stress, is often seen as a positive reaction to stress. There is generally some form of communication of this stress to others. Recognition strategies include crying or seeking advice.
3 *Distraction,* when the individual involves her/himself in activities to 'let go' of the stress. Taking up a hobby or exercise is often a distraction technique. Sometimes this might be a helpful strategy, but there is a danger that this might result in denial of the cause of stress. Denied stress can manifest itself later in life.
4 *Self-destruction* is another classic negative reaction and can be considered an inwardly violent reaction to stress. Self-destructive behaviour can range from not doing homework to self-mutilation or suicide.
5 *Endurance,* living with the stress, which is a strategy with both potentially negative and positive outcomes. Whilst such a reaction can overburden the young person, it can also be a time for reflection. Examples of endurance strategies are 'holding something in' or attempting to be alone.

Other authors have described similar phenomena in different terms. The classic 'fight' and 'flight' reactions to stress, for example, are similar to the aggressive/self-destructive and distracting behaviours respectively (Allen and Green, 1988). Certain coping strategies have been associated with possible physical and psychological problems. Adoption of aggressive or self-destructive coping strategies in youth, for example, positively correlates with depression in adulthood (Dise-Lewis, 1988).

Coping is situation-specific (Lazarus and Folkman, 1984) and it is, therefore, not easy to predict how young people will cope in any given stressful situation. They may adopt more than one strategy in working through a particular stressful event. It is also common for young people to use certain strategies for one sort of problem and others for a different problem. As a result, pupils will not always react in a given manner, although it is probable they will major in a particular coping strategy. The teacher's expectations of their pupils may also influence their behaviour.

Pupils' actions are often an enactment of what their teachers expect of them (Rosenthal and Jacobson, 1968). So their stress reactions might be a similar response to expectation.

Whatever strategy a young person adopts to cope with stress, there will be implications for school life. Some stress reactions can be more problematic for school life than others. Aggressive or self-destructive behaviour, for example, can disrupt teaching, undermine discipline or endanger the young person concerned, her/his peers or school staff. Staff may need to maintain discipline by reacting to such behaviour. However, addressing the reason for the stress is the only way effectively to deal with the problem (Jones, 1984). Even positive stress reactions can cause problems for the school. Stress-recognition might be a generally positive reaction to stress, but may put staff in a position where pupils want to talk to them about their problems. If staff are unable or unwilling to deal with this appropriately, then the reaction might have a negative outcome. One can see that whatever the stressor is, whatever the reaction is, teachers should listen and react to their pupils' needs.

WHAT AFFECTS COPING?

If coping strategies can be learned then the school should have a potential role in encouraging the adoption of successful coping mechanisms. Therefore in looking at how a young person reacts to a situation, it is valuable to explore why they are acting in a certain way. If nothing else, understanding the reason for a type of behaviour can help teachers react to the behaviour itself, rather than judge the young person involved. It can also be valuable for planning interventions. How a young person copes in stressful situations will be dependent on several factors. The literature on stress and coping suggests that these are almost as many and diverse as are the causes of stress. However, they do seem to fall into several broad categories.

Many authors believe that gender can influence how a young person will react to stressors. It is believed, for example, that female adolescents experience higher levels of depression than their male peers do (Avison and McAlpine, 1992). However, young men are significantly more likely to commit suicide than young women (Harrington, 1994). This discrepancy may be due to the tendency of a male-dominated medical system to diagnose women's health problems as psychological rather than physiological in origin (Burns, 1990). Then again, young men appear to have more access to materials for suicide. Alternatively, it could be a result of societal expectations on males not to directly show their stress or seek support (Arnold, 1990).

Even in the pre-adolescent period, boys under stress typically react aggressively, while girls are more likely to become self-destructive (Allen and Green, 1988). This gender difference might be a response to sociocultural influences and can have enormous implications for the health and well-being of young people. Some authors consider eating disorders, for example, to be the manifestation of a self-destructive stress reaction (Hunt, 1993). These predominantly affect females, and there is growing concern over the numbers of pre-adolescent girls exhibiting eating disorders. Gender-stereotypical behaviour may also have repercussions for how teachers respond to stress reactions in the classroom environment. Purely because of the disruption that it may cause, aggressive reactions may be noticed more often than internalised stress. It follows that girls may receive less support because their stress is more likely to go unrecognised.

The *nature of the stressful event* can also affect coping. The severity of a stressor will naturally have an impact on the individual's coping reaction. In addition, previous successful conclusions to stress events will influence coping, as this will increase the individual's sense of self-efficacy. This refers to the ability to deal with unpredictable situations. Self-efficacy is a significant determinant in how people cope with stressful events (Turner and Avison, 1992).

It is, perhaps, unsurprising that *personal resources* may have a significant bearing on young people's appraisal of potential stressors and adoption of stress-coping strategies. Important issues are self-esteem and locus of control. Self-esteem is the individual's sense of her/his own self-worth. Individuals with high self-esteem are less likely to adopt maladaptive coping strategies (Blom *et al.*, 1986). Locus of control concerns how people view their influence over their own destinies. People with an internal locus of control see themselves as responsible for their own destinies. Individuals with an external locus, on the other hand, believe they have little dominion over their futures (Rotter, 1966). An internal locus of control is associated with more effective coping (Lau, 1988).

Other people can also influence how a young person copes in a stressful situation. Their perceptions of how much *social support* they can rely on is an important factor (Holahan and Moos, 1987). Young people who feel incorporated into and supported by their social network often cope better than those who feel excluded from it. As a part of social support, *familial support* is also an important element in determining the young person's ability to cope in stressful situations. The help and encouragement that young people get from their families will affect their coping skills. It is also quite likely that how parents cope with stress influences how their children cope. Coping strategies can be learned at a very young age. Parents will model these for their children, who may learn both appropriate and inappropriate behaviour from them (Holahan and Moos, 1987).

At present there is some debate over whether the structure of the family can shape young people's ability to cope with stress. Some commentators have suggested that young people from one- or step-parent families are more likely to suffer from stress (Gore *et al.*, 1992). However, similar findings have been recorded for families with poor parental health. This suggests that the effect of family structure on coping may be, in part, due to the adverse economic conditions that often accompany ill health or one-parent family status. It is not necessarily the result of alternative family structures.

Coping is strongly influenced by *socioeconomic/demographic characteristics*. Perceived low standard of living relates to distress, and can play a major part in how a young person copes with problems (Gore *et al.*, 1992). Relative poverty itself is a major stressor for young people of all ages, but low socioeconomic status may result in a lack of coping resources. It is significantly associated with an external locus of control (Wallston and Wallston, 1981). Factors such as parental unemployment, poor housing and the general social disadvantages associated with poverty will increase the number of stressors in a young person's life and may undermine her or his ability to cope with them. Race can be another factor, with young people from ethnic minority backgrounds experiencing more stressors in their lives (Cronkite and Moos, 1984). This is probably due to the combined effects of poverty, which is more prevalent within ethnic minority groups, and racism.

Finally *age* is linked to how the young person copes with stress (Compas *et al.*, 1992). Young people of different ages will differ in their social, emotional, cognitive and biological development. Younger children are more likely to focus on the problem in coping with a stressor. They will try to alter or control the person, environment or relationship that is causing the problem. As adolescence approaches there is an increase in the use of emotion-focused coping strategies. Here, the young person will attempt to deal with her or his feelings about the situation. In addition, with age, young people's sense of self-efficacy tends to improve as they gain more life experiences. How young people appraise their stressors will change with age too. Very young children have an egocentric view of the world which is challenged as they grow older. In line with this, they come to reassess their responsibility for problems and their power to change situations (Arnold, 1990). Although few primary school age children will experience the problems of adolescence, part of the responsibility of primary school education is to equip them to deal with these problems later on.

Examination of the above shows that how a young person copes with a life crisis will be dependent on a variety of other factors. Moreover, coping strategies may be learned responses to life events (Holahan and Moos, 1987). A young person may employ one strategy because she/he is not permitted, or able, to deal with stress in another manner.

WHAT CAN THE SCHOOL DO?

Young people spend a high proportion of their lives at school. As a result, the influence of school on their lives is far-reaching. There are various ways in which the school can help. For the sake of clarity these have been categorised into passive action, teaching pastoral care and reactive interventions.

Passive action

Sometimes, just being there is enough. School is a vital social network for most young people. It often provides the social support that is so important in helping young people to cope with stressors. To young people living with extreme stress, simply going to school can be helpful. It can provide a source of stability, comfort and support away from the turbulence of family life (Blom *et al.*, 1986). In this way, the school is essentially a passive resource.

If the school is to provide such support there must be an understanding and nurturing environment. Some commentators argue that teaching staff are often more preoccupied with maintaining discipline than providing support. They suggest that this may be due to the often hostile 'hidden curriculum' of schools (Bulman and Jenkins, 1988). The hidden curriculum sends unconscious messages to pupils and staff about what the school expects of them and what they can expect from it. A hostile hidden curriculum can pre-judge and alienate pupils. It dismisses their concerns and ambitions, and reflects the hierarchical nature of society through a system of status and stereotyping (Bulman and Jenkins, 1988).

The pastoral care system can encourage the school to challenge an inhospitable hidden curriculum. Pastoral work can develop pupils' self-esteem, encouraging them to question the assumptions made about their lives and futures. In other words, it enables them to challenge the factors that determine how they cope with stress.

Teaching pastoral care

The role of education for young people is effectively to prepare them for adult life. Therefore, there is a strong argument for stress management techniques to be taught in schools. In recent years, innovations in pastoral care have sought to fulfil this aim. This involves the notion of teaching pastoral care to pupils through personal and social education (PSE). The aim of PSE is the development of skills that will enable the pupil to move from dependence to interdependence – it has been argued that this is about pupil empowerment (Tones, 1988). PSE can be a discrete subject or integrated into other syllabuses as a cross-curricular topic. Various schools have adopted Active Tutorial Work (Baldwin and Wells, 1983) as an approach to the delivery of PSE. Active Tutorial Work involves using those areas of the timetable set aside for form activity. Some teachers feel that this detracts from their capacity to communicate with their pupils, as this time is useful for one-to-one discussion (Tall and Langtree, 1988). Unfortunately, it appears that, for many pupils, this period is traditionally one for exchanging news and catching up on homework (Bell and Maher, 1986).

Despite a statutory requirement on schools to teach PSE (NCC, 1990), in many schools it remains a poor relation to traditional academic subjects. Furthermore, in Key Stages 1 and 2 it is often squeezed out by the curriculum demands of these subjects (Dearing, 1993). However a well-planned and resourced PSE programme can enable young people to deal with stress. PSE can be used to encourage the development of specific coping skills, such as time management and assertiveness training. In addition, it can help raise pupils' self-esteem and self-efficacy (Rogers, 1978). This will give young people a sense of control over their circumstances, as well as the skills to deal with their problems. Of course, such a programme cannot undo the structural forces that may lead to stress in the first place. It could not, for example, transform a young person's socioeconomic status. However, it can present them with the ability to deal with its potentially stultifying effects (Hopson and Scally, 1988). This concurs with teachers' belief that their role is not to help pupils, but to help them help themselves (Carey, 1992).

Improving self-esteem and self-efficacy requires that the school respects and values its pupils. Part of this process is that teachers promote the appropriate expression of feelings by their pupils. To do this, staff require the skills to enable them to explore their feelings. Counselling skills training can achieve this. As Collins (1986, p. 23) says of counselling in schools: 'Counselling allows people to discover things about themselves and articulate and explore their future development.' Therefore, counselling and coping skills development is part of a preventive strategy towards dealing with stress. The school is arming the pupil to deal with future stress. This makes a natural assumption that everyone will experience potentially stressful situations at some point during their lives.

Reactive interventions

Occasionally the school must deal with a pupil's stress in the 'here and now'. Blom *et al.* (1986) call this a 'reactive intervention'. They suggest that this will involve a teacher's cognitive understanding of the pupil's situation. This necessitates that teachers allow pupils to express their feelings. They should provide support, and possibly modify their, and the school's, expectations of the young person for a time. In addition, interventions should include an element of skill development, enabling the pupils to improve their mastery of stressful situations.

In the first instance, dealing with stress involves the identification of the stressor (Carey, 1993). Research suggests that teachers are ineffective at predicting what their pupils' stressors are (Taylor and Spiess, 1989). This indicates that, rather than assuming what pupils' problems are, teachers should seek relevant information from the pupils themselves. To do this, teachers must not only be able to encourage their pupils to talk, but listen to what they are saying as well. In addition, part of their role is to enable pupils to develop crisis management skills. This is similar to Carl Rogers' view of a 'helping relationship', which he defines as:

> one in which one of the participants intends that there should come about, in one or both of the parties, more appreciation of, more expression of, more functional use of the latent inner resources of the individual.
>
> (Rogers, 1961, p. 40)

Therefore, in developing reactive interventions, teachers must respect their pupils and listen and respond to their needs. Counselling skills will enable them to do this as they promote a pupil-centred approach. Furthermore, the development of a nurturing hidden curriculum and worthwhile PSE programmes will benefit from the use of these skills. In light of this, it seems that if the school is to build an effective pastoral system, its staff need counselling skills.

WHAT ARE COUNSELLING SKILLS?

In many ways, the most important of these relate to the teacher's attitudes to the pupil concerned. Carl Rogers calls these the 'core conditions' and says that these are sufficient for an effective counselling relationship. The core conditions are:

1 *'Unconditional positive regard'* or acceptance. According to this, the teachers should value the intrinsic worth of their pupils, no matter what they have done. Effectively, the teacher must distinguish between the sin and the sinner.
2 *'Empathy'*, or the ability to understand another person's situation and reactions as if you were that person. To be empathic, the teacher has to abandon, or at least be very aware of, his or her own prejudices and assumptions.
3 *'Congruence'* or genuineness, which is being honest. Teachers will have to surrender their professional or personal 'masks' and allow themselves to be real. Young people are very good at spotting a fake, so part of this process is ensuring that responses match feelings. Therefore, if

a teacher feels sad or angry she/he should show that and not pretend to feel something else, or nothing at all.

Rogers (1961) cites the work of Halkides as evidence for the importance of the core conditions. She found that in therapeutic exchanges each of these three qualities was significantly associated ($p < 0.001$) with a successful conclusion to therapy. It also appeared that the therapeutic methods adopted were less important than the therapist's ability to display the core conditions. Rogers says:

> it is the attitudes and feelings of the therapist, rather than his [sic] theoretical orientation, which is important. His procedures and techniques are less important than his attitudes. . . . It is also worth noting that it is the way in which his attitudes and procedures are perceived which makes the difference to the client, and that it is this perception which is crucial.
>
> (Rogers, 1961, p. 44)

Displaying the core conditions can be enormously threatening to some teachers (MacMillan, 1993). They undermine the traditional view of teaching which is often about didactic methods and a disciplinarian style. Yet this is a completely inappropriate method for dealing with pupils' problems.

A growing awareness of this has led to the growth of the humanistic movement in education. In *Freedom to Learn for the '80s*, Carl Rogers (1983) presents an abundance of evidence to prove that the humanistic style of teaching is effective. Whatever criteria are chosen, be they academic, social or emotional, pupils taught humanistically compare favourably with those who are not. To the humanist educator, there is no distinction between a teacher's teaching role and her/his caring role. Therefore, the core conditions are a necessary part of the teaching process, as the following quotation illustrates: 'teachers who show a high level of respect [unconditional positive regard] and empathy, and feel secure enough to be themselves in the classroom [congruence], have greater success' (Anderson, 1986, p. 21; author's additions in brackets).

There are also valuable techniques that teachers can use to facilitate a counselling relationship (Truax and Carkhuff, 1967). These are:

1 *Concreteness* which encourages the speaker to be definite about what they are saying and feeling. In doing this, the teacher should discourage the pupil from vagueness and generalisation. This will help the pupil to focus on their feelings.
2 *Confrontation* or the challenging of discrepancies and contradictions in what the speaker is saying or doing. In challenging pupils, teachers should adopt a tentative and exploratory approach. Being too direct and confrontational could be destructive.

3 *Immediacy* involves encouraging the speaker to concentrate on what is happening in the 'here and now'.

The specific micro-skills teachers can use in counselling situations include:

1 *Attending*, which requires the teacher to communicate, verbally or non-verbally, that they are listening. Attending indicates to the pupil that their feelings are valid and helps them to feel secure in the counselling situation. When talking to pupils, teachers should be aware of, and attempt to avoid, possible distractions, for example the needs of other staff or pupils. If they allow themselves to become distracted, this may undermine the pupil's sense of security and trust.
2 *Paraphrasing* means reflecting back to the pupil what she or he has said. This indicates to them that the teacher has listened accurately. It also provides an opportunity for the pupil to clarify and focus what they are saying. Paraphrasing helps teachers confirm that they have understood what the pupil is saying.
3 *Identifying and reflecting feeling*. Pupils will not just recount facts, but how they feel about the facts. Often the feeling is more important than the problem itself. Therefore, it is helpful for pupils to explore their feelings. The teacher can help them do this by reflecting back what they perceive the feeling to be.
4 *Summarising* at the end of a session can be useful because it will help both the teacher and the pupil to clarify the situation. It is also a useful way to draw an end to the session and decide on future action.

The presentation of counselling skills in this chapter is cursory, and may seem to some to be too superficial to be of any value. No apologies are made for this as these are not skills that one can learn from a book, no matter how thoroughly they are described. Anyone interested in exploring and developing their counselling skills is advised to seek some form of training. The British Association of Counselling[1] can provide details of suitable courses.

TEACHER TRAINING AND COUNSELLING SKILLS

It is reasonable to argue that teacher education should include counselling skills training. The value of such training in pastoral care would be to enable teachers to communicate more effectively with their pupils. Rogers (1983) argues that this will only occur when teachers have addressed their personal development. Teachers need to be confident of their abilities, and comfortable with themselves, to redefine traditional power relationships. Chapter 13 gives more consideration to this. McGuiness (1989) claims that teacher training for pastoral care needs to address this. Training must encourage self-reflection and an exploration of what McGuiness calls the 'real me'.

There is concern over the paucity of initial teacher education for the pastoral role (Grant, 1992). Training generally deals with cognitive and not affective issues (Williams, 1986). Therefore, newly qualified teachers are far more confident about teaching subjects than they are about their pastoral role. Yet, Her Majesty's Inspectorate has expressed particular concern over the inadequacy of induction for pastoral care (HMI, 1993). Despite this, within one year of qualifying, two-thirds are teaching PSE and over half have become form tutors (Calvert and Henderson, 1994). This is a cause of some disquiet among those concerned with the provision of pastoral care. Teacher training does not appear to prepare teachers adequately for a pastoral role. Despite this many new teachers take on that role as soon as they qualify.

There is an argument that initial teacher education is not an appropriate place for pastoral care training. After all, there is barely sufficient time in a 36-week Postgraduate Certificate of Education course to cover this in addition to subject teaching. Furthermore, can college provide the real-life situations that are valuable for learning about pastoral care? However, initial education can expose the student to innovative ideas and influences that they may not encounter in their working life (Lunt *et al.*, 1993). Furthermore, some schools' pastoral care systems appear, at best, as erratic and ineffective. It therefore follows that relying solely on these schools to prepare the new teacher for their pastoral role does little to challenge existing poor pastoral practices in some schools. Finally, there is some apprehension over the expectation on practising teachers to train student teachers. First, they may be too busy with their own work to provide complete training and, second, teachers will not necessarily have command of the skills required to train adults (Williams, 1994).

There is also some misgiving over the level of in-service teacher training afforded to pastoral issues. A 1980s survey revealed that approximately 40 per cent of teachers with up to 10 years experience had no in-service training in pastoral care (Maher and Best, 1985). Again, the shortage of appropriate training may be inhibiting the development of pastoral care. Recent years have seen the inclusion of a specific pastoral care qualification in some university prospectuses. The Institute of Education, for example, offers a diploma in pastoral care (Watkins, 1992). However, whether this will be enough to meet demand, or whether it will encourage other institutions to offer similar courses, remains to be seen.

Improving the provision of training at initial and in-service level should enhance the status and practice of pastoral care in British schools. But simply providing training is only part of the answer and other problems will remain. Teachers themselves have identified the lack of space for counselling pupils as a setback to pastoral care. Many find themselves in the position of dealing with distressed pupils in corridors or classrooms. They also believe that there should be more time for all aspects of pastoral care work (Maher and Best, 1985).

There is a strong case for improving pastoral care and counselling skills training. The remainder of this chapter considers how the teacher can use these skills for developing interventions to help pupils in crisis situations. All the ideas presented in the following pages are the result of discussions with practising teachers from primary, middle and secondary schools.

ACTION FOR INTERVENTION

Just as the school can be a source of support for pupils, it can also hinder the coping process. Life crises can be emotional minefields and teachers need to negotiate interventions carefully. If possible, they should consider all the possible implications their plan of action might have for their pupils. Ill-advised policy or interventions can be destructive (Blom *et al.*, 1986). Teachers also require accurate information if they are to develop appropriate interventions. The most obvious source of information is the young person concerned. Teachers can only access relevant information if they can communicate with their pupils. So, if possible, the teacher should always attempt to talk to the pupil involved. This reinforces the need for counselling skills. There are, however, other factors that might indicate that there is a problem. These can be gleaned by observing pupils or talking to their family and friends.

Observation

Broadly speaking this falls into three categories:

1 *Behavioural changes.* Stress can often be manifested as a deviation from normal behaviour. Consequently, if pupils adopt uncharacteristic behaviours, this might be a reaction to their problems. Long-term behavioural changes are often more valuable indicators of stress than short-term changes or one-off events. The latter may have a variety of causes, not necessarily linked to a major life stressor. In primary and middle schools, teachers generally work closely with their pupils. This means that they are in an ideal position to notice behavioural changes. These might be:

- Emotional – the pupil might become easily upset or display wide 'mood swings'. There might be exhibitions of aggression, withdrawal, attention-seeking or disruptive behaviour.
- Work-related – many teachers expect stress to result in a deterioration in academic standards. However, sometimes stress can result in an unexpected improvement in the standard of a pupil's work. They

might be using school work as a distracting coping strategy. Therefore, teachers should be aware of any changes in performance, be it in assessed work, examinations, homework, the pupil's participation in lessons or their school activities. Teachers should also look out for pupils who become generally less attentive or responsive, or express attitudes to issues or people that are out of keeping with her/his character.

- Social – this relates to the pupil's peer relationships. These may become suddenly altered, the pupil may become isolated or abandon one social group in favour of another.

2 *Appearance*. Changes may result from a life crisis. Various physical changes are possible. Those to be aware of include rapid weight loss or gain, bruises, cuts or signs of pain. Pupils may also seem tired, or may be unusually untidy or unclean.
3 *Covert messages*. These are 'hidden' themes expressed by the pupil. They will require some form of analysis to determine their actual meaning. The pupil may express these through play, art, drama or creative writing. In primary schools, this is particularly important. Children might express in a drawing, for example, what they cannot express in words. Some teachers will use art in a proactive manner to encourage children to open up and explore their feelings (Williams *et al*., 1989).

Teachers should also be aware of:

1 *Deceit* – if pupils are lying about some area of their life, it may indicate that they have a problem in that area. Alternatively, they might be attempting to deflect interest from a related issue.
2 *Displacement* – this occurs when pupils over-react to a minor incident (perhaps to gain attention), when in reality there is a more serious problem in their lives.

If a pupil is displaying stress-related behaviour, observing the behaviour of any siblings in the school may indicate if the problem is family-related. Very young children might experience difficulties articulating their problems. Therefore, many primary school teachers see observation as a valuable tool for exposing pupils' problems.

Talking to the family

Vital information about a pupil's well-being can be provided by the family, usually the parents. The use of the term 'parent' refers to the pupil's social parent. It does not imply any necessary biological relationship. Ideally, if a pupil is experiencing a life crisis, her or his parents may inform the school about it. Whether this occurs is often dependent on the nature of the problem, and the family's relationship with the school. Parents might not want to tell a member of school staff if they feel the problem is a personal, family matter, or if it relates to their treatment of their child. Alternatively, parents may be unaware that their child is experiencing a problem.

Similarly, parents might feel uncomfortable talking to the school, or unwilling to do so. However, if there are good channels of communication between parents and staff, they will come to know and (hopefully) trust the teachers. When this occurs, parents will be more likely to warn the school of any potential problems. This will be further enhanced if parents understand how the school can help. If there is a sudden change in the relationship between particular parents and the school, then this may indicate a problem.

Other people to talk to

There are other people who may tell the teacher if a problem exists for a particular pupil. These include the pupil's friends, relatives, neighbours, other pupils and other staff.

School records

Teachers can use these to assess whether a problem is long term or recent. An examination of records is particularly useful for a new teacher, one who is unfamiliar with the pupil or if a pupil has changed school. Teachers should look for:

1 *Absences* – an increase in absences, sometimes a pattern of absences may develop. This might suggest that a pupil has a problem with certain lessons or members of staff.
2 *Lateness* – the teacher should be aware of the extent of lateness or any patterns that may emerge. If possible, excuses for continued lateness should be scrutinised.
3 *Illnesses* – teachers might suspect that the pupil is not really unwell, or that the illnesses maybe stress related. Alternatively, existing conditions might deteriorate because of the pupil being under stress.

All these possible means of problem identification require some intuition by the teacher. It is quite possible that the teacher could misread the signals. This could have damaging consequences for the pupil's relationship with the teacher and even the whole school. It is therefore important that these signals are only used as indicators and that staff take care to talk to the pupil to find out her or his needs.

Another issue of concern is confidentiality. Many of the identification techniques noted above involve discussing the pupil's situation with others. In addition, the use of counselling skills will inevitably put the teacher in a position where they will hear sensitive information. Teachers should negotiate the limits of confidences before the pupil discloses information. It is unlikely that this will prevent the young person talking, but there will be boundaries for both the teacher and the pupil. Failing to follow these might destroy the trust between the teacher and pupil. Furthermore, it might devalue the whole notion of confidentiality and respect within the school.

Teachers need to handle all information appropriately. They should ask themselves, who needs to know and how much do they need to know? Some teachers will need to be aware that a problem exists if they are to react appropriately. However, all that many staff will need is a broad outline of the problem and not specifics. There are problems with confidentiality. It may limit the potential for action, but the teacher should respect the rights of the pupil involved. More problematic is the reaction of other staff. Some may feel alienated or angry, and may see this as colluding with the pupil. Therefore, confidentiality is best addressed within the confines of a clear whole-school policy. All staff should see it as a professional responsibility to follow a set procedure. Of course, new and temporary staff should be aware of the policy when they start.

OUTSIDE AGENCIES

Confidentiality procedure is particularly relevant when dealing with outside agencies (see also Chapter 5). However, this should not dissuade teachers from contacting such groups for advice or support. Many different agencies exist that can help teachers and pupils. Some of these are problem-specific, providing detailed information and possibly therapeutic services such as counselling for young people. Unfortunately, no single teacher could reasonably be expected to know of all relevant organisations. As a result, when a problem arises they may be unsure of who to contact. What is needed is some networking – perhaps schools should draw up a handbook or list (regularly updated) identifying which groups provide information or help for particular issues. Consequently, if a problem then arose, a relevant organisation could be contacted immediately. It might also be valuable if the school could keep a 'bank' of relevant resources that teachers, pupils or parents could consult if they wanted to.

Outside the school there are various agencies that can help, these could include:

- social services
- medical services
- police

- educational psychologists
- support groups
- specialist groups
- community groups

Teachers should not overlook the voluntary sector in seeking outside help.

This chapter has attempted to describe a theoretical basis for how the teacher can provide a good pastoral care service to pupils. It also suggests some practical steps a school can take to improve this service. There is a clear rationale for the provision of counselling skills training for teachers. Helping young people cope with crises, whatever they may be, is an important factor in attending to their general well-being. When a young person does not, or is not allowed or helped to cope with crisis situations, this can have serious implications for their health. They might exhibit social, academic, psychological or behavioural problems in both the short and the long term (Avison and McAlpine, 1992). Research has shown, for example, that high stress may result in overuse of legal or illegal drugs (Dise-Lewis, 1988). Therefore, dealing with life crises can be considered mental health promotion. It is possible that teachers can act as health promotion agents by helping their pupils cope with stress.

Furthermore, this will complement the schools' academic syllabus. The available evidence suggests that young people are more receptive to learning if they feel that they are listened to (Rogers, 1983). Hence, by using counselling skills teachers could have a dual role of preventing stress-related illness and facilitating a learning environment. If this is to occur, teachers cannot simply use counselling skills in a crisis situation. They must integrate the skills into their day-to-day teaching.

NOTE

1 British Association of Counselling, 37a Sheep Street, Rugby, Warwickshire, CV21 3BX.

REFERENCES

Allen, D.P. and Green, V.P. (1988) Helping children cope with stress, *Early Childhood Development and Care*, 37, 1–11.

Anderson, J. (1986) Health skills: the power to chose, *Health Education Journal*, 45, 1, 19–24.

Arnold, L.E. (1990) *Childhood Stress*, New York: John Wiley & Sons.

Avison, W.R. and McAlpine, D.D. (1992) Gender differences in symptoms of depression among adolescents, *Journal of Health and Social Behaviour*, 33, 77–96.

British Association of Counselling (BAC) (1992) *Directory of Training in Counselling Skills*, London: BAC.

Baldwin, J. and Wells, H. (1983) *Active Tutorial Work*, Oxford: Blackwell.

Bell, L. and Maher, P. (1986) *Leading a Pastoral Team*, Oxford: Blackwell.

Blom, G.E., Cheny, B.D. and Snoddy, J.E. (1986) *Stress in Childhood: An Intervention Model for Teachers and Other Professionals*, New York: Teachers' College Press.

Bulman, L. and Jenkins, D. (1988) *The Pastoral Curriculum*, London: Blackwell.

Burns, J. (1990) Psychological aspects of women's health issues, in P. Bennet, J. Weinman and P. Spurgeon (eds) *Current Developments in Health Psychology*, New York: Harwood Academic Publishers.

Calvert, M. and Henderson, J. (1994) Newly qualified teachers: do we prepare them for their pastoral role? *Pastoral Care in Education*, 12, 2, 7–12.

Carey, P. (1992) *How Teachers Deal with Pupils' Life Crises*, Cancer Research Campaign Education and Child Studies Research Group, University of Manchester, Manchester.

Carey, P. (1993) Dealing with pupils' life crises, *Pastoral Care in Education*, 11, 3, 12–18.

Collins, N. (1986) *New Teaching Skills*, Oxford: Oxford University Press.

Compas, B.E., Davies, G.E., Forsythe, C.J. and Wagner, B.M. (1987) Assessment of major and daily stressful events during adolescence: The Adolescent Perceived Events Scale, *Journal of Consulting and Clinical Psychology*, 55, 4, 534–541.

Compas, B.E., Worsham, N.L. and Ey, S. (1992) Conceptual and developmental issues in children's coping with stress, in A.M. La Greca (1992) *Stress and Coping in Child Health*, New York: Guilford Press.

Cronkite, R.C. and Moos, R.H. (1984) The role of predisposing and moderating factors in the stress–illness relationship, *Journal of Health and Social Behaviour*, 25, 372–393.

Dearing, R. (1993) *The National Curriculum and its Assessment: Final Report*, London: School Curriculum and Assessment Authority.

Dise-Lewis, J.E. (1988) The life events and coping inventory: an assessment of stress in children, *Psychosomatic Medicine*, 50, 484–499.

Gore, S., Aseltine, R.H. and Colton, M.E. (1992) School structure, life stress and depressive symptoms in a high school aged population, *Journal of Health and Social Behaviour*, 33, 97–113.

Grant, D. (1992) From coping to competence? Teaching practice, stress and the professionalisation of student teachers, *Pastoral Care in Education*, 10, 2, 20–27.

Harrington, R, (1994) Depression in adolescence, paper presented at Adolescent Mental Health Conference, Trust for the Study of Adolescence, Manchester, 30 September.

Her Majesty's Inspectorate (HMI) (1993) *The New Teacher in School*, London: HMSO / Ofsted.

Holahan, C.J. and Moos, R.H. (1987) Risk, resistance, and psychological distress: a longitudinal analysis with adults and children, *Journal of Abnormal Psychology*, 96, 1, 3–13.

Hopson, B. and Scally, M. (1988) *Lifeskills Teaching Programme No. 4*, Leeds: Lifeskills Associates, University of Leeds.

Hunt, L. (1993) Five hundred years of eating disorders 'reflect women's lack of power', *Observer*, 12 September.

Jones, A. (1984) *Counselling Adolescents* (2nd edn), Essex: The Anchor Press.

Lau, R. (1988) Beliefs about control and health behaviour, in D.S. Gochman (ed.) *Health Behavior: Emerging Research Perspectives*, New York: Plenum Press.

Lazarus, R.S. and Folkman, S. (1984) *Stress, Appraisal and Coping*, New York: Springer Publishing.

London, P. (1987) Character education and clinical intervention: a paradigm shift for US schools, *Phi Delta Kappan*, May, 667–673.

Lunt, N., McKenzie, P. and Powell, L. (1993) 'The right track'. Teacher training and the New Right: change and review, *Educational Studies*, 19, 2, 143–161.

MacMillan, M. (1993) Education and counselling, in B. Thorpe and W. Dryden (eds) *Counselling: Interdisciplinary Perspectives*, Milton Keynes: Open University Press.

Maher, P. and Best, R. (1985) Preparation and support for pastoral care: a survey of current provision, in P. Lang and M. Marland (eds) *New Directions in Pastoral Care*, London: Blackwell.

McGuiness, J. (1989) *A Whole-school Approach to Pastoral Care*, London: Kogan Page.

National Curriculum Council (1990) *Curriculum Guidance 3: The Whole Curriculum*, York: NCC.

Rogers, C.R. (1961) *On Becoming a Person: A Therapist's View of Psychotherapy*, Boston: Houghton Mifflin.

Rogers, C.R. (1978) *On Personal Power: Inner Strength and its Revolutionary Impact*, London: Constable.

Rogers, C.R. (1983) *Freedom to Learn for the '80s*, New York: Merrill Press.

Rosenthal, R. and Jacobson, L. (1968) *Pygmalion in the Classroom*, New York: Holt, Rinehart & Winston.

Rotter, J.B. (1966) Generalized expectancies for internal versus external control of reinforcement, *Psychological Monographs: General and Applied 80*.

Southern, S. and Smith, R.L. (1980) Managing stress and anger in the classroom, *Catalyst for change*, 10, 4–7.

Tall, G. and Langtree, G. (1988) Pastoral education, evaluation and GRIST, *Pastoral Care in Education*, 6, 2, 17–23.

Taylor, R.D. and Spiess, G.A. (1989) Effect of age on congruence between adults' and youths' rating of life event stressors, *Psychological Reports*, 65, 1017–1018.

Tones, K. (1988) The role of the school in health promotion: the primacy of personal and social education, *Westminster Studies in Education*, 11, 27–45.

Truax, C. and Carkhuff, R. (1967) *Towards Effective Counselling and Psychotherapy*, Chicago: Aldine.

Turner, R.J. and Avison, W.R. (1992) Innovations in the measurement of life stress: crisis theory and the significance of event resolution, *Journal of Health and Social Behaviour*, 33, 36–50.

Wallston, K.A. and Wallston, D.S. (1981) Health locus of control scales, in H.M. Lefcourt (ed.) *Research with the Locus of Control Construct. Volume 1: Assessment Methods*, London: Academic Press.

Watkins, C. (1992) *Pastoral Care* (information sheets), Advisory Centre for Education, Coventry.

Williams, A.E. (1994) Roles and responsibilities in initial teacher training – student views, *Educational Studies*, 20, 2, 167–180.

Williams, M. (1986) *Human Relations in Education 6: Training in Counselling and Human Relations*, University of Nottingham: School of Education.

Williams, T., Wetton, N. and Moon, A. (1989) *A Picture of Health: What Do You Do that Makes You Healthy and Keeps You Healthy*? London: Health Education Authority.

8

MANAGING BEHAVIOUR

Tony Charlton and Kenneth David

INTRODUCTION

All schools, in differing degrees and diverse ways, encounter some pupil behaviour which staff (and pupils) find difficulty in coping with. Such behaviour can emanate from factors centred, for example, upon the home, the peer group, the school, the classroom and the individual's biological make-up, or any combination of these and yet other factors. Herculean attempts can be made by individuals – as well as a whole staff – to prevent the onset of problem behaviours. However, events still arise when prevention initiatives flounder and teachers' efforts have to be directed more towards intervention strategies, recognising of course, that there will be times when this intervention should focus upon the teacher and the institution, rather than the pupil.

In the school context, prevention and intervention practices are linked strongly with pastoral care responsibilities and routines. With the management of behaviour in mind, we include in this chapter some strategies and techniques which teachers and schools may wish to consider in their work for pupils' personal, social and academic development. Many of these management techniques are inevitably associated with a healthy school ethos.

Behaviour modification and management has a whole library of appropriate books, and is a wide-ranging and specialised area. We can only summarise here a limited amount of material as a reminder and checklist of pastoral care matters. The references to this chapter include suitable books for deeper study.

SCHOOLS DO MAKE A DIFFERENCE

Over the last two to three decades, teachers have wisely become more accepting of notions that many behaviour problems in school can best be understood, and resolved, in the context where they occur. This endorses views that, on most occasions, the *context* holds the clue to factors which cause and/or maintain problem behaviour. The context facilitates not only an understanding of many school-based problems; it offers, also, the appropriate setting for intervention. In support of this thinking Frude and Gault (1984, p. 36) reported in their school-based enquiry into pupil misbehaviour that:

> Many of the incidents reported to us indicated some weakness in the school organisation, sometimes in the use of buildings, sometimes in the curriculum, or timetable, and sometimes in the teaching or pastoral context.

In a very similar vein Galloway *et al.* (1982, p. 63) had already argued that:

> a knowledge of a school's policies and its teachers' attitudes is often as important in understanding disruptive behaviour as knowledge about family stress and intellectual weakness.

When confronted by children whose behaviour challenges our teaching skills to the limit, it can be convenient – and therapeutic, at times – to externalise the causes of such behaviour away from factors associated with the classroom and school (and even the home) and, instead, direct them upon the individuals themselves. We have in mind the cartoon showing a large teacher towering over a miscreant, roaring:

> Some people will blame your genes, some people will blame your environment, some people will blame your teachers, but I blame you, Wimpole, pure and simple.

Clearly, assumptions of this kind are uncommon in schools, for we appreciate – though at times we may find it far from easy to admit – that causes of problem behaviour often do arise from the very setting where they occur. Experienced teachers already know this. Their time in school will have shown them that whilst some classes behave impeccably with certain teachers, they misbehave with others; and that there are children who function healthily and competently at school, but not in the home (and the reverse). Research strengthens, and informs, this experience and knowledge (e.g. Rutter *et al.*, 1979; Mortimore *et al.*, 1988; Reynolds and Cuttance, 1992; Charlton *et al.*, 1995). Implications from such enquiry submit the following school-based factors as important determinants, or mediators, of pupils' good behaviour:

- good leadership by senior management in consultation with colleagues, and sensitive to the opinions of parents and pupils;
- shared staff policies on expectations to do with pupils' academic and social behaviour as well as teachers' professional behaviour;
- a curriculum which is matched to pupils' present and future needs;
- academic expectations which are high, though not unreasonable;

- an emphasis upon effective use of rewards for good work and (in particular) good social behaviour, rather than the application of punishments;
- high professional standards by teachers in terms of planning, setting and marking work; starting and ending lessons on time, and supporting – rather than undermining – the work of their colleagues;
- pedagogical skills which arouse pupils' interests in the subject material, and motivate them to work well;
- classroom management skills which help prevent problem behaviours from arising;
- healthy, supportive and respectful relations between teachers, between teachers and pupils, between pupils, between school and home, and between school and outside agencies.

Supportive of these 'good school attributes', was the admission within the Elton Report (DES and Welsh Office, 1989a, p. 88) that:

> some schools have a more positive atmosphere than others. It was in these positive schools that we tended to see the work and behaviour that impressed us most. We found that we could not explain these different school atmospheres by saying that pupils came from different home backgrounds . . . these differences had something to do with what went on in the schools themselves.

Our experience of working with schools suggests that schools can gain from considering each of the above factors when appraising their own performance. Self-appraisal exercises require schools and teachers not only to check their professional work, and their pupils' welfare, but also to evaluate their weaknesses as well as their strengths. We should not undervalue the commitment and conviction that this exercise demands; yet the benefits can be considerable. In our experience most schools can, and do, conduct these evaluations with professionalism. However, there may be schools where morale is low, leadership is weak, the staffroom ethos is depressed and staff feel too threatened to 'expose' themselves in this way. In this situation, the school may not always merit censure and condemnation. Directions for improvement are to be preferred, and good Ofsted practices will be directed towards providing this type of positive support.

Whilst it is nonsense to claim, or assume, that schools and teachers are perfect, we know that:

- the great majority of teachers make considerable efforts to succeed in their professional endeavours;
- these efforts do not always lead to success. All of us, therefore, to a greater or lesser degree, derive benefit from continually reflecting upon and evaluating our teaching. These efforts help us to keep 'in touch' with the reality of our performance;

- self-appraisal will work best when it has the support of the school and colleagues;
- efforts to enhance our teaching and management skills will be more likely to succeed if we have access to 'guidelines for good practice' for reference and comparison.

SOME GUIDELINES FOR GOOD PRACTICE

We now list a number of guidelines for teachers to consider as they reflect upon practices in their own classrooms and schools. The list is not definitive, but highlights areas that our own pre- and in-service teachers have found informative and useful.

Reinforcement skills

When using positive reinforcement skills we need to consider the following:

- Do I reinforce (reward) good social behaviour as much as I do good academic behaviour? This is an important area of our teaching to consider. Research has shown consistently that teachers tend to give far more approvals to good academic behaviour than good social behaviour. Regrettably, most good social behaviour goes unrewarded, whilst misbehaviour attracts a surfeit of negative comment (see Merrett and Wheldall, 1987; Charlton *et al.*, 1995).
- Am I overzealous in my use of reinforcement? Keep in mind, 'teachers who reinforce everything, reinforce nothing'. Young children need reinforcements for their industry, their persistence as well as their achievements. Until such times as they become proficient at self-reinforcement, they are dependent upon our reassurances and approval. We can best help them if we are not overgenerous in our use of rewards, or reinforcers. Put more simply, do not be too generous.
- Do I reward effort and persistence, as much as outcomes (i.e. achievements)? Without effort and/or persistence, achievement becomes less likely.
- Do I vary my reinforcer 'menu' to match individual needs and settings? We can become over-reliant upon verbal rewards. Used prudently, and with understanding, a whole range of non-verbal reinforcers can be very effective. Non-verbal reinforcers such as touch, proximity, gestures and facial expressions can help not only to give variety to our teaching and management skills but can also be more effective in certain settings. A nod of encouragement to a shy pupil, for example, can be a confidential and very acceptable way for the pupil to be given praise.

- We underestimate the power of our non-verbal communications. Mehrabian (1972) claims that only 7 per cent of a message is concerned with the content (the words); 38 per cent is to do with voice tone and an overwhelming 55 per cent radiates from body language.
- Do I reinforce groups as well as individuals? Group reinforcers can be more effective, at times; they allow a number of pupils – perhaps the whole class – to share the teacher's pleasure about some aspect of their behaviour or achievement.
- Do I make clear to the pupil(s) what I am rewarding? 'Well done' may not always make clear to the pupil what is being praised. It might be more appropriate, at times, to comment 'I am pleased with your good work. You must have worked extra hard. Well done.'
- Do I forget to reinforce some pupils; the forgotten ones? Compared to their more personable and extroverted peers, quieter and more introverted children may attract far less attention and praise. It's easy to forget them, and so easy to become insensitive to our neglect. (Make a list of your pupils' names, and place a tick against each name as you deliver a verbal reinforcer to her or him. Try to maintain this recording for a day; you could be surprised; *and* concerned.)

Negative reinforcements

Negative reinforcements can help stop misbehaviour. However, their administration requires caution. In effect, they are threats which are used by the teacher with the intention of curtailing or preventing, misbehaviour. Individuals or groups can avoid the threat only if they behave as required. Here is one common example, 'If you don't stop talking, you will all stay in at breaktime!' (Mind you this could be a welcome reward on a cold, wet day!)

If used infrequently – and alongside an acceptable number of positive reinforcements – problems may not arise. Trouble (for the teacher as well as pupils) often looms when the teacher makes inordinate use of them, and develops the habit of controlling children's behaviour with negative reinforcers.

Using punishments

When using punishments to quell some unwanted aspect of classroom behaviour, we need to be mindful that their effects can be harmful, unproductive and counterproductive. Often they serve only to suppress the behaviour; by itself their application does not teach alternative, and more desirable behaviours. Punishments may also generate fears and anxieties within the punished, which then generalise to other settings (e.g. a punishment administered in the classroom can precipitate fears not only of the classroom, but of the school, too). Additionally, as Clarizio and McCoy (1983) point out, there is always the possibility that such behaviour on the teacher's part will serve as an unhealthy model for children.

There is a role for punishment as long as it is applied sparingly, prudently and alongside other more positive teacher behaviours (e.g. reinforcements for good behaviour). It can be reasoned, also, that the 'world outside' operates (although not always equitably and prudently) on a system of rewards and punishments, and that children should become familiar with the reality of the 'outside world'.

Given the above reservations, Clarizio and McCoy (1983) offer the following guidelines for teachers on the use of punishment:

- first, try to identify, and remove, unhelpful reinforcers (or antecedents) which elicit, or sustain, the problem;
- always try to warn – not threaten – a pupil about her/his unacceptable behaviour; this action, by itself, may deter the problem;
- it is often better to punish early, than to delay until the problem behaviour has escalated;
- make it clear why the punishment is being administered;
- punishments should be given fairly and judiciously;
- they should not be employed as a cathartic experience for the teacher, and should be used in a rational, systematic and 'mood free' manner;
- do not over-use punishments and, finally,
- ensure that your classroom is not suffering from a reinforcement 'famine' (ask yourself how frequently your rewards are available to *all* pupils).

Sound advice is also included in the Elton Report (DES and Welsh Office, 1989a) where mention is made of doing all that you can to avoid:

- humiliating . . . because it breeds resentment
- shouting . . . because it diminishes you
- over-reacting . . . because the problems will grow
- blanket punishments . . . because the innocent will resent them
- over-punishment . . . because it is wiser to keep your powder dry, never punish what you can't prove
- sarcasm . . . because it damages you

Clearly, the message is: punishments should be used sparingly and prudently if they are to be effective, and not counterproductive.

The self-concept

Working on the self-concept is becoming more and more a focus for our work in school. The self-concept is the sum total of all of the views a person holds about her or himself; views which are linked to perceptions the person holds about her or himself, socially, personally, physically and academically. Whilst it has a descriptive element (I am tall), it has also an implicit evaluative aspect (I am taller than most others). This evaluative aspect is often important when undertaking (unconscious or conscious) comparisons between our 'perceived' self and what we call our 'ideal' self (i.e. what we would like to be). For example, some adolescents (particularly girls) would like to be slim, yet perceive themselves as being fat (although this may be untrue). This difference between *what they would like to be, and what they think they are,* can be so substantial – and important to them – that it causes a great deal of unhappiness. At times, this dissatisfaction can lead to an enforced diet or, in more extreme cases, an eating disorder.

Our self-concept, then, is fashioned not by our experiences but our interpretations (or *perceptions*) of them, which affect the views we hold of our 'self' and, consequently our behaviour. In *The Centre of the Cyclone* the author writes appositely and cogently: 'Whatever one believes to be true, either is true or becomes true in one's mind.' It can be argued that our self-concepts provide an indication of our emotional health. For example, some children perceive themselves as being so insignificant, so unloved, so neglected and so incompetent that it is hardly surprising that they come to the learning setting ill-equipped (emotionally and cognitively) to cope successfully with the demands of classroom work.

Unsurprisingly, these perceptions which individuals hold about themselves, are largely responsible for their behaviour. In the past when education was first becoming sensitive to the importance of the self-concept in learning, Snygg and Combs (1949, p. 78) emphasised this causal link by contending that: 'What a person does and how he behaves are determined by the concept he has about himself and his abilities.' Since those times, a plethora of research has highlighted the important role a pupil's self-image has in motivating her, or him, to employ effort and industry in order to achieve well (see Lawrence, 1972; Burns, 1982; James *et al.*, 1991). Although some dispute exists about the causal direction (i.e. does achievement affect self-concept or does self-concept determine achievement), few dispute that there is a strong reciprocal link between self-concept and behaviour (e.g. academic performance). Apart from the educational value of using this link to good effect in the school, it seems important that the educational process should always aim to help pupils feel good about themselves. With this 'feel good' factor in mind, Elias and Maher (1983) echoed the concerns of many others when they cautioned that schools were in danger of becoming learning factories, with little or no attention being given to pupils' social and affective development. Perhaps, at school level, we need to remind ourselves from time to time, that children are thinking and feeling as well as active individuals. This line of neglect was pursued by Charlton and Jones (1990, p. 24) who argued that whilst much school time is given to working on literacy and oracy skills:

> whether or not time is allocated to work on children's affective functioning too often depends on adventitious encounters with teachers who have been converted to the need to address such areas. It is time – as a profession – that we all recognised, for example, the need to give adequate time to 'working on the self'.
>
> It is iniquitous for us not to undertake this task. As educators, are we called upon to help educate the 'whole' child? If not, who looks after the neglected parts?

Whether or not you are in agreement with the above comment, no one would dispute that a good self-image is associated not only with scholastic benefits, but is linked also to better adjustment as well as greater happiness in later life (see Rogers, 1983). It is unlikely that those who are satisfied with their achievements, their families, their work, their contributions to society are the ones who spend inordinate and protracted periods of time being helped by counsellors, therapists and psychiatrists; rather, it is those – perhaps through no fault of their own – who feel unwanted, unloved, unsatisfied and dissatisfied.

Methods of raising, or enhancing, our pupils' self-concepts are neither esoteric nor difficult. Research studies (many of them classroom-based) suggest we can do so:

- by tailoring our teaching to meet individual needs, and so making success more likely than failure;
- by helping pupils to feel supported and valued. Often we can achieve this by finding time to listen to them, by learning about – and understanding – them, by showing an interest in them and by giving them unconditional positive regard (we may not like their behaviour, but this need not stop us liking them);
- by encouraging realistic self-praise. As we become older, we have to become less dependent upon others' praise. If we are to survive healthily we need self-praise; to tell ourselves that our achievements are something we should be proud of. This practice is an important one in our increasingly selfish society where people are too often unmindful of others, and their needs for constant reassurance, recognition and praise;
- by giving them opportunities to recognise, and publicise, their own achievements as well as other positive aspects of their lives;
- by helping them to appreciate that others have feelings. By doing this we can assist them to socialise more competently, and the 'worlds' of the classroom and school can become better and healthier places to live in;

- by challenging them; 'this work is harder than the last piece, but I think you can do it';
- by encouraging them to understand that they have more control than they think over what happens to them (this refers to their locus of control: see Charlton, 1985). It is important to help youngsters realise that *their* efforts and their persistence are often the key factors which lead to their successes.

Teacher expectations also seem to be influential in shaping the self-concept and, thereby, affecting performance. Rosenthal and Jacobsen reasoned that pupils' academic gains in their Pygmalion research, occurred as a consequence of the teachers' changed behaviour (particularly their expectations) towards them. With reference to the teacher(s) they claimed that:

> By what she said, by how she said it, by her facial expressions, postures and perhaps by her touch, the teacher may have communicated to the children that she expected improved academic performance. Such communications together with possible changes in teaching technique may have helped the child to learn by changing his self-concept, his expectations of his own performance and his motivation as well as his cognitive skills.
>
> (1968, p. 217)

In a similar manner, the role of significant others in shaping the self-concept is stressed within Combs's book *The Human Side of Learning*. He makes this comment:

> The student takes his self-concept with him wherever he goes. . . . Are we influencing that self-concept in positive or negative ways? We need to ask ourselves these kinds of questions. How can a person feel liked unless someone likes him? How can a person feel wanted unless someone wants him? How can a person feel accepted unless someone accepts him? How can a person feel he's a person with dignity and integrity unless someone treats him so. And how can a person feel that he is capable unless he has some success.
>
> (1969, p. 37)

From a more practical standpoint, Canfield and Wells (1976) have produced 100 exercises which teachers can use to help enhance pupils' self-image. One of our in-service students used thirty of these exercises in assemblies, over a period spanning one term. In her written assignment, at the end of the term, she wrote – with much emotion – about the outcomes of their use:

> There were times when I felt like crying, because the effects of the exercises upon the children were so moving. It began with the

children, but then spread to the staff. The whole school changed, for the better. Parents wrote to the Head, they rang her, and some came to see us. They couldn't believe what had happened. One of the mid-day supervisors said to me 'It's a miracle'. Yet I feel that all we had done, was to open a door so that the light gave the children a glimpse of a more considerate and caring world. They needed to learn about this, as much as they did about arithmetic and reading.

The link between the 'self' and academic performance has received much attention in the work of Lawrence (1971, 1972). In a number of his research studies he demonstrated how pupils' academic improvements could be outcomes of teachers' successful attempts to enhance children's feelings about their self. These attempts were based largely around three relatively simple, yet effective, counselling skills; unconditional positive acceptance, genuineness and empathy.

- *Empathy* implies an understanding of another person, as if you were in their shoes. No one can empathise totally with another's feelings and thoughts; but effective teachers (like effective counsellors) seem to get close to it. If you can begin to empathise with pupils' thoughts and feelings you become better able to understand them. Whilst this understanding is important at all times, it becomes crucial when you try to help them deal with a problem. Comments like 'I am beginning to understand how you feel' can provide much needed reassurance and comfort to one who is experiencing anxieties or concerns.
- *Unconditional positive regard* requires us to communicate an affection and respect for a person which is differentiated from any dislike we may hold about their (mis)behaviour. 'I don't like your behaviour, but I like you.' This is not always an easy task; but it is made easier if we can look for positive, rather than negative, aspects in a person, particularly a young one. Everyone has a positive 'side'; though it may be the case that with some we need to search hard.
- *Genuineness* is a quality people value and search for in their relationships with others. It implies a sense of honesty which encourages trust. Pupils, even very young ones, are very adept at assessing their teachers, and it is to the 'honest' one whom a troubled child is likely to turn to for help. Burns (1982) lists the characteristics of the genuine teacher including the following where:
    - her verbal and non-verbal behaviours are congruent with each other;
    - she is willing to be reasonably open about herself;
    - she does not draw attention to her status.

Protecting pupils' self-worth, or at least taking steps to ensure that we do not reduce it, should be an automatic concern of ours. However, some children are unfortunate to be in classrooms where their self-worth is reduced (unintentionally or otherwise). A few years ago we asked PGCE students, many of whom were adults with considerable experience of working in industry or commerce, to reflect upon their early school experiences and remember teacher comments which reduced their self-concept. These are some of them;

- Where did your parents get *you*? Your brother was really bright.
- With your black skin you don't have to worry about sunburn.

Clearly, there can be times when thoughtless comment has lasting impact upon our thoughts and feelings. If we remember them, then they must have made (unfavourable) impressions in our 'hearts and minds'. In the classroom we need to be ever mindful of this

Controls from without

Some years ago Fritz Redl was confronted by his staff at his residential special school in America. They did not question his philosophy, which derived from a psychodynamic approach. A key factor of this approach is that the disturbed children should be given a type of environment which – in time – helped them to control their own behaviour 'from within'. The staff agreed with this long-term aim. However, they stressed that they needed some guidelines (or external controls) which would enable them to manage the children's behaviour until such times as the youngsters could control it themselves. With this support in mind, Redl and Wineman (1953) devised a short list of techniques for his staff. These techniques are invaluable to all teachers (and parents) in their management of behaviour; so we repeat some of them here:

- Ignore misbehaviour, as far as is practicable. Much of it will disappear if you do.
- Use your sense of humour, if you can, to defuse tensions and challenges to your authority.
- Signal interference can be a subtle, yet effective, controller (a raised eyebrow, a finger to the lips, or a wink).
- Proximity, or touch, control can be an invaluable technique (e.g. the teacher moves towards the misbehaviour to quell it).
- Involvement of interest relationships, where the teacher notes that a pupil is encountering difficulties in remaining on-task and moves towards him, or her, to express interest in the work and help to re-ignite the lost interest.

Relationships

Relationships can be the key to success in the classroom and the school. In order to relate to individuals and groups it is necessary to make 'contact'. Once again, the Elton Report (DES and Welsh Office, 1989a) has simple yet invaluable advice about how to help arrange this. The report talks about the teacher taking the initiative and being required to:

- greet and be greeted
- speak and be spoken to
- smile and relate
- communicate

More often than not, the building of relationships is a lengthy process, and can be achieved in many ways; getting to know – really know – your pupils is one way of doing this. To know them we need to listen to them talk, for example, about their out-of-school lives, their fears and concerns, their holidays and their home, and about what they do with their leisure time. Knowledge of this type can help us to understand better the individual, and her/his behaviour.

It is helpful, too, if we have glimpses of parts of their world, such as their TV viewing preferences. Knowing something about their viewing tastes gives us a point of contact so that we key in to conversations, for example, about *Eastenders*, and *Home and Away*. Programmes such as these can also be used in pastoral care discussion focusing upon such matters as the break-up of friendships, family responsibilities and AIDS. In Chapter 11, Tony Charlton talks more about the value of using pupils' television viewing in school. The teacher's training will enable her or him to decide what is age-appropriate for their pupils.

Preventive approaches

Preventive approaches are always to be preferred to intervention, for many reasons. First, it is better if problems do not arise; concerns, stresses, unhappiness and conflicts are better avoided for they can cause untold misery for youngsters and teachers. Second, a great deal of time and energy can be saved if problems are avoided; teacher resources can then be directed elsewhere. The PAD material (Preventive Approaches to Discipline) has been devised along these lines by Chisholm *et al.* (1986) and is based upon the following premises:

- pupils' behaviour is influenced by the teacher's behaviour;
- teachers with effective classroom control are skilled at avoiding and de-escalating problem behaviour;
- specific techniques of classroom management and control can be described, practised and acquired by teachers;

- teachers should take responsibility for developing their skills and should be supported in doing so by their schools.

The common sense rules within PAD are worthy revision points for teachers; there are times when we forget the obvious! PAD talks, for example, about teachers:

- positioning themselves in classrooms so that they can oversee, and regulate, behaviour;
- adequately preparing lesson content making sure materials and equipment are appropriate, adequate and easily utilised;
- using unobtrusive and subtle management skills such as proximity control;
- helping to ensure lessons are less likely to encourage misbehaviour by refining their non-verbal skills so that they:
  - avoid speaking in a monotonous way
  - make regular eye-to-eye contacts with pupils
  - use gestures to support their teaching, and
  - avoid communicating feelings of anxiety or tenseness;
- organising lesson materials before pupils arrive;
- supervising pupils' entrance into, and exit from, the classroom;
- giving clear instructions concerning lesson activities;
- making sure that lesson changes are planned carefully and run smoothly;
- constantly, yet surreptitiously, monitoring behaviour around the classroom;
- intervening promptly where problems occur;
- marking classwork promptly and thoroughly;
- employing teaching techniques which are varied, in order to maintain (or arouse flagging) interest;
- anticipating lesson endings so that the lesson concludes smoothly; and,
- making sure that the classroom layout facilitates, rather than impedes, smooth-running lessons.

Peer support practices

Such practices can help members of tutor groups to become more personally, socially and academically competent. Peer tutors also stand to gain from this involvement, as does the school.

By 'peer support' we refer to those instances (usually planned and under the supervision, or guidance, of a teacher) where young pupils are directly involved in organising and delivering experiences to help maximise some aspect of their peers' functioning (i.e. their affective, social, physical and cognitive performance). Such help can refer to cross-age as well as same-age learning systems and may refer to diverse practices where pupils are given roles, for example, as peer counsellors, peer tutors, bully line counsellors or peer buddies. This assistance can involve pupils in listening to others read, attending to them whilst they talk about their personal problems, 'teaching' some aspect of a curriculum area (e.g. arithmetical computations), or providing sympathetic support to someone who is encountering difficulty in adjusting to the demands of school. Whichever practice is employed, it usually includes a type and degree of interaction which is uncommon in classrooms which omit this support. There are strong indications, too, that 'the instructional, social and cost effectiveness of (peer) tutoring is mounting' (Gartner and Lipsky, 1990, p. 84).

Interestingly, peer support can effect 'gains' which are equally apparent for those *giving* the help (e.g. the tutors) as those *receiving* it (e.g. pupils). Additionally, it has been suggested that occasions arise when the peer tutors' contributions appear even more productive than those given by the teacher (Good and Brophy, 1987). This effectiveness seems to stem from youngsters' use of:

> more age-appropriate and meaningful vocabulary and examples; as recent learners of material being taught, they are familiar with the tutee's potential frustrations and problems; and they tend to be more directive than adults.
>
> (Thousand and Villa, 1988, p. 166)

Charlton and Jones (in press) describe in some detail a number of studies using peer support practices in primary and secondary schools, and those seeking more detailed discussions on these practices can turn to them. In these studies, children in receipt of peer support made significant academic as well as social gains. Overall, the studies suggest the following advantages:

From the teacher's perspective

- It frees their time so they can become more watchful over, and more supportive of, individuals' learning tasks and outcomes. This type of role provides additional opportunities for teachers to orchestrate pupils' success. By making their classroom duties more manageable, this freedom may also help reduce teachers' stress levels.
- Evidence shows that by harnessing peer support practices the teacher helps to improve pupils' all-round performances. Teaching becomes more individualised, and perhaps more 'needs oriented'.
- Peer support practices can help redress the imbalance between teacher talk and pupil talk which currently seems to be 'weighted in favour of the teacher' (Kyriacou, 1986, p. 145).
- Some of the pupils involved: 'who had formerly been aggressive and argumentative in their behaviour towards their peers showed remarkable patience and commitment when in the 'teaching role' (Atherly, 1989, p. 151).

From the peer tutors' perspective

- Tutors also gain from 'learning by teaching'. Their involvement helps to improve their own academic competence, a long-held belief which has now been established empirically.
- Hamblin (1978) reminds us that peer counselling can raise the counsellor's feelings of worth. He suggests, also, that as peer support practices become more widespread within a school they can contribute to a healthy ethos. Related to this, there is evidence that tutors can gain in self-assurance and willingness to assume responsibility.
- Without access to adequate instruction and good example, it is not difficult for children to grow up to become selfish and uncaring. The notion of helping others, and feeling that their help is valued, is a commendable practice. Peer support offers meaningful classroom opportunities to promote the development of healthy pro-social attitudes.

Listening

Listening to children can reap many benefits for the classrooms, the school and children. Unfortunately, however:

> Active listening (in an interpersonal context) is rarely given the recognition, and time, it deserves in classrooms and schools, or elsewhere. This is regrettable for a number of reasons as this chapter has sought to make clear. Children stand to derive much benefit from being listened to; their academic success can be enhanced, their personal problems can be reduced, their self-esteem and motivation can be enhanced. Schools benefit too.
>
> (Charlton, 1996, p. 57)

Children usually respond favourably and successfully when adults find time to listen to them. On their part, adults have much to gain. In the counselling or tutorial setting, the teacher can often best help the individual through the use of the listening skill, one which is central to non-directive counselling. From a wider perspective, the teacher can learn a great deal from attending to children in this way. This knowledge helps deepen their understanding of children as well as personalise their relationships, qualities which contribute to good teaching. Elsewhere, children's voices can provide invaluable feedback about a whole range of school-centred matters.

In their enquiry Wade and Moore (1994) demonstrated how well children can remind us of these types of experience, if we listen to them. They consulted over 150 children with a wide range of special needs about their views of changing schools. Responses showed that over half of the sample expressed fears about being lonely, not being able to make new friends, being bullied or picked on, not coping with academic work or about harsh teachers. Children with visual impairments expressed fears about finding their way in unfamiliar buildings. From a more positive perspective the children suggested ways in which the transfer could be less anxiety-provoking. Their comments demonstrate a sensitivity and sensibility which may shame some schools. Pupils suggested that before pupils move to a new school the teachers at the new school should:

- tell you what it is like
- have things ready
- show you around
- be aware that you're coming
- let you have a day there
- let you meet the teachers
- know what a difficult and painful experience it is

Other potentially profitable opportunities for the teacher to listen to pupils, occur when:

- formulating classroom or school rules
- counselling
- assessing pupils' (and teachers'!) progress in school
- asking for self-assessments
- wanting to learn more about their 'inner' and 'outer' worlds.

There are many instances in classrooms where the 'teacher's ear' provides help for children's learning; thus listening by the teacher supports learning by the pupil. Of course this link is probably true in many areas of the teacher's work, but here we are concerned with occasions where pupils' anxieties, low self-image and fears handicap their learning. In these instances instructional work is unlikely to succeed until therapeutic intervention removes the handicap (or emotional block, as it is sometimes called). More often than not, this intervention incorporates skills more readily associated with non-directive counselling strategies than teaching practices. Whilst these strategies require teachers to empathise with the pupil, it is the listening facility which anchors them (Burns, 1982). During the last twenty years or so the value of this 'listening and talking' therapy has become clearly established. Teachers use their listening skills to encourage children to talk about themselves in ways which help remove blocks to learning. More innovative, perhaps, are those instances when peer counsellors have been involved in this work. Experiences have shown that peer counsellors are often as successful as their adult counterparts in undertaking non-directive support work with pupils (James *et al.*, 1991).

It has been a practice in schools – though not a common one – to heed pupils' self-assessments on such matters as their emotional functioning (e.g. their feelings about their self and their anxieties). However, the practice of listening to pupils' self-assessments in academic (and academic-related) areas is more recent and more embryonic. Within the past few decades there has been a trend towards pupil profiling of one type or another. In accord with the DES policy statement on records of achievement (DES&WO, 1989b) these innovations offer opportunities for older pupils to become involved in 'self-assessment and in the discussion of their assessment with their teachers' (Murphy and Torrance, 1988, p. 36). It is worth noting that Rogers (1983) suggests this involvement necessitates an unlearning process – rather than being a *learning* one – where pupils are encouraged to become less dependent upon external sources for evaluations (e.g. from teachers, through peer comparisons), and more inclined to look 'inward for signs of progress and growth' (p. 62).

There is little evidence that the wide range of organised peer support practices are common in classrooms. Regrettably, their absence from the teaching scenario may withhold from teachers and pupils opportunities to become involved in relatively uncomplicated – yet effective – methods of helping to manage pupils' learning and behaviour, more effectively.

CONCLUSION

In this chapter we have outlined proven, and valued, practices which teachers and schools can profit from. These practices hint strongly at the complexities and perplexities of teaching, and in doing so stress the need for on-going professional development to enhance the behaviour management skills which underpin both healthy pastoral care, and classroom teaching practices.

Appraisals of our own practices can confirm their effectiveness; they can also suggest the need for modifications to them. Three considerations follow. First, as part of teachers' endeavours to refine their pastoral care practices, this chapter may encourage them to *appraise* their own behaviour management expertise. Second, dealing constantly with challenging behaviour is not easy; at times the stress from these encounters can be considerable, even for more experienced teachers. It may be the case, therefore, that consideration of the chapter's contents will prove therapeutic in that they *confirm* the adequacies of many existing practices in the classroom and wider school, yet suggest that relatively minor 'tinkerings' are needed. Third, they may also encourage teachers to consider modifications to their approaches by testing out 'new' ones, for there are times when we all, unintentionally (and, perhaps, unwittingly) stray away from good professional practices.

REFERENCES

Atherley, C.A. (1989) Shared reading: an experiment in paired tutoring in the primary classroom, *Educational Studies*, 15, 2, 145–154.

Burns, R. (1982) *Self-concept Development and Education*, Eastbourne: Holt, Rinehart & Winston.

Canfield, J. and Wells, H.C. (1976) *100 Ways to Enhance the Self-concept in the Classroom: A Handbook for Teachers and Parents*. Englewood Cliffs, NJ: Prentice Hall.

Charlton, T. (1985) Locus of control as a therapeutic strategy for helping children with behaviour and learning difficulties, *Maladjustment and Therapeutic Education*, 3, 1, 26–32.

Charlton, T. (1996) Listening to children in school, in R. Davie and D. Galloway (eds) *Listening to Children's Voices*, London: David Fulton.

Charlton, T., Essex, C., Lovemore, T. and Crowie, B. (1995) Naturalistic rates of teacher approval and disapproval and on-task levels of first and middle school pupils in St Helena, *Journal of Social Behaviour and Personality*, 10, 4, 1023-1030.

Charlton, T. and Jones, K. (1990) *Working on the Self*, Cheltenham: College of St Paul and St Mary Press.

Charlton, T. and Jones, K. (in press) Peer support practices, in K. Jones and T. Charlton (eds) *Overcoming Learning and Behaviour Difficulties*, London: Routledge.

Chisholm, B., Kearney, D., Knight, H., Little, H., Morris, S. and Tweddle, D. (1986) *Preventive Approaches to Disruption*, Basingstoke: Macmillan Education.

Clarizio, H.F. and McCoy, G.F. (1983) *Behaviour Disorders in Children*, New York: Harper & Row.

Combs, A. (1969) *The Human Side of Learning*, Boston: Allyn & Bacon.

Department of Education and Science and Welsh Office (1989a) *Discipline in Schools* (Elton Report), London: HMSO.

Department of Education and Science and Welsh Office (1989b) *Records of Achievement*, National Steering Committee Report, London: HMSO.

Elias, M. and Maher, C. (1993) Social and affective development of children: a programmatic perspective, *Exceptional Children*, 49, 4, 339–345.

Frude, J. and Gault, H. (1984) *Disruptive Behaviour in Schools*, Chichester: John Wiley & Sons.

Galloway, D., Ball, T., Blomfield, D. and Seyd, R. (1982) *Schools and Disruptive Pupils*, London: Longman.

Gartner, A. and Lipsky, D. (1990) Students as instructional agents, in W. Stainsback and S. Stainsback (eds) *Support Networks for Inclusive Schooling*, Baltimore, MD: Paul H. Brookes Publishing.

Good, T.L. and Brophy, J.E. (1982) *Educational Psychology: A Realistic Approach*, New York: Holt, Rinehart & Winston.

Hamblin (1974) *The Teacher and Counselling*, Oxford: Blackwell.

James, J., Charlton, T., Leo, E. and Indoe, D. (1991) A Peer to Listen, *Support For Learning*, 6, 4, 165–170.

Kyriacou, C. (1986) *Effective Teaching in Schools*, Oxford: Blackwell.

Lawrence, D. (1971) The effects of counselling upon retarded readers, *Educational Research*, 13, 2, 119–124.

Lawrence, D. (1972) Counselling of retarded readers by non-professionals, *Educational Research*, 15, 1, 48–54.

Mehrabian, A. (1972) *Silent Messages*, Belmont, CA: Wadsworth.

Merrett, F. and Wheldall, K. (1987) Natural rates of teacher approval and disapproval in British primary and middle school classrooms, *British Journal of Educational Psychology*, 57, 95–103.

Mortimore, P., Sammons, P., Ecob, R. and Stoll, L. (1988) *School Matters – The Junior Years*, London: Open Books.

Murphy, R. and Torrance, H. (1988) *The Changing Face of Assessment*, Milton Keynes: Open University Press.

Redl, F. and Wineman, D. (1952) *Controls from Within*, London: Collier-Macmillan.

Reynolds, D. and Cuttance, R. (1992) *Effective Schools*, London: Cassell.

Rogers, C. (1983) *Freedom to Learn in the '80s*, New York: Charles Merrill.

Rosenthal, R.R. and Jacobsen, L.L. (1968) *Pygmalion in the Classroom*, Eastbourne: Holt, Rinehart & Winston.

Rutter, M., Maugham, B., Mortimore, P. and Oustan, J. (1979) *Fifteen Thousand Hours: Secondary Schools and their Effects on Pupils*, London: Open Books.

Snygg, D. and Combs, A.W. (1949) *Individual Behaviour: A New Frame of Reference for Psychology*, London: Harper & Row.

Thousand, J.S. and Villa, R.A. (1988) Accommodating for greater student variance, in M. Ainscow (ed.) *Effective Schools for All*, London: David Fulton.

Wade, B. and Moore, M. (1994) Good for a change? The views of students with special educational needs on changing school, *Pastoral Care in Education*, 12, 2, 23–27.

9

BULLYING IN THE PRIMARY SCHOOL

Everyone's concern

Sonia Sharp

Social acceptance and involvement is an important feature of child development. Research into the friendships of primary age pupils suggests that pupils who fail to establish successful relationships with their classmates and who are rejected by their peer group are more likely to experience adjustment problems in school and later in life (Cowen *et al.*, 1973; Rubin, 1985). Although there will always be some children who naturally prefer to be alone, the majority of children enjoy social contact with their peers. Breakdown in friendship may lead to depression, loneliness, resentment and anger. Poor peer relationships can arise for a variety of reasons, and bullying is one of these.

ABOUT BULLYING BEHAVIOUR IN THE PRIMARY SCHOOL

Bullying behaviour is an anti-social phenomenon which can occur in any group context. It involves at least two people, usually more. It is persistent aggressive behaviour which is intended to dominate and intimidate. It can be direct or indirect, physical, verbal or psychological; and includes behaviours such as name-calling, social exclusion, extortion and rumour-mongering. It usually reflects an imbalance in power between the parties involved. It is distinct from occasional disagreements or fights between two people of groups of equal status or strength. Bullying can take very subtle forms and can be difficult for those not directly involved to detect. The fearfulness which bullying can cause can be maintained by threatening glances or innuendo, creating in the victim an anxiety of what *might* happen rather than actual physical or verbal contact.

Bullying behaviour is a common feature of school life, especially in the primary years. At any one time, as many as one in four primary-aged pupils may be experiencing bullying at school. Research into bullying in UK schools (Whitney and Smith, 1993) provides insight into the nature and extent of bullying behaviour. In a study of 2,623 primary-aged pupils attending sixteen primary schools in Sheffield, Whitney and Smith found that on average 27 per cent of pupils had experienced bullying more than once or twice in the term leading up to the survey; 10 per cent of these pupils were being bullied regularly throughout the term. Name-calling and physical aggression were the most frequent forms of bullying. Many pupils also reported that they were being isolated and deliberately left out, had nasty rumours spread about them, had their possessions taken, damaged or stolen. Both boys and girls reported that they had experienced bullying behaviour. Girls were more frequently subjected to verbal and indirect bullying; boys experienced more physical violence and threats. Some bullying reported in this study occurred on the way to and from school, but most took place in school – 75 per cent happened during playtimes and lunch breaks.

Any pupil can be the victim of bullying behaviour. Those pupils who are more socially isolated, who are noticeably 'different' in some way from the majority of pupils, have special educational needs or who have poor social skills are more at risk of experiencing bullying behaviour. Pupils who join a class part way through the academic year can also become the targets of a bullying group. Pupils are more often bullied by a group of pupils in the same class or year group.

Pupils who bully others are often supported by a close-knit group of peers. These pupils can come from any social background. They can be very able, articulate pupils and may have little empathy for their victims. These powerful and cohesive groups of pupils may even intimidate some members of staff. Alternatively, some bullying pupils may be favoured by individual teachers. Pupils who bully others can be perceived to be popular by peers. This does not mean they are necessarily liked by their classmates but that other pupils are seen to obey the bullying pupil and conform to their wishes.

Teachers often remain unaware of the extent of bullying behaviour in their classes. This is partly because of the conspiracy of silence which bullying encourages. About half of all pupils who are bullied are reluctant to tell an adult. Other pupils who witness bullying may also be afraid to tell. Parents are often the first adult to know their son or daughter is being bullied. The deliberate nature of bullying means that it is usually planned and orchestrated to remain hidden from adult view. When teachers are informed about a bullying incident by a pupil or parent, they may be surprised or even disbelieving because they have had no awareness of the bullying relationship. When teachers encounter a bullying incident, they may only be aware of the final sequence of events. The retaliation of a victim can be misinterpreted as provocation.

Bullying behaviour has an immediate impact upon pupil well-being and happiness. Although some pupils may seem to provoke bullying reactions in their peers, nobody likes to be bullied. About 20 per cent of pupils will take time off school to avoid being bullied. Some children are even driven to hurting themselves. Both boys and girls find rumour-mongering the most stressful (Sharp, 1995).

Bullying behaviour can also reduce the learning potential of some children. One-third of pupils report that their concentration is impaired by the anxiety caused by bullying. The management of social relationships is central to establishing a co-operative climate for learning. A constructive climate enables pupils and teachers to get along with each other and attend to the business of education. Discord detracts from the possibilities of learning.

So what can schools do about bullying? The very nature of bullying behaviour can make it difficult for teachers to respond effectively. Teaching staff may well be unaware of the extent of bullying behaviour within the school. It may seem as though 'bullying is not a problem'. But how do you know that? Staff may be suspicious that relationships are not good, but have no evidence upon which to act. When actually aware of some bullying, staff may find themselves faced with a dilemma when one pupil gives one account of the situation and two or three give another conflicting but equally plausible version. Staff are required to treat all pupils with respect and dignity and so finding a way to tackle such evasive behaviour in a fair and effective manner can be challenging. Fortunately, school-based research into bullying behaviour has begun to identify solutions and the remainder of this chapter will outline some of these.

SCHOOLS DO MAKE A DIFFERENCE

Norway has led the way in helping schools deal with bullying. In 1983, spurred on by public pressure following three child suicides and evidence produced by Dan Olweus that bullying was a widespread problem, the Ministry for Education funded a nation-wide campaign against bullying in all 3,500 Norwegian schools.

A survey on bullying was carried out in all schools, and a package of materials was provided for teachers, including a video for classroom discussion of the issue, and a folder of advice for parents. There was also considerable national discussion of the problem. Each class of pupils developed its own anti-bullying charter which was backed up by parent and staff agreement about sanctions should bullying occur. Attention to bullying was maintained by regular class discussions about social issues. These class meetings provided a forum for pupils who were being bullied, or who knew of someone being bullied, to talk.

Olweus (1992) evaluated the effectiveness of this campaign in forty-two schools in Bergen. He compared levels of bullying at three time points – just before the intervention started, one year later and two years later. Olweus found that over the two-year period rates of reported bullying had fallen by about 50 per cent.

A second evaluation was carried out by Erling Roland in the Rogaland county of Norway around Stavanger (Roland, 1993). Roland monitored thirty-seven schools, over three years between 1983 and 1986. He only found decreases in levels of reported bullying in those schools which had systematically and consistently taken action against bullying. These findings suggest that schools can reduce levels of bullying but these changes will only continue if schools maintain their efforts over time.

In 1990, the Department of Education agreed to fund a similar project to the Norwegian one in Sheffield, directed by Peter Smith (Smith and Sharp, 1994). The project aimed to identify effective intervention strategies for preventing and responding to bullying. The project ran from 1991 to 1993 and involved sixteen primary schools and seven secondary schools. Schools tried out various intervention strategies and the effects of these were monitored. A questionnaire survey carried out in 1990 and repeated in 1992 demonstrated the extent of reductions in bullying behaviour. All of the schools involved developed whole-school anti-bullying policies. They supported these in practice through a range of additional interventions.

ESTABLISHING A WHOLE-SCHOOL ANTI-BULLYING POLICY

A whole-school anti-bullying policy is a document which states the aims of the school and which defines practice within the school. Through implementation of the policy, everyone within the school should be clear about how bullying behaviour is defined and about how it can be prevented and responded to.

Schools which had involved most of their staff (including non-teaching staff) in the process of policy development had the largest reductions in levels of bullying. In these schools, all staff had been involved in debate and discussion about what bullying is and how it should be tackled as part of an awareness-raising programme. Consultation about the actual content of the policy was widespread and thorough. Schools which consulted with pupils as well as staff about policy content were more successful in encouraging pupils to tell a teacher when they were bullied and increased confidence amongst pupils that 'this school does take action against bullying'.

The anti-bullying policy needs to relate to other social policies, such as general behaviour, equal opportunities and pastoral care. Indeed, the pastoral policy provides a framework within which the anti-bullying policy can be implemented.

Policy content

Each school will develop a policy which reflects its own needs. Within the Sheffield anti-bullying project, schools included:

- the aims and objectives of the school in relation to bullying;
- a clear definition of which behaviours are considered to be bullying within the school (this may differ from school to school);
- a description of how bullying would be prevented;
- procedures for staff, pupils, parents and governors who become aware of a bullying situation;
- procedures for bullying situations which persist even after initial intervention by the school.

Preventing bullying

Preventative measures can most effectively be achieved in three ways:

- through the pastoral curriculum;
- through staff behaviour;
- through enhancing the quality of playtimes and lunch breaks.

The pastoral curriculum

Within the context of personal and social education, the curriculum provides a forum for:

- educating pupils about the problem of bullying;
- introducing the school's policy on bullying;
- challenging attitudes about bullying;
- teaching pupils how to respond effectively to bullying and how to manage difficult situations constructively;
- teaching pupils how to support peers who are being bullied;
- engaging pupils in the development of strategies for preventing bullying;
- facilitating the development of an anti-bullying ethos within the school.

Through the curriculum it is possible to explore a wide range of issues about the problem of bullying behaviour. These include practical issues such as:

- What is bullying?
- What motivates people to bully?
- How does bullying affect others?
- How does it feel to bully/be bullied?
- What can you do about bullying?

Important moral issues can also be explored safely through the curriculum. In exploring these kinds of issues pupils would consider:

- Why does bullying occur?
- What would our society be like if bullying were acceptable?
- What moral dilemmas do we face as bystanders in a bullying situation?
- Can bullying ever be justified?

Challenging bullying

Teaching children to challenge bullying behaviour is essential as they are more likely to witness bullying occurring than adults. Some pupils are inclined to intervene spontaneously if they see someone being hurt. Many pupils, however, may feel intimidated and helpless when witnessing a peer being picked on. Pupils who witness bullying can unintentionally socially reinforce the pupils who are carrying out the bullying by co-operating with them, being friendly towards them or by ignoring the bullying behaviour. They can even help to enhance the reputation of the bullying pupil by spreading rumours about bullying incidents. The consequences of these kinds of behaviour can be explored with pupils through role play and discussion.

In the same way, more challenging behaviours can be taught and encouraged. Pupils who witness bullying taking place can get help from an adult; align themselves with the victim; indicate disapproval non-verbally; assist the bullied pupil to escape the bullying situation; directly challenge the bullying by making statements such as 'That's not fair', 'Leave her alone', 'If you don't stop I'll tell the teacher'.

By making it explicit how pupils can respond effectively when they witness a peer being bullied and by rehearsing these responses through role play, we increase the likelihood of pupils supporting each other when bullying does occur. Once pupils have understood how collusion reinforces bullying behaviour and how low-level resistance can prove extremely effective in stopping the bullying, they are more confident in taking an active role in tackling the problem. The long-term effect of this kind of peer intervention is the development of an anti-bullying peer ethos which operates alongside adult intervention and hinders the establishment of classes or groups where high levels of bullying behaviour are the norm.

Quality circles

Quality circles (QCs) can be introduced to provide a structure for involving pupils themselves in the development of anti-bullying strategies. A quality circle is a small group of individuals who meet regularly to follow a structured problem-solving process. The members of the quality circle brainstorm concerns and problems which directly or indirectly affect their work. One of these is selected, and the nature and extent of the problem is explored and investigated. The pupils collect data, through observation or questionnaire so that they fully understand the nature of the problem they have chosen to explore. Once they have identified how extensive the problem is and how it is caused, they begin to develop a solution. This solution is presented to management and if appropriate is implemented.

For example, one quality circle group thought that most bullying took place in the toilets at playtime. They investigated by taking it in turns to enter the toilets at 5-minute intervals during each playtime over a one-week period. They entered a cubicle and noted down what they had observed on their way in. At the end of the week they had collected evidence which suggested that a particular group of older pupils were persistently hanging around the toilets and teasing anybody who came in. Their solution was to present the information they had collected to the class teacher of this group. The teacher confronted the pupils and the bullying stopped. Another quality circle identified that nobody was praised for being considerate to their peers. Their solution was to establish a weekly merit system for pupils who had been co-operative with other pupils. This was incorporated into the school behaviour policy.

The success of the quality circle work relates to the participative nature of the approach. The pupils are engaged in working collaboratively with peers on real problems and their solutions are implemented throughout the school. To enable the QCs to be successful, both the school and the class teacher needed to be committed to enabling the pupils to take a participative role in school management. This means that the adults in the school community have to be prepared to share power and decision-making with the pupils by respecting and recognising the value of their solutions.

There is no evidence to suggest that QC work will stop bullying behaviour on its own, but the research indicates that it enables pupils to investigate the issues meaningfully and provides them with a clear structure to formulate and implement their own solutions. It raises awareness about the problem of bullying and helps the pupils to understand and reflect upon their own behaviour and attitudes towards others. Its basis in a co-operative learning style promotes a non-violent, constructive approach to problem-solving.

There are a wide range of resources available to schools who wish to address the issue of bullying with pupils. Some are specifically designed to tackle bullying; others relate to areas already within the curriculum which relate to bullying.

Generally speaking, short-term projects or lessons on bullying and related issues will have a limited effect on pupil behaviour. Immediately after the piece of work, pupils may be more considerate of each other. Reports of bullying behaviour may increase. After a week or so, their behaviour may have resumed its normal pattern. For more long-lasting change, longer-term programmes of work are required which engage the pupils in sharing responsibility for tackling bullying with adults in the school community. Problem-solving approaches which enhance communication skills and emphasise co-operative working and constructive conflict resolution are more likely to be effective here. Teaching pupils how to interact with peers in an assertive manner can provide pupils with strategies for handling bullying situations and for expressing their own views and wishes without dominating others. Assemblies and collective worship can be used to re-emphasise teaching points.

Staff behaviour

Constructive methods of behaviour management and classroom control model positive behaviour. Teachers and other staff can be directive and firm without being aggressive and cruel. If pupils see and hear bullying behaviour used by adults they may copy it. Some schools have begun by developing a staff code of conduct before beginning to work with pupils on the issue of bullying.

The playground

Bullying is more likely to occur when pupils are overcrowded or bored. The structure and design of the playground can increase or reduce the possibility of bullying behaviour. Playgrounds which offer a diverse range of areas and activities can provide pupils with a variety of activities to suit their needs. Some pupils will enjoy active, challenging opportunities; others will prefer to sit and talk with friends or spend time alone reading, digging, building. The wider the range of opportunities, the more likely pupils are to be positively engaged.

Supervisors need to be sensitive to the problems of bullying and know how to respond. Unfortunately, in some schools supervisors themselves can be the target of bullying behaviour. This is exacerbated if supervisors are seen as low-status workers by other staff, pupils and parents. Schools can help supervisors to improve the quality of supervision by being clear about the role and status of supervisors, by ensuring that the supervisors know the school behaviour policy, and by offering training in behaviour management techniques. Supervisors can be invited to attend any in-school events relating to bullying and can be helped to distinguish between bullying, other types of aggressive behaviour and rough and tumble or imaginative play which may look like fighting. Supervisors and teaching staff can be encouraged to develop their playground management skills. Effective supervision involves moving around the school grounds, engaging pupils in brief conversation and continually scanning the area to pick up on potential problems. If an aggressive incident does arise it should be approached calmly and responded to in line with school policy. If a teacher and supervisor are present at the same time, it should be clear who will do what. It can help maintain the status of the supervisors if, at such times, the teacher supports the supervisor rather than taking over from him or her.

Peers can provide a support network for bullied pupils at lunch time in primary schools. This can be achieved by setting up 'activity groups' or by training pupils as mediators or buddies. An activity group or club is run by pupils for pupils and allows opportunities for structured games which anyone can join in. For those pupils who feel left out or who find it difficult to build relationships with others, activity groups provide a safe and easy way of becoming involved with other pupils. Activity groups can be indoor or outdoor and can involve active, physical games, board games, art or computer activities.

Pupils can be trained to intervene when there is conflict between peers. Even the younger primary school pupils can learn the skills of mediation and conflict resolution. Pupils who are in conflict with each other can be given the option of sorting the problem out with a mediator or going to see a member of staff. The mediator then works with the pupils through a series of problem solving steps. These include:

1 Identifying what each person wants.
2 Identifying what each person needs.
3 Exploring possible ways of meeting both parties needs.
4 Agreeing a solution.

Older pupils can also be trained in active listening skills and ways of helping others to identify their own solutions. These pupils are then 'on duty' at lunch times and pupils who are worried, upset or angry can have a chat with them about their concerns. Listening and mediation services do not replace staff support for bullied pupils but they do allow pupils to contribute positively to the school community and they do acknowledge that some pupils will prefer peer support to adult support.

Responding when bullying occurs

All staff must take bullying seriously, even if they are not sure what exactly has happened and who was involved. They should listen carefully to what each pupil has to say. Any potential bullying situation which is ignored can be interpreted as acceptance by pupils. Pupils will only report bullying behaviour if they feel that they will be taken seriously and that helpful action will be taken. If we take action when bullying is reported this will reduce the duration of the bullying and reduce the likelihood of it re-occurring.

Usually in a situation where bullying is reported, the version of events will differ from one pupil to another. It may be difficult for staff to know who is telling the truth. There will rarely be neutral witnesses to verify accounts. If at all possible, try a problem-solving approach as a first step. This requires the teacher to focus on finding a solution rather than discovering the sequence of events leading to the problem. A typical 'problem-solving' discussion with a group of pupils who seem to have been involved in bullying might go as follows:

Teacher: I've listened to what each of you has to say. What is clear to me is that there is a problem here. The problem is about how you all get on with each other . . .

Jack: But, Miss, it's not me . . . it's him!

Zack: It's not! It's not! That's unfair!

Phil: It's not, Miss. It's Jack. He's lying . . .

Teacher: Now listen to me. All of you are involved in this. We are going to put aside who has done what to whom for a few moments. You all agree that you are not getting on with each other?

All pupils: Nod or shrug. 'I suppose so.'

Teacher: OK. So let's think about what we can do to improve this situation. We don't want you to be 'best friends', just to let each other be. What can each of you do to make sure this happens?

SILENCE.

Phil: Well, I suppose we could share the ball at lunch time.

Teacher: An excellent idea.

Zack: We could stop cussing each other.

Teacher: Very good.

Phil: We could leave Jack alone.

Jack: I could find some other people to be with.

Teacher: All good ideas. Let's see if you can put them into practice. Now, I am going to make a note of what we have agreed here. We will meet again in a week's time to see how things have improved. I will mention this to your parents so they know what has been going on and how you are going to sort it out. Off you go now.

If the bullying stops at this point, the teacher will have made a constructive and low-key intervention. For many pupils this kind of discussion is sufficient to deter future bullying. For some, however, the bullying will continue. Parents should always be involved at this point. Sanctions may be required. If damage to personal possessions or injury has occurred, parents may wish to press charges against the bullying pupils.

Supporting the bullied pupil

Bullied pupils are often very quick to blame themselves for being bullied. They may believe that they deserve some of the nasty things which have happened to them. Their social self-esteem is likely to be poor. A first step will be to help the bullied pupil to feel better about themselves. The second step will be to help the pupil to identify how they can respond to the bullying themselves and who can support them in doing this. Sometimes this may involve teaching the pupil specific strategies.

Some of the most effective strategies for standing up to bullying come from work on assertiveness. By teaching pupils to be assertive, we teach them to stand up for their own rights without violating the rights of others. Assertiveness work teaches us that we are equal, rather than inferior or superior to our peers. It provides a set of 'scripts' which can be used in situations where we are not being listened to, where someone is trying to manipulate, threaten or hurt us. An assertive statement expresses calmly and simply what you do or do not want to happen. For example:

'I don't like it when you call me names. I want you to stop.'
'I don't lend my bike.'
'I won't give you my dinner money.'
'No. I don't want to.'
'I want you to leave me alone.'

Assertiveness training attends to how you speak as well as what you say. Teachers can help pupils to stand and speak with confidence. This requires the pupil to stand in a relaxed manner, with shoulders back, arms by their side, maintaining eye contact with the main tormentor. They should not smile or laugh, maintaining a serious expression. If they speak they should keep their voice low and controlled. If you are working with bullied pupils you should teach them to:

- be assertive;
- enlist support wherever possible and certainly tell an adult afterwards;
- leave the situation at the earliest possible moment.

Assertive strategies may not always work. The pupil him or herself will have to make a decision about what is the best course of action in any situation. The pupil should always attend to his/her own personal safety first.

Supporting the pupils to make their own response is more effective than making a response on their behalf. By not leaving an opportunity for the pupils to respond to the bullying behaviour themselves, the teacher may reinforce the helplessness and powerlessness the bullied pupil might be feeling. Teachers can and should challenge the behaviour of the bullying pupils whilst supporting the bullied pupils in contributing to the solution.

EVALUATING THE EFFECTIVENESS OF THE WHOLE-SCHOOL POLICY IN PRACTICE

The more thoroughly and extensively the whole-school policy is implemented, the more likely you are to achieve success. The rate at which this can be achieved and the way in which these changes can be identified will vary from school to school. You should see a reduction in the number of pupils who are being bullied. This reduction may be quite large and may occur soon after you begin to implement your whole-school anti-bullying policy.

The most efficient way of identifying changes in levels of bullying is to carry out an anonymous survey. You should do this before you begin to work on bullying and then repeat it on an annual or bi-annual basis once you have begun to implement your policy. You can buy survey materials or you can design your own. If you design your own you may want to ask:

- background information about the pupil (age, gender, cultural background, etc.);
- how often they have been bullied that term / that week – a shorter time span is better for younger pupils; specify types of bullying behaviour;
- where the bullying took place;
- who bullied them;
- who they told about it;
- how often they have bullied someone that term / that week;
- whether they would help someone who was being bullied;
- whether they feel that bullying is taken seriously by the school.

Surveys which are based solely on reading and writing discriminate against some children. Younger pupils or pupils who experience difficulty with literacy will need support or access to alternative methods of gathering information. Translations into community languages may also be required.

By comparing your whole-school results on an annual basis you will identify progress made and areas for further development. By analysing results class by class you will become aware of classes where bullying is a particular problem and respond appropriately.

SUMMARY

Bullying behaviour is a pastoral concern for all primary schools. It affects the educational and social well-being of those pupils directly involved. It also impacts upon the pupils who witness the bullying or who know it is happening. If unchallenged it can shape the social relationships within a class and even the ethos of the school as a whole. In the absence of skills to manage difficulties within their relationships with others, children become anxious and worried.

Schools can do many things to reduce levels of bullying. The most effective interventions involve staff and pupils in tackling the problem together. Interventions which do not include the pupil population are unlikely to promote change. A whole-school anti-bullying policy provides a framework for tackling the problem and it is the process of developing and implementing this which enables change to occur.

REFERENCES

Cowen, E.L., Pederson, A., Babigian, H., Izzo, L.D. and Trost, M.A. (1973) Long-term follow up of early detected vulnerable children, *Journal of Consulting and Clinical Psychology*, 41, 438–446.

Olweus, D. (1992) Bullying amongst school children: intervention and prevention, in R.D. Peters, R. McMahon and V.L. Quinsey (eds) *Aggression and Violence throughout the Life Span*, Newbury Park, CA: Sage.

Roland, E. (1993) Bullying: developing a tradition of research and management, in D. Tattum (ed.) *Understanding and Managing Bullying*, Oxford: Heinemann Educational.

Rubin, K.H. (1985) Socially withdrawn children: an at risk population? In B.H. Schneider, K.H. Rubin and J.E. Ledingham (eds) *Children's Peer Relations: Issues in Assessment and Intervention*, New York: Springer-Verlag.

Sharp, S. (1995) How much does bullying hurt? The effects of bullying on the personal well-being and educational progress of secondary aged pupils, *Educational and Child Psychology*, 12, 2, 81–88.

Smith, P.K. and Sharp, S. (eds) (1994) *School Bullying: Insights and Perspectives*, London: Routledge.

Whitney, I. and Smith, P.K. (1993) A survey of the nature and extent of bully/victim problems in junior/middle and secondary schools, *Educational Research*, 35, 3–25.

10

STARTING SECONDARY SCHOOL

An account of a collaborative enquiry and development process

David Frost

I cannot pretend to have a neutral, academic perspective on this subject. My interest in the transition from primary to secondary school first arose from the fairly painful experience of parenting a child who had to make that exciting and challenging journey. When my daughter was in the primary school, her mother and I were accustomed to being protective and having considerable influence and control over her experience outside the home. Having been a secondary school teacher I was also well aware of the way in which some adolescents can become disaffected when confronted by the particular demands of secondary schooling. So, the transition was for us a time of considerable anxiety and I became very sensitised to the issues involved. At the end of the first term I sat down to reflect on the difficulties we had experienced as a family and wrote to the head teacher about them, thus beginning a fruitful dialogue covering a wide range of issues.

During my daughter's second year of secondary schooling I found myself in a position to provide some support to another school where the primary–secondary transition had been identified as a development priority. I was a tutor with a higher education institution and had been attached to the school as a professional development consultant. I was approached by the head teacher with a request to meet the school's primary–secondary liaison teacher and to devise a development project which would address the concern. This chapter provides an account of that development project, and deals with some of the lessons we learned both about the primary–secondary transition and the process of development and change. First however, I would like to summarise the issues arising from my experience as a parent.

THE PARENTS' PERSPECTIVE

What follows is an outline of the concerns I reflected on in some detail at the end of my daughter's first term of secondary school.

The school uniform There was no such thing at primary school so this was the first new challenge. The guidelines provided by the school were helpful but still left room for interpretation. We found that the High Street shops were less than helpful in that they tended to promote items which had a strong fashion dimension. As parents, we struggled to reconcile what we thought would be acceptable to the school, what was acceptable to us and what was desirable from our daughter's point of view.

Wanting to be normal Our daughter's overriding concern was to fit in, to be seen to be 'normal' and inconspicuous. Her way of coping with the complexity of this new school life was to try to 'go with the flow' which meant that she would use her peers as reference points rather than consult school guidelines or ask her teachers or parents. She would tend to avoid drawing attention to herself by being the only one to do something 'properly'. This set up considerable tension within the family.

The timetable In primary school it hardly existed. You go to the same place every day and on Thursdays you take your PE kit. On arrival at the big school our daughter had to copy out a complicated matrix with abbreviations which stood for the names of subjects such as 'creative and performing arts' and the names of at least a dozen different teachers and the numbers of over fifteen different teaching rooms. Everyday she had to try to work out which books to take and where to go, relying on her handwriting and her memory of what these abbreviations stood for. It was a nightmare.

Homework This was probably the most significant area of difficulty. In primary school there was no homework as such, but from the first day of secondary school it was a daily problem. My daughter was issued with a small record book into which she was to enter the details of her homework each day. The fundamental problem was that she really did not want her parents to know what homework she had been set because she would then have to deal with their expectations and demands as well as those of the teacher who had set the homework. Again, it was easier and felt safer to follow the perceptions and standards of her classmates. The actual entry in the record book, hastily scribbled down as the end-of-lesson bell was ringing, was invariably inadequate. The space provided was tiny and my daughter's ability to encapsulate the teacher's instructions in a few words was not very advanced.

Even if the description of the homework task could be determined, the nature of the learning objective was often elusive and it is very difficult to support an anxious child without knowing what she is meant to be learning. There were further problems because of the lack of skills for independent learning. In order to cope with homework you need to be a good planner, being able to make decisions about when to do each assignment and when to do the preparation. Very often the task would demand some library work or a practical investigation which could not easily be done the night before the homework was due to be handed in. More complex is the question of how to pursue an assignment: my daughter did not know how to conduct an investigation or write an essay – she needed to be taught these skills.

The presentation of the homework was endlessly problematic. It was often unclear as to whether first or final draft was required and my daughter was reluctant to see the distinction. We were also unclear about the appropriateness of using the home computer to present homework and my daughter's desire to remain inconspicuous meant that she was reluctant to use it. When we asked the Year Head about this he said that the school was very keen to promote IT; the difficulty was that most of my daughter's classmates worked on the basis of a one-off draft written with a pen, mistakes being 'Tipp-Exed', and 'being normal' had become the main priority for her.

Information about the curriculum The question of homework was most crucial because it centred on what our daughter was actually learning. As parents we wanted to get involved in our daughter's education but, without reliable information this is very difficult. Even as well informed educationists, we still found it hard to get a clear picture of the syllabus for each subject and the curriculum as a whole. We were very anxious to know for example, which modern language our daughter would be pursuing and which history topics she would be picking up during Key Stage 3. Unfortunately, the school tended to communicate in a piecemeal fashion leaving us without a coherent picture of the course of our daughter's education.

Care of school equipment The range of equipment needed at secondary school is greater than at primary school and far more expensive; a mathematical calculator was included for example. Once we had overcome the difficulty of being sure about exactly what was required and the not inconsiderable cost, there remained the problem of preserving it all and maintaining it in an acceptable condition. For the first time we had to contend with the problem of things being 'borrowed' permanently and books being marked with endless fashionable slogans. Again, we felt that standards were being set, not by teachers and parents working together, but by the peer group – 'everybody does it' tended to be our daughter's claim.

Access to the school Safety had never seemed to be a problem in primary school but now we found that we were anxious because our daughter was not allowed into the school building until a few minutes before morning registration. We were not happy with the idea of her spending up to half an hour unsupervised in a school playground shared by 1,200 young people between the ages of 11 and 18.

A fuller account of our experiences as parents can be found elsewhere (Frost, 1993) but it must be clear from this brief outline that, running throughout this experience is a great deal of parental anxiety which is a problem in itself. The child is operating in two worlds and is striving for independence. The school is trying to nurture a sense of responsibility in the adolescent but may not necessarily be able to facilitate it as effectively as some parents might expect. But what about the child's problems?

THE CHILD'S PERSPECTIVE

I do not propose to examine in any great depth the question of whether transition from primary to secondary school is problematic for the children making that transition; my assumption is that it is. As secondary teachers, we have all seen classes of young students arrive in September looking relatively enthusiastic and positive and, by the following July we see that they have sorted themselves out into those who will succeed and those who will fail. In discussing the notion of the hidden curriculum and the way it can have a negative impact on the self-esteem of young children, Richard Pring quotes David Hargreaves from his book, *The Challenge for the Comprehensive School* in which he says that:

> our present secondary school system, largely through the hidden curriculum, exerts on many pupils, particularly but by no means exclusively from the working class, a destruction of their dignity which is so massive and pervasive that few subsequently recover from it.
>
> (Hargreaves in Pring, 1984, p. 103)

Current research by Jean Rudduck (1996) under the title of 'Making Your Way Through Secondary School' provides fresh insights into the experiences and perceptions of secondary school students, and previous studies (see, for example, Jennings and Hargreaves, 1981 and White and Brockington, 1983) have noted the impact of transfer on student attainment. There seems to be substantial evidence that transfer at the age of 11 tends to cause something of a setback for many students who then have to catch up. And for some, of course, the catching up never comes. In the early stages of our development project at St Andrew's School someone read out the words of a youngster, recorded as part of a research project. The student had been interviewed as part of White and Brockington's study and Gorwood (1986) had used the quotation to conclude his book on curriculum continuity. The child's words illustrate how the transition to secondary school can simply put a stop to learning: 'I still don't understand it. I was enjoying myself in the juniors and I went to senior school and everything stopped. I suddenly didn't want to go to school.'

There are clearly a significant number of children who never recover from the shock of going up to the big school and, instead of embracing new challenges with enthusiasm and determination, set themselves on a career path of negativity and disaffection. This in turn affects the value added to their education in the primary school and is increasingly likely to be of serious concern to secondary schools as the climate of market forces brings pressure to measure and publish indicators of 'value added'.

ADDRESSING THE CONCERN

When I was asked to help St Andrew's School address this as a development priority it was suggested to me that I might provide a 'course', the implication being that, if the primary–secondary liaison teacher were to be better informed about the issues then he would be able to improve the situation. We discussed the matter and quickly identified 'collaboration' as a key concept in the development of a more effective transition. It seemed unhelpful therefore for a single individual to undertake a course even if a suitable one could be found. Instead we decided to set up an enquiry and development project which would draw colleagues into a collaborative relationship within which they could work together to evaluate current practice and take steps to improve it. By virtue of my role as a tutor in higher education, we were able to offer accreditation which we hoped would help to motivate colleagues through recognition and support for their active development work. The model we adopted I refer to as 'reflective action planning' which essentially involves individuals engaging in a process of personal development planning leading to a portfolio of evidence of their contribution to this common endeavour (see Frost, 1995, for a fuller account of the model).

The primary–secondary liaison teacher and I agreed on the wording of a proposal which we set out in a leaflet and sent to all members of staff within St Andrew's School, all Year 6 staff in the primary feeder schools and anyone with special responsibility for liaison or continuity in those schools. The leaflet set out the aims of the project:

Box 10.1 Project aims

Specific aims would need to be explored and refined by members of the group but in broad terms the purpose of the group would be to improve practice in this area by:

- producing materials and guidelines which would provide support for students, parents and other colleagues in order to ensure a smooth transition from primary to secondary school;
- sharing experience and ideas about strategies for the maintenance of curriculum continuity for years 6–7;
- exploring organisational and pastoral issues related to the management of the primary–secondary transition;
- identifying good practice and building on it through an action research process.

It is also suggested that such a project is likely to make a major contribution to the professional development of individuals involved and will also foster an enhanced level of collaboration between the institutions taking part.

The leaflet also described the process which would involve three after-school meetings per term organised by the primary–secondary liaison teacher in consultation with all members of the group. As the college tutor, I would be responsible for the provision of materials and guidance on the accreditation process, and for facilitating enquiry and discussion, but the content of the programme would be determined collectively by the group as would the choice of any guest speakers we might wish to invite. Although the actual agenda would be the product of discussion and negotiation we nevertheless thought that it would be helpful to set out in that initial leaflet the sort of areas which we thought might be relevant:

Box 10.2 Possible areas for enquiry

Participants will be invited to engage in research and development in the following areas:

- parents and the community;
- assessment and record keeping;
- teaching and learning styles and strategies;
- the curriculum (e.g cross-curricular themes, IT, technology);
- pastoral care and special needs;
- resources for learning;
- progression in the foundation subjects.

It is suggested that initial sessions should enable the group to explore their concerns and to identify a range of issues which should be addressed collaboratively by the group as a whole. Individuals will be asked to enquire into particular issues and report back to the whole group.

The purpose of the leaflet was to attract at least one representative from each subject area in the secondary school and at least one teacher from each feeder primary school. This part of the process was crucial since the project depended for its success on the involvement of all those who were in a position to affect practice. The management of the transition is the concern of the whole educational community and cannot be compartmentalised.

ACTION PLANNING FOR ENQUIRY AND DEVELOPMENT

At the first meeting of about fourteen teachers we discussed the themes suggested in the leaflet and members of the group volunteered to tackle areas of particular interest. Within the meeting we formed separate subgroups to begin the process of action planning; in most cases a teacher from St Andrew's joined up with a colleague from one of the primary schools. The guidance on reflective action planning suggested that participants should first clarify and write down the particular focus they had decided to tackle, second, to describe the possible enquiry strategies which might be most appropriate, and then to describe any changes or improvements in practice which could be implemented immediately and subsequently monitored. These general intentions, it was suggested, should be translated into specific targets with names against the various tasks and dates for completion. Finally, it was suggested, partners should agree and write down the way in which they intended to report the outcomes of their enquiry activity. The latter would turn out to be rather problematic as the project progressed and we discovered the extent to which change can lead to conflict. Box 10.3 shows an example of the action plans generated at that first session.

The headings and prompts used for the interviews are set out in Box 10.4. The student teachers needed some discussion to overcome their doubts about the approach to the interviews but they readily agreed to the project because it helped them to fulfil the requirements of their initial training course.

Once action plans were drawn up, we discussed them as a group and helped each other to refine the tasks in detail. We also took decisions as a whole group, for example on the question of inviting individuals into the group to speak to us about their special area of interest or expertise. Some of the action plans were quite narrowly focused, simply enabling individuals to become better informed, others enabled primary and secondary colleagues to carry out subject-specific tasks. Some plans had far-reaching and more fundamental consequences as I hope to make clear below. It could be said that, through the collaborative action planning activity, we effectively explored our general concerns and translated them into more

Box 10.3 Action plan

Focus for development
We need to know more about the experiences of our Year 7 students and the way the school's induction arrangements ease the transition.

Enquiry strategies
A series of interviews with groups of Year 7 students at the end of their first term would tell us a great deal about the effectiveness of induction arrangements but could also provide us with insights into matters concerned with curriculum continuity. We will ask student teachers currently on serial practice in the school to help us by conducting semi-structured interviews with groups of three Year 7 students. One group from each form should suffice. We will provide a set of thematic headings and prompt questions.

Proposals for change
We do not propose any changes at the moment but would want to see what arises from the interviews.

Targets
We will draft the interview schedule within a week and ask the primary–secondary liaison teacher to arrange for the student teachers to carry out the interviews during the first week of December.

Reporting
We will analyse the interview notes and present a summary to the group at our first meeting after the Christmas vacation.

concrete objectives designed to bring about real improvement in practice. These objectives can be summarised in the following way:

- arrange for a mutual shadowing/observation exercise for all members of the group;
- review the induction programme in the light of the feedback from Year 7 students;
- contact the advisory teacher responsible for a project to develop modern languages in primary schools and investigate ways in which teachers from St Andrew's could best support such endeavours in the locality;
- set up a science group to discuss the National Curriculum and share expertise;
- invite a deputy head from another secondary school to speak about the research she had done on the primary–secondary interface;
- ask myself (the college tutor) to make a presentation based on my reading of a number of journal articles dealing with good practice in this area;
- investigate what transfer documentation was in use in all the primary feeder schools and evaluate bought-in systems such as the Modbury Record Book;

Box 10.4 Going up to the big school: Year 7 interviews

Below are categories of questions or headings which could be used to structure the interview which should be conversational. The prompts should be used merely as ideas to get the conversation going rather than a list of questions to be asked in order.

Introduction to the school
Did you get lost when you first came to St Andrew's?
How did you find your way about? Did you have a map?
Did older students look after you?
Who told you what to do when you first came?

Making friends
Did all your friends come up with you or did some of them go to other secondary schools?
Did you make new friends easily? Did you get bullied by the older students?

The school day
How did you feel about having different teachers for everything?
How did you manage the changing of lessons?
When do you have lunch? Is that easy to manage?
Did you forget your timetable at first?

Curriculum
Is the work you do at secondary school different? How?
Have you found that you have repeated things that you did in the primary school?
Are the lessons more interesting or more boring?

Teaching approaches
Do you tend to work in a different way at the secondary school?
What sorts of things did you do in an average day at the primary school?
Is there a difference in the way the teachers teach?
Do you do more writing now?
Did you work with other students when you were at the primary school?
What about homework? Did you have any help in getting organised for it?

Advice to new students
What advice would you give to Year 6 students who will be coming up next year?
How can the school make it better for new students?
What would you have liked to do before coming to the secondary school?
Did you visit the school before you came?

General
How long did it take you to settle in here? Do you enjoy secondary school?
Do you have any worries about going into Year 8?

- invite the assessment co-ordinator to explain St Andrew's assessment policy;
- conduct an audit of the ways in which Year 7 form tutors use the information passed up from the primary feeder schools.

Clearly, these action plans were only the beginning of a cycle of evaluation and action and, with hindsight, I think that it added up to a fairly ambitious programme of activity. However, as the following account should make clear, the process of working through these concerns and action plans was of itself very instructive and served to raise the group's awareness of the complexity of the problem. It was also the case that some of these plans emerged as priorities as the project progressed.

Mutual observation and shadowing

First then the mutual observation/shadowing exercise: one of the most direct benefits of the group was that colleagues from across 'the great divide' had a forum within which to meet and explore their different worlds. The action planning discussions in small groups led to a desire to explore these different worlds more directly. These exercises were relatively easy to arrange although quite costly in terms of the supply cover which enabled partners to visit each other's schools for at least half a day. These short visits provided useful insight into differences in teaching and learning styles and led to a very useful discussion about curriculum continuity. The most interesting point to emerge was that, when talking about curriculum continuity we need to talk about the 'received curriculum' rather than a series of written statements about the content or the learning objectives. This discussion led to a longer-term plan to look closely at the students' experiences of teaching and learning in both Year 6 and Year 7.

Evaluating the induction arrangements

After further discussion it was agreed that both the liaison arrangements and the induction programme were quite satisfactory and time would be better spent on other matters. However, it emerged later that not all members of the group shared this view and evidence from the Year 7 interviews suggested that a more thorough evaluation would be worthwhile. This raises the difficult question of the politics of collaboration in a climate of market forces. It takes courage for a large secondary school to open up its practices to scrutiny but, I would argue, it is precisely this willingness to evaluate which is likely to impress colleagues in the feeder primary schools.

Subject-focused work

The modern languages enquiry raised an interesting question about how the expertise in the secondary school could be shared with colleagues in the primary school in such a way that curriculum continuity could be best served. There were clearly two alternative approaches; one involves the secondary teachers visiting the primary schools to teach occasional French lessons and the other involves the provision of materials and support to primary colleagues so that they can develop their own expertise and, more importantly, the confidence to have a go. This raised the question of whether the subject departments in the secondary school could provide Inset for primary colleagues.

This question of subject-focused Inset had already been tackled by the science department and was seen as an on-going project. St Andrew's had valuable equipment to lend and materials to share as well as a wealth of understanding in what has tended to be a weak area for the primary schools. Colleagues reported that these sessions were very useful but we did discover a problem in that primary colleagues saw themselves, quite rightly, as having much to contribute in terms of their understanding of the children as individuals and their preferred learning styles, whereas many of the members of the secondary school science department saw the interaction as a one-way street in which expertise was passed down and expectations were made clear. This somewhat arrogant position can lead to difficulties. One difficulty for us was that many of the secondary science teachers simply did not bother to attend, leaving the Head of Science to carry out what we imagined they perceived to be a low-priority task.

Drawing on previous research

The invitation of a guest speaker to talk about her research was very helpful in introducing us to ideas from the literature and to good practice from elsewhere. In pursuing her own master's degree Janet Hubble had delved into the available literature and was able to save our group a lot of time by sharing what she had found (Hubble, 1992). First, Janet provided us with a clear vocabulary which she had derived chiefly from Derricott (1985). It was important for us to distinguish between 'transition', 'liaison' and 'curriculum continuity' because it helped us to think about the practice which these terms describe.

An historical overview helped us to think about how the recurring problems associated with transition had been identified and tackled in the past. In the 1960s, for example, the Plowden Report (DES, 1967) had made clear recommendations about cross-phase conferencing and on the transfer of a portfolio of evidence of a child's attainment at the point of transition. We also learnt that HMI (HMI and DES, 1989) had put forward some sound guidance on matters which are now fairly commonplace. They recommended that:

- school prospectuses should be distributed at least one term in advance;
- open days for prospective students and their parents should be organised;
- Year 7 tutor groups should consist of a mix from all the feeder primaries;
- detailed transfer documentation should be produced;
- written statements about the transfer procedures should be agreed and adopted by all schools affected;
- there should be a designated member of staff responsible for liaison and transfer in each secondary school;
- primary teachers should be invited to visit their ex-students during their first year in the secondary school;
- Year 6 students should be taken to visit their secondary school in the summer term prior to transfer.

This presentation also introduced us to practices tried elsewhere such as those organised by Abbey Woods School in the 1960s. Their initiatives included:

- joint primary/secondary drama productions and concerts;
- joint social functions for members of staff;
- staff exchanges;
- common resource facilities.

Although this presentation was wide-ranging and generally thought-provoking we found that, as a group, our discussions tended to focus increasingly on assessment and the recording of information about student attainment.

Focusing on curriculum continuity

Following this general seminar I circulated notes from my reading of a journal article entitled 'Primary–secondary transfer after the National Curriculum' (Gorwood, 1991). The discussion which followed increasingly focused on assessment issues which we felt were crucial to curriculum continuity. Gorwood had started by examining the false assumption that the introduction of the National Curriculum had solved the problem of curriculum continuity. The nature and purpose of transfer documentation became a central concern. Gorwood had carried out substantial research in this area and accounts of good practice suggested that the business of achieving curriculum continuity should not be the sole responsibility of the Year 7 and Year 6 co-ordinators but it should be adopted as a responsibility by each subject department in the secondary school and as a whole-school matter in the primary schools. Secondary school subject departments needed to designate a person to keep the department briefed on such matters as transition, developments in primary education, the use of transfer documentation and possibilities for cross-phase collaboration.

The importance of transfer documentation

The action plan to investigate the variety of approaches to transfer documentation used by the primary feeder schools emerged naturally from our discussions about assessment and transfer. It became clear that it was not possible for the Year 7 form tutors to make reliable decisions about so many new students when the information about their achievement at primary school was recorded and disseminated in so many different ways. It became immediately clear that the standardisation of transfer documentation would be costly. Some of the primary schools represented in our group had already invested in the 'Modbury' scheme which was not computer based but, nevertheless represented a significant investment. As a group, we examined the Modbury scheme and considered suggesting that all the primary schools adopt it. However, the attempt to audit the ways in which transfer records were being used in the secondary school raised further problems.

The members of the group who had agreed to take on this investigative task found that colleagues were reluctant to discuss the issues, but it became clear that many tutors did not use the records at all. The primary school members of the group were angered and dismayed to learn that the portfolios of children's work so painstakingly put together, annotated and sent up to the secondary school might not even be looked at by the child's new teachers. It also emerged that subject departments were not taking into account the attainment of individual students but instead were basing their curriculum planning on the assumption that all students were at the same level. This had major implications, not only for the specific issue of the form in which transfer documentation should be constructed, but also, more generally, for curriculum planning in the secondary school. We came firmly to the conclusion that the secondary school needed to adopt a more individualised approach which recognises the actual attainment of the new intake of students.

Assessment and teaching and learning styles

We were aware that St Andrew's was in the middle of a review of their assessment policy and that this might have implications, not only for the kind of information passed on at the point of transfer, but also for teaching and learning styles. We therefore asked the school's Assessment

Co-ordinator to visit our group and tell us how that new policy was shaping up. His talk was most illuminating and threw up issues which were to prove controversial. The school was moving towards a systematic, computer-driven approach to the recording of achievement which would facilitate the monitoring of individual students' progress as well as the recording and reporting of achievement. As a group we were impressed with these proposals and saw in them the possibility that curriculum continuity could be furthered and the good primary practice of matching the curriculum to the individual's needs could be supported and promoted by this scheme. The emergent policy had been influenced by advice from a visiting consultant, Ruth Sutton, who has always argued that assessment is essentially about teaching and learning (Sutton, 1991). We noted that she had prefaced her book with the following quotation from the Report of the Task Group on Assessment and Testing:

> Promoting children's learning is a principal aim of schools. Assessment lies at the heart of this process. It can provide a framework in which educational objectives may be set, and pupils' progress charted and expressed. It can yield a basis for planning the next educational steps in response to children's needs. By facilitating dialogue between teachers, it can enhance professional skills and help the school as a whole to strengthen learning across the curriculum and throughout its age range.
>
> (TGAT, 1986)

There still remained a central difficulty however: the development of St Andrew's assessment policy had not yet taken into account the question of what was being recorded and reported on in Year 6. It emerged that the Assessment Co-ordinator had not yet seen the important document from the Department of Education, Circular 14/92, *Reports on Individual Achievement*. Our next step, therefore was to request that we make our own presentation to St Andrew's Assessment Working Party.

One of the members of our group, a deputy head from one of the primary feeder schools, volunteered to make the presentation with the rest of the group present to enter into the discussion. The presentation was a robust one and had something of an edge to it. She began by putting forward key questions that had arisen in our earlier discussions.

KEY QUESTIONS AND RECOMMENDATIONS ON ASSESSMENT

1 How is attainment recorded in all of the schools concerned?
2 In what form is information about students' attainment and achievement transferred to the secondary school?
3 Can a common format for information transfer be agreed upon?

4 How do subject teachers at St Andrew's currently use information derived from transfer documentation?
5 How can more effective use be made of the information transferred?
6 How can we co-ordinate schools' responses to Circular 14/92?
7 How can the new assessment policy currently being developed at St Andrew's be matched with the assessment policies of the primary feeder schools?

Our spokesperson went on to argue that these concerns should be regarded as whole-school issues which had to be taken on, not only by the assessment working party, but by the senior management of the secondary school. She then put forward our recommendations which were as follows:

- the questions outlined above should be discussed by the assessment working party as a matter of urgency;
- the process of assessment policy development should take into account the issues identified by the primary–secondary group to ensure that records of achievement in the primary schools are effectively dovetailed into St Andrew's assessment system;
- heads of subject departments should be asked to review their practice in relation to these issues and to ensure that they find their place on their departmental agendas and that proper use is made of transfer documentation;
- a formal evaluation of the transition and induction arrangements should be agreed and put in place for the forthcoming academic year;
- the schools concerned should explore the possibility of organising joint staff development activities as part of a Development Day;
- links need to be established between each subject department and each primary feeder school to facilitate the sharing of ideas about the curriculum at the interface of Key Stages 2/3 and to avoid repetition in curriculum delivery;
- there should be immediate consultations concerning a concerted response to Circular 14/92.

The discussion which followed this presentation was not an easy one. The assessment working party had worked hard on the new policy and had now to face the challenge of what was taken to be unfair criticism from colleagues from within the school and from the primary feeder schools. It was clear, however, that the issues could not be ducked. This meeting served to remind me that the process of change is necessarily a journey which is unpredictable and problematic. Conflict is inevitable and can lead to creativity. This is what Michael Fullan was recognising when he said that 'problems are our friends' (Fullan, 1993).

CONCLUSION

The year-long process of enquiry and development had led us to the point where the issues were clear and the obstacles to improvement were being actively confronted. It would be very neat and tidy to be able to describe the actual improvements which flowed from these events, but my purpose here was not to provide a blueprint for the effective management of the transition but rather to illustrate how such a collaborative, developmental process can be effective in bringing about change. I have also shared what we discovered along the way about the primary–secondary transition and hope that this will be of help to other groups who may wish to undertake a similar journey.

REFERENCES

Department of Education (1992) *Reports on Individual Achievement*, Circular 14/92, London: HMSO.

Department of Education and Science (1967) *Children and their Primary Schools* (The Plowden Report), London: HMSO.

Derricott, R. (ed.) (1985) *Curriculum Continuity: Primary to Secondary*, Windsor: NFER/Nelson.

Frost, D. (1993) Starting secondary school: the parents' perspective, *Pastoral Care in Education*, 11, 4, 6–11.

Frost, D. (1995) Reflective action planning: a model for continuing professional development, in D. Frost, A. Edwards, and H. Reynolds (eds) *Careers Education and Guidance*, London: Kogan Page.

Fullan, M. (1993) *Change Forces*, London: Falmer Press.

Gorwood, B. (1986) *School Transfer and Curriculum Continuity*, London: Croom Helm.

Gorwood, B. (1991) Primary–secondary transfer after the National Curriculum, *School Organisation*, 11, 3, 283–290.

Her Majesty's Inspectorate and Department of Education and Science (1989) Curriculum Continuity at 11 Plus, *Education Observed* 10, London: HMSO.

Hargreaves, D. (1982) *The Challenge for the Comprehensive School*, London: Routledge & Kegan Paul.

Hubble, J. (1992) Factors which have encouraged or hindered inter-school relationships since 1965, unpublished Masters dissertation, Canterbury: Christ Church College.

Jennings, K. and Hargreaves, D.J. (1981) Children's attitudes to secondary school transfer, *Educational Studies*, 7, 1, 35–39.

Pring, R. (1984) *Personal and Social Education in the Curriculum*, London: Hodder & Stoughton.

Rudduck, J. (1996) *Transitions in the Secondary School*, London: Routledge.

Sutton, R. (1991) *Assessment: A Framework for Teachers*, London: Routledge.

Task Group on Assessment and Testing (TGAT) (1996) *Report of the Task Group on Assessment and Testing*, London: DES.

White, R. and Brockington, D. (1983) *Tales Out of School*, London: Routledge.

Part III

VIEWPOINTS

11

TELEVISION VIEWING

Tony Charlton

TELEVISION: A PLUG-IN DRUG?

Given that broadcast television is the world's most frequently used mass entertainment and information medium (Gunter, 1987) it is hardly surprising that children are among the more regular and persistent viewers; although difficulties are encountered in determining the exact number of hours they spend *watching* television. Some of these difficulties arise because children – like adults – can engage in other activities whilst viewing, including talking with peers and adults, daydreaming, undertaking homework, reading and playing games. Moreover, parental estimations of children's viewing often correlate poorly with children's accounts, whilst children themselves often fail to report accurately on the programmes they watched.

Despite these measurement difficulties, the following figures seem to represent median viewing hours reported in USA and UK research studies. In the USA, Anderson and Collins (1988) reported weekly viewing hours for 2–5-year-olds (27.8 hours), for 6–11-year-olds (24.3 hours) and for teenagers (23 hours), whilst 4–15-year-olds viewed for an average of 19.2 hours per week in the UK (Social Trends, 1990). By the time youngsters reach 18, most will have given more time to watching television than to any other activity apart from sleeping (Sprafkin *et al.*, 1992). Furthermore, high school graduates in the USA will leave school having viewed TV for a period in excess of their time spent in school (up to 20,000 against 14,000 hours). With such figures in mind, it comes as no surprise that television viewing occupies more time than any other single out-of-school activity, and accounts for in excess of half of all leisure time.

Given the National Commission on Education's (1993) estimate that soon, viewers may have a choice of some 200 television channels, any concerns now held about the extent of current viewing hours are likely to heighten in the foreseeable future.

TELEVISION EFFECTS: GOOD OR BAD?

Clearly, TV is a time-consuming leisure pursuit for many children. Whilst it is also a compelling conduit for their social, affective and cognitive development (Comstock and Paik, 1991), some claim television serves only to spawn unwanted, and possibly harmful, effects upon children's development. Part of this thinking derives from considerations of the powerful influences of television commercials upon children. At times (particularly at Christmas), these 'hidden' persuaders can entice children to generate incessant (and often unrealistic) demands upon parents. Forceful attacks have been made, also, upon what some perceive as an almost constant menu of gratuitous violence on television. Elsewhere, television has been labelled a 'plug-in drug' (Winn, 1977) which succeeds only in sedating pupils' minds as well as their bodies.

It is hardly surprising, therefore, that over the past few decades, television has been berated as a contributor to a wide range of undesirable traits, including aggressive behaviour, unsociable attitudes and lowered academic performance. The causes underlying these concerns emanate from two distinct influences: 'displacement' and 'content' effects.

From a *displacement* standpoint Royes (1980) claimed that TV viewing diminishes levels of 'culture-ness' by abducting viewers from community-based activities. Where studies have monitored the arrival of broadcast TV there is broad agreement that time given to television is taken away from other more traditional and more cultural activities (Williams, 1986). Displaced pastimes include listening to the radio, participating in clubs and socials, visits to the cinema and reading, as well as engaging in conversation with peers and adults. Viewing may also block communication among family members (Walters and Stone, 1971), eroding familial interactions essential to children's healthy emotional, social and intellectual development. On other occasions, some parents seem intent on using the television as a surrogate parent. Winn (1977), for example, is critical of adults who encourage excesses in children's viewing because it pacifies them, and comments, 'Surely there can be no more insidious a drug than one that you must administer to others in order to achieve an effect for yourself' (p. 12).

From another perspective, Singer (1992) has argued that excessive viewing interferes with the development of the social skills, and mental capacities, which children need to acquire socially approved behaviours. Equally disconcerting are findings which insinuate that heavy viewers – compared to light ones – risk having their cognitive performance impaired, so that their reading and homework progress is discouraged (e.g. Anderson and Collins, 1988). In other words, heavy viewers risk becoming cognitively passive.

Whilst many are understandably concerned about displacement effects associated with watching television, it is the area of *programme content* which has attracted most research attention. Many of these studies have maintained that viewing violent behaviour encourages children to model aggression. This connection is supported by findings from Williams's (1986) naturalistic study in a small township in Canada, where children's aggression levels increased once television was introduced. Concerns like these are heightened by the American Psychological Association's calculations that, by the age of 11, children will have watched 8,000 televised murders and 100,000 lesser acts of brutality, in addition to real-life mayhem in news bulletins. Findings of low levels of problem behaviour on the South Atlantic island of St Helena prior to the introduction of broadcast television provide further, tentative support for this link (Charlton *et al.*, 1995).

In fairness, the case for claiming that viewing violence encourages violent behaviour, has not been clearly established. Fontana (1981), for example, suggests television violence only sanctions violent inclinations a person already has; although it can also suggest specific ways in which these inclinations can be put into practice. Whether or not inclinations become practices seems to depend upon a number of influences, including the prestige of the person practising television violence; the more prestigious the 'character' the more likely this is to happen. Fontana also makes the point that these inclinations are less likely to be translated into deeds if the child has a well-developed value system. Wiegman and Kuttschreuter (1992), are more questioning about the TV–behaviour connection. In their longitudinal study, they claimed that once adjustments were made for 'starting' levels of aggression and intelligence, the notion that 'television violence viewing leads to aggressive behaviour could not be supported' (p. 147). The same study, giving an infrequent consideration to pro-social behaviour, likewise reported non-significant positive correlations between viewing pro-social behaviour and pro-social behaviour.

Despite conflicting views on the connection between viewing violence and consequent behaviour, a moderate and plausible claim seems to be that: 'the depiction of violence in television programmes increases the chance that children in the audience will act aggressively themselves' (Vooijs and Van Der Voort, 1993, p. 139). However, more general claims that television affects behaviour, are bolstered when considering the effects of commercials upon people's purchasing habits. If television is ineffective in influencing behaviour, then advertising agencies the world over have been misleading their clients for years.

TELEVISION COMMERCIALS AND BEHAVIOUR

Commercials are frequently regarded as generating untoward effects upon children's behaviour. Adler (1977) estimated that youngsters observe some

20,000 of them yearly, and Ward and Wackman (1972, p. 152) caution that in homes where levels of hostility are high, the youngster is 'likely to besiege the adults in his life for advertised products'. In an equally disturbing manner, Fowles (1992, pp. 223–224) acknowledges that commercials for children are:

> pitched to deep-lying needs and longings. . . . Advertisers learn how to engage children's attention through proprietary research done by special companies that test and interview children. Texaco determined it could sell more gas if nagging children directed their parents into filling stations where toy fire trucks were given out at each fill-up.

The obvious success of TV commercials offers impressive evidence that viewing can, and does, affect behaviour. Perhaps the principle difference between 'ordinary' programmes and commercials (which can be the more engaging at times) is that the latter tend to be designed and produced by people proficient in using television as a 'persuader' rather than as an 'entertainer'.

MAKING GOOD USE OF TELEVISION

Whilst there is disagreement about ways in which television affects youngsters' behaviour, its influence 'on social processes is undisputed' (Williams *et al.*, 1992, p. 19); although – as already mentioned – discussion around this subject has tended to be one-sided. More often than not, it is television violence which has been the focus of enquiries, consequently sparse attention has been directed towards the effects of viewing pro-social behaviour. However, television is not always regarded negatively; on occasions it is accepted that it can influence behaviour in positive ways. Along these lines, Gunter (1984, p. 152) reminds us:

> Some programmes, for example, deliberately emphasise pro-social themes of generosity, helpfulness and co-operation between people, and even those action-dramas in which violence is most commonly and vividly portrayed often feature positive, socially desirable behaviour.

Likewise, he remarks that research studies have shown that children can, and do, learn pro-social behaviours from their viewing. More recent comment suggests that pro-social content may even counteract anti-social content to some extent (Gunter and McAleer, 1990).

These comments remind us that television can be used to encourage positive influences upon children's, and young adults', behaviour. If this is the case, then, given that children spend 15,000 hours or more in school, it makes sense that teachers should be skilled in making effective use of the television medium for the benefit of their pupils' all-round development. Although there is only limited evidence of this thinking being incorporated within the National Curriculum, such neglect has not stopped others from making pleas that:

> The school curriculum must cater for this new and exciting area. . . . As it is, television viewers could be quite badly misled by what they see on television. The matter could become worse as we go into the 21st Century. We must carry out our main duties as educators, that is, we must prepare the children to be able to function effectively (and healthily) in the future society.
>
> (Naidu and Wallace, 1993, p. 10)

In reality, like most other electronic 'gadgets' in our lives, television is neither good nor bad. Its effects stem largely from the use individuals make of it. In the case of television, this use refers to more than just the number of hours, and the type of programmes, children view. Perceptions matter also. For example, a tendency has been noted for young viewers to have difficulty distinguishing between fantasy and reality (Drew and Reeves, 1980) and Greenberg and Reeves noted that where television content is seen as real: 'the child's attitudes and behaviours are more likely to be consistent with the content of that exposure' (1976, p. 87). This comment is reinforced by Hearold's (1986) findings. After examining over 200 studies dealing with television's effects upon behaviour, he concluded that the degree of perceived realism about a programme was a significant factor in determining whether or not the viewer would model behaviours. If programmes perceived as fantasy (cartoons are an extreme example) are less likely to affect viewer's behaviour, then it may benefit children to have early help to discern differences between real life and 'fictional' events. If 'fictional' violence in a film is perceived as real, there are greater risks of imitation occurring, than if pupils understood that it was 'make believe'. This point will be considered again, later in the chapter.

Other important mediators of the television–behaviour connection appear linked to the degree and quality of parental mediation, the development of critical viewing skills, opportunities to discuss programmes with people who are responsible and mature, and parental viewing habits. With these factors in mind, benefits of television viewing seem likely to accrue where:

- parents exercise prudent supervision over their children's viewing
- parents' viewing habits serve as good models for their children
- schools encourage the development of children's critical viewing skills and
- where schools draw upon children's viewing experiences to help advance their personal and social development.

Whilst accepting that parents have the major responsibilities and obligations to help their children profit from their TV viewing, this chapter is now concerned with examining ways in which *schools* may utilise children's viewing habits and preferences in order to advance their personal and social development.

PERSONAL AND SOCIAL EDUCATION: AND TELEVISION

In his research in Northern Ireland, Collins (1990) discovered that more than 50 per cent of first- and third-year pupils preferred programmes such as *Neighbours, Home and Away* and *Roseanne* or *Cheers*. Their least favourite programmes included the *News* and *Coronation Street;* whilst their most admired TV characters were Scott and Charlene (from *Neighbours*). These tastes are unlikely to match those of most teachers. Consequently, if teachers intend to capitalise upon their pupils' viewing habits and preferences, they will need to watch, and try to understand (even empathise with) the characters, the plots and the settings. Equipped with this knowledge and understanding, teachers have scope to establish 'contact' by listening to, and engaging in, their pupils' conversations about such programmes; they can also initiate discussion with them. In other words, teachers can learn to use television for fundamental educational purposes. The Elton Report also had this in mind.

In their deliberations upon pupils' (mis)behaviour the Elton Report recommended that:

> teachers and parents should make active use of television as an educational resource, reinforcing the positive messages presented by programmes and encouraging children to become more discriminating and critical viewers.
>
> (DES and Welsh Office, 1989, p. 162)

There are, of course, different ways in which these tasks can be undertaken, one of which is to incorporate pupils' viewing within 'lessons' linked to personal and social education. (It is worth noting that, since 1990, schools can record off-air terrestrial channels for educational purposes, as long as the school is covered by the licensing scheme operated by the Educational Recording Agency; see Appendix to this chapter.)

Occasions are not uncommon in classes where the teacher labours ineffectively with a particular point. The point might involve matters from any of the components from the cross-curricular themes of 'Education for Citizenship' and 'Health Education' (e.g. sex education, family-life education, safety, substance use and misuse). With older pupils, reactions can often indicate frustration or boredom, whilst younger children may still manage to maintain a polite – yet distanced

– expression. Despite well-intentioned and well-informed attempts to get the point across, the adult fails to capture the hearts and minds of the youngsters. This is where television can come in handy. Every week there are numerous incidents on television programmes which can be used to illustrate a point in question. Pupils, for example, can be asked how they viewed the break-up between two youngsters in an episode from *Home and Away*. Did it have to happen? Was it undertaken correctly? Could it have been handled better? If one partner was rejected how could (s)he be helped? Who could provide this help and how would it be given? How would you feel if it happened to *you*? Similarly a death in *Neighbours* can provide a 'safe haven' for discussions on bereavement and the psychological impact of loss.

What makes these 'television' discussions invaluable – despite being fictional – is that the situations under scrutiny are not necessarily perceived as unreal. The televised drama – or at least the particular matters under discussion – are often 'real' ones (to some pupils). Many pupils will have shared similar experiences. It may be the case that they have separated from close friends, they were bullied, their parents were divorced or they have first-hand experience of domestic violence. Whatever the testing event, their experiences may have left them lost in an adolescent world, and needing help. They may have needed help to understand, to cope with, to learn from and come to terms with *their problem*. Peer groups are not always equipped to provide this help. This is where the television and the teacher can work together effectively. Managed skilfully by the teacher, classroom discussions centred upon pupils' viewing can make valuable contributions to pupils' affective health and competences. Because many pupils will have viewed the programme under discussion, most of them already will be familiar with the incidents; consequently, the discussion has topicality, relevance and appeal. With the teacher's guidance, an almost limitless range of matters can be discussed openly and productively in this way; and outcomes are likely to be far more successful than if raised in a more traditional and impersonal way, without the help of the television.

On other occasions, more adult-oriented soaps such as *Eastenders*, and *The Bill* and *Roseanne* introduce areas which not all teachers feel easy talking about with (or to) youngsters. These areas can include drug-taking, smoking, solvent abuse, gambling, racism, ageism, pregnancy, peer pressure, abuse, religion and sexual relationships. In contrast to the experiences of many teachers, most pupils have been reared on a television diet which deals with these matters in a fairly routine and rather bland manner. However, whilst children may be familiar with such matters, there is no guarantee that they comprehend them. Drawing upon the happenings in a television programme can offer opportunities for teachers and pupils to capitalise upon. Against this backcloth – and where appropriate – matters can be raised and discussed sensitively, sensibly and informatively. However, even in the best-run lessons, plans can take a wrong turn; particularly where the lesson is focusing upon areas which involve emotions (relationships in particular). At all times, the teacher will need to be vigilant so that (s)he can intervene in order to prevent, or redress, hurtful, harmful or misleading comments.

The *Grange Hill* series is another favourite of youngsters. Although not to everyone's taste, the series has managed to raise a number of school-based concerns such as bullying (by teachers as well as peers), extortion, stealing, peer-pressure, loneliness and loyalty. If the teacher and pupils are well-versed in the programme then a ready-made series of PSE topics is available through a medium which most pupils are motivated to watch, attend to and (given an appropriate forum for discussion) learn from. With younger children, incidents of this kind can be used, at the very least, to remind children that all people have feelings. It is too easy, perhaps, for young viewers to side with the macho bully who gets what she wants by intimidation and aggression. It's not difficult, either, to learn that if violence and intimidation are practised, desirable rewards such as money, power and admiring onlookers seem to be there for the picking. Some children may well come from homes where this faulty 'learning' is reinforced daily; consequently they have few opportunities to learn otherwise and develop more acceptable behaviours. Some years ago there was a news report about a teenage girl who endured years of sexual abuse from her father. Her years of abuse had taught her to believe that her experiences were typical. It needed a social worker to explain this was not the case.

Opportunities to capitalise upon youngsters' TV viewing are not confined to any single area of the curriculum. Components from the 'Health Education' and 'Education for Citizenship' cross-curricular themes can be incorporated into most areas of the timetable for this purpose (see NCC, 1990). They can be incorporated, for example:

- across the whole curriculum
- as a separately timetabled subject
- as part of a defined PSE course, and
- as part of a pastoral/tutorial programme

DEVELOPING CRITICAL VIEWING SKILLS

So far in this chapter, consideration has been given to ways in which teachers can integrate some of their pupils' viewing experiences into a broad-based curriculum for personal and social education. There are other areas, as well, which teachers can address to help their pupils become more 'television literate', or 'mediate'. The development of critical viewing skills is a further step in this direction.

The news (local news programmes might, at times, be more appealing and appropriate) can be used to highlight a variety of PSE themes. Conflicts, tragedies, joys, discoveries, disenchantments, achievements and disappointments feature regularly and can be capitalised upon. Programmes such as *Right to Reply* can show that people do not always agree with what has been said or has been shown; they can indicate, as well, how people can make their points of view known. Whilst there is a tendency to regard news reporting as accurate and without distortions, these programmes are produced by people, who – as individuals or groups – share a propensity to perceive events subjectively. This subjectivity can induce biased reporting. Vested interests, also, can result in biased reporting; and our own experiences of news reporting during the Falklands conflict helps remind us how this can happen. With these frailties in mind, there is a strong case for educating children to be questioning about what they see on news and news-related, programmes. This task was dealt with by Vooijs *et al.* (1995) in Holland. They designed a six-programme schools' television series intended to: 'teach children . . . that television news broadcasts give a selective and thus subjective and incomplete impression of the news' (p. 23).

Whilst their study's outcomes showed pupils became more insightful about such matters as selection processes involved in news broadcasts, they did not show decreased credibility levels about the broadcasts. However, a similar instructional programme was designed and evaluated by Kelley *et al.* (1985) in the UK. They reported that pupils *did* develop a more critical attitude towards television news. In their research, pupils were involved in analyses of specific news broadcasts. The programme also included a practical element: pupils were required to plan, prepare and produce their own programmes using video recording and editing equipment. The discussions, together with the practical work, seemed to provide pupils with insight into news broadcasting. They became able to understand better the constraints which producers can be exposed to. In turn, this awareness enabled them to become more critical of news productions.

Initiatives such as these are part of a wider exercise designed to help pupils become more discriminating in their viewing. The chapter now considers some of these other exercises.

BECOMING MORE DISCRIMINATING CONSUMERS OF TELEVISION

What of the violence content in some programmes? Whilst some think violence on television should be restricted others, along the lines advocated by the USA Surgeon General's report on television, have claimed:

> Recognition of the importance of television as a part of a child's growing-up experience has led in recent years to the view that children need to learn something about how to watch television and how to understand it. Much as they are taught to appreciate literature, to read newspapers carefully, and so on, they need to be prepared to understand television as they view it in their homes.
>
> (Pearl *et al.*, 1982, p. 81)

In this context a number of researchers have demonstrated that parents can alter the effects upon children of viewing television violence by discussing programmes with them (e.g. Leyens *et al.*, 1982). Some studies have indicated that parental co-viewing, with its opportunities for prudent censorship and discussion, provides opportunities for parents to maximise beneficial potential of television, and moderate negative effects. Of course, one of the problems here is that parents are not always around to 'educate' their children's viewing. St Peters (1989) reported that parents co-viewed with their children during children's programmes, for only 22–25 per cent of the time. Nevertheless, the notion is appealing that if parents can do this, so can teachers.

A number of investigations have examined this notion. One successful school project was conducted by Vooijs and Van Der Voort (1993) in Holland. Their enquiry was based around a six-programme television series designed to help 10–12-year-old children to become more discriminating consumers of violence on television. The project, which also included a student workbook and teacher's manual, aimed to reduce approval of unjustified violent actions, and to focus upon pro-social actions on TV. This was undertaken through the use of six 20-minute programmes. The programmes, for example, showed violent TV programme excerpts and then involved real policemen to explain how they were allowed to use only reasonable force when struggling with law-breakers. Interviews with victims of violence were incorporated also, to put across the emotional, as well as physical, experiences of violence. As mentioned earlier in this chapter, one of the programme's aims was to show youngsters that much of the violence they viewed was unreal. For example, blood was really dye, huge rocks were sponges, weapons were 'toys' and smashed windscreens were made of sugar. The project achieved successful outcomes in that it:

> led to an increase in factual knowledge of differences between violence as depicted in crime series and real-life violence, and a decrease in the perceived realism of violent television programmes.
>
> (Vooijs and Van Der Voort, 1993, p. 139)

In the USA a number of sophisticated programmes have directed their energies towards making children 'more literate consumers of television'

(Sprafkin *et al.*, 1992, p. 118). Many of these have been designed to include exceptional children (e.g. CESSMA and Kidvid Critical Viewing Curriculum). The 'Curriculum for Enhancing Social Skills through Media Awareness', more often known as CESSMA (Sprafkin *et al.*, 1986) comprises fourteen 30-minute lessons based upon brief videotaped segments from popular children's television shows. Like the Dutch study, the first five lessons aim to develop children's awareness of distinctions between reality and fantasy on television. However, the next five lessons focused upon puppetry, make-up, costumes and other special effects, to show how violent actions are 'faked'. Among the success indicators of the programme was the finding that, compared to their peers in a control group, those who completed the programme identified less with characters who used violence. This outcome seems important given that in a similar programme, Huesmann *et al.* (1983) reported that those who reduced their identification with aggressive characters were also those who reduced their own levels of aggression the most.

A unique element of the Kidvid programme (Abelman and Courtright, 1983) is its focus upon a number of pro-social behaviours including altruism, empathy, co-operation, reparation, sympathy and sharing. During a 3-week programme, these behaviours were discussed and included in excerpts from television programmes. In week 1, pupils were encouraged to become aware of their own viewing habits and the pro-social and anti-social components within programmes viewed by them. Week 2 then focused upon motives and consequences of behaviour in televised programmes, and compared them to real life settings. In the final week alternatives to aggressive behaviour were considered, and demonstrations were given concerning the different ways of resolving conflict situations. Evaluations of the Kidvid programme showed that 'graduates' became better at recognising and labelling pro-social behaviours in their viewing.

Of course CESSMA and Kidvid are not the only programmes available to teach critical viewing skills. Others are available in Europe, and elsewhere (e.g. Kelley, 1991; Vooijs and Van Der Voort, 1993). However, it appears that many countries, and many schools, have yet to be recruited into the ranks of those who believe that television 'literacy or mediacy' is an important area in which there is a need to invest considerable interest and energy if pupils are to be educated to maximise benefits from television viewing, whilst being aware, too, of potentially unhealthy influences.

CONCLUSION

Despite the volume of studies investigating the television–behaviour connection, there is still disagreement over the nature, and strength, of the connection. Regrettably, for many, television is seen as a negative influence, socially and culturally, and is often considered a poor medium for learning. This viewpoint is both unfounded and misleading. Few dispute that television has the capacity to exercise influence, of one kind or another, over viewers' behaviour; but, like so many of life's experiences, outcomes are largely determined by individuals. In this sense the television experience is not different. It seems that children can be helped to become 'television literate' and, in turn, this literacy can enable them to profit from their viewing. Some of this help may reside in the home; some can be provided for at school. National Curriculum documentation (e.g. NCC, 1990, p. 1), for example, stresses the value of involving parents 'so that what is learned in school can be supported by appropriate experiences at home'. Regrettably, whilst there is some control over what happens in school, there is little direct control over what goes on in the home. As with so many other areas of 'shared' responsibility between home and school, schools not only have to undertake their own share of those responsibilities, but have to be prepared to compensate, also, for those homes which are unable, or unwilling, to provide this support.

With these obligations in mind, this chapter signalled some ways in which children's television viewing can be capitalised upon within the PSE curriculum. One of the ways involved incorporating some of the issues and concerns from pupils' viewing experiences into discussions during personal and social education. Others focused upon helping pupils become 'television literate' by assisting them to become more critical in their viewing, more able to distinguish between reality and fantasy and being less accepting of viewpoints transmitted, for example, in the news.

Hopefully, some of the points discussed in the chapter will offer guidance to schools and teachers in their endeavours to help their pupils to become more proficient socially and emotionally. What is irrefutable is that electronic technology is becoming an almost obligatory (and sometimes unavoidable) element within our working and leisure hours. If we accept that we need to spend time in schools helping pupils to become literate and numerate, arguably we should spend as much time helping pupils to become 'mediate'. Personal and social education offer schools areas within which contributions to this 'education' can take place.

APPENDIX

How does it affect you with regard to off-air recording?

Since May 1990 any off-air recording (television and BBC Radio) of terrestrial channels for educational purposes *must* be covered by the licensing scheme operated by the Educational Recording Agency, whose members represent the copyright owners of such material. The only exception to this is Open University programmes.

Most schools in the state sector are covered with a blanket licence held by their Local Education Authority. Schools in the independent sector are licensed individually; Grant Maintained Schools may be covered by a Grant Maintained Schools Centre or may be licensed individually. Other establishments, such as universities, colleges and language schools, are also licensed by the ERA.

(Printed with the kind permission of the Educational Recording Agency Ltd, 74 New Oxford Street, London WC1A 1EF, tel. 0171 636 2402.)

BIBLIOGRAPHY

Abelman, R. and Courtright, J. (1983) Television literacy: amplifying the cognitive level effects of television's prosocial fare through television curriculum intervention, *Journal of Research and Development in Education*, 17, 46–57.

Adler, R. (1977) *Research on the Effects of Television Advertising on Children*, Washington, DC: National Science Foundation.

Anderson, D.R. and Collins, P.A. (1988) *The Impact on Children's Education: Television's Influence on Cognitive Development*, Working Paper 2, US Department of Education.

Charlton, T., Abrahams, M. and Jones, K. (1995) Prevalence rates of emotional and behavioural disorder among nursery class children in St Helena, South Atlantic: An epidemiological study, *Journal of Social Behaviour and Personality*, 10, 1, 273–280.

Collins, J. (1990) Television and secondary school children, *EMI*, 27, 2, 128–134.

Comstock, G. and Paik, H. (1991) *Television and the American Child*, San Diego: American Press Inc.

Department of Education and Science and Welsh Office (1989) *Discipline in Schools. Report by the Committee of Enquiry chaired by Lord Elton*, London: HMSO.

Drew, D.G. and Reeves, B.B. (1980) Children and television news, *Journalism Quarterly*, 57, 45–54.

Fontana, D. (1981) *Psychology for Teachers*, London: British Psychological Society.

Fowles, J. (1992) *Why Viewers Watch: A Reappraisal of Television's Effects*, Newbury Park: Sage Publications.

Greenberg, B.S. and Reeves, B.B. (1976) Children and the perceived reality of television, *Journal of Social Issues*, 32, 4, 86–97.

Gunter, B. (1984) Television as a facilitator of good behaviour among children, *Journal of Moral Education*, 13, 3, 152–159.

Gunter, B. (1987) *Poor Reception: Misunderstanding and Forgetting Broadcast News*, Hillsdale, NJ: Lawrence Erlbaum.

Gunter, B. and McAleer, J.L. (1990) *Children and Television – The One-eyed Monster*? London: Routledge.

Hearold, S. (1986) A synthesis of 1043 effects of television upon social behaviour, in G. Comstock (ed.) *Public Communication and Behaviour*, Vol. 1. New York: Academic Press.

Huesmann, L.R., Eron, L.D., Klein, R., Brice, P. and Fisher, P. (1983) Mitigating the imitation of aggressive behaviours by changing children's attitudes to media violence, *Journal of Personality and Social Psychology*, 44, 899–910.

Kelley, P. (1991) Failing our children/The comprehension of younger viewers, *Journal of Educational Television*, 17, 3, 149–158.

Kelley, P., Gunter, B. and Kelley, C. (1985) Teaching television in the classroom: results of a preliminary study, *Journal of Educational Television*, 11, 57-63.

Leyens, J.P., Herman, G. and Dunand, M. (1982) The influence of an audience upon the reactions to filmed violence, *European Journal of Social Psychology*, 12, 131–142.

Naidu, B.R. and Wallace, B. (1993) Television's effects on cognitive development, *Gifted Education International*, 9, 5–11.

National Commission on Education (1993) *Learning to Succeed*, London: Heinemann.

National Curriculum Council (1990) *Curriculum Guidance 5: Health Education*, York: NCC.

Pearl, D., Bouthilet, L. and Lazar, J. (1982) *Television and Behaviour: Ten Years of Scientific Progress and Implications for the Eighties (Vol. 2)*. Washington, DC: US Government Printing Office.

Royes, H. (1980) Television and traditional culture: a survey of Afro-American women on St Helena Island, South Carolina, *Dissertation Abstracts International*, 41/12-A, 4876–93.

St Peters, M. (1989) Television and families: parental coviewing and young children's language development, social behaviour and television processing, paper presented at the Biennial Meeting for Research in Child Development (Kansas City, MO, 27–30 April).

Social Trends (1990) Television and radio: average viewing and listening per week, by age, *Social Trends*, 20, 153.

Singer, R.S. (1992) Childhood, aggression and television, *Television and Children*, 5, 57–63.

Sprafkin, J., Watkins, L.T. and Gadow, K.D. (1986) Curriculum for enhancing social skills through media awareness, unpublished curriculum, State University of New York at Stony Brook.

Sprafkin, J., Gadow, K.D. and Abelman, R. (1992) *Television and the Exceptional Child: A Forgotten Audience*, Hillsdale, NJ: Lawrence Erlbaum.

Vooijs, M.W. and Van Der Voort, T.H.A. (1993) Teaching children to evaluate television violence critically, *Journal of Television*, 19, 3, 139–152.

Vooijs, M.W., Van Der Voort, T.H.A. and Hoogeweij, J. (1995) Critical viewing of television news: the impact of a schools television project, *Journal of Educational Television*, 21, 1, 23–35.

Walters, J.K. and Stone, V.A. (1971) Television and family communication, *Journal of Broadcasting*, 15, 409–414.

Ward, S. and Wackman, D. (1972) Family and media influences on adolescent consumer learning, in E.A. Rubenstein, G.A. Comstock and J.P. Murray (eds) *Television and Social Behaviour: Volume 4. Television in Day-to-Day Life: Patterns of Use*, Washington, DC: US Government Printing Office.

Wiegman, O. and Kuttschreuter, M. (1992) A longitudinal study of the effects of television viewing on aggressive and pro-social behaviours, *British Journal of Social Psychology*, 31, 147–164.

Williams, P.A., Haertel, E.H., Haertel, G.D. and Walberg, H.J. (1992) The impact of leisure-time television on school learning: a research synthesis, *American Educational Research Journal*, 19, 1, 19–50.

Williams, T.M. (1986) *The Impact of Television: A Natural Experiment in Three Settings*, Academic Press: New York.

Winn, M. (1976) *The Plug-in Drug: Television, Children and the Family*, New York: Viking Books.

Winn, M. (1977) *The Plug-in Drug*, New York: Bantam Books.

12

TAKING OUR CHILDREN SERIOUSLY

Core values for teachers and parents

Richard Whitfield

INTRODUCTION

We live in a culture in which it is difficult for us to take each other sufficiently seriously in the light of what we know about optimum human development. Technological, social and economic changes have been so rapid that it is hard for us to catch our breath to reflect upon three key issues:

1 the meaning of our lives – questions of purpose;
2 who we are and what we would like to become – questions of identity; and
3 how we might get there, given both constraints and opportunities – questions of tactics.

Yet for all of us who hold responsibility for rearing the next generation, particularly as parents and teachers, these reflective questions ought to be faced. Sadly we often avoid them because there are always other things with which to busy ourselves, and they raise complex and demanding questions about fundamental values. In defence of such avoidance we may reason that even if we had a carefully worked out set of values for ourselves, which had implications for children, then this would make very little difference to our professional and their social worlds. Such cynicism and avoidance of engagement is understandable when educational systems are in practice funded by rather distanced bureaucracies, and much of the curriculum seems prescribed.

But the vocation – yes, vocation – of parenthood or teaching is predicated upon the reality that here are these unique children at this never-to-be-repeated time in my or our care. These children need to, indeed long to – yes, long to – learn useful knowledge, skills, insights, values, ethics and wisdom and to develop reliable relationships. And they so often have those incessant 'why?' questions. It is our task – indeed privilege – in collaboration with others, to help them shape a coherent and worthwhile life in a complex and perplexing world. In so doing we create, and help them to create, a better world in which there is a greater sense of purpose, more meaning, greater fulfilment and less pain.

So we do have the potential to make a difference – worthwhile changes but not necessarily entirely predictable ones – for these children now and into their futures. And if we do not influence them, then there are likely to be a host of others who might exploit their vulnerabilities and damage their lives and potential. This chapter is therefore concerned with child-centred values, their nature in the light of research evidence, their pursuit and their fulfilment.

US FOR THEM

As teachers and parents at best we nurture and catalyse the in-part self-creation of persons by opening up the world and its deposits of human experience in a responsible and structured way. The roles are demanding, the enterprises are essentially ethical, and we are only as good at the tasks of mediating personal growth in children as our distilled total experience and techniques of prompting learning allow.

When I was involved in teacher education more continuously than I am now I used to tell my students that teaching is akin to the 'hokey-cokey' – you put your 'whole self in' (to the classroom) 'and shake it all about'. So the richer and more intriguing we are, the more able we can be to open up young minds and hearts to the richness of human experience, capability and insight. Life, wisdom, well-being and a sense of security in us transmits to the young. Conversely, so do dullness, superficiality, depression, arrogance and insecurity.

So who we are matters, and if we are to love our children, enabling them to stand on our shoulders, then as adults we need to be continually growing ourselves. As parents and professionals we can only hand on and prompt development from what we ourselves have learned.

HOPE, MUTUALITY AND VULNERABILITY

Our children are above all symbols of hope that at least bearable and better futures are possible. The planned, longed-for, wanted baby is above all an extension of faith in the future of human-kind. Given nurture, baby, then child, becomes a living message into the future, only part of which we are likely to see.

Recently I attended the opening of a new extension to a church-affiliated (voluntary controlled) primary school. The extension enables the rising 5–11-year-olds of the community to be educated on one site in modern premises after many years of coping with infants and juniors on a split site. The project, like so many of its kind, was overdue. Achieving it was a team effort by diocesan and local authority officials, governors, parents, teachers, the architect and building contractors.

So this now integrated building is both an investment and a symbol of hope in the future, and in the capacity and potential of a community's children. Its success over the ensuing years will be a matter of curriculum content and processes, the skills and dedication of the teaching and support staff, and, crucially, the social and psychological richness and stability of the homes from which the pupils come.

As part of the school's opening ceremony, held in the playground area on a lovely summer afternoon, all the school's children (some 120 of them) joined hands in a large circle around all the assembled adults, enfolding us, as I felt it, in their love, gratitude, yearnings and hope. Here was an 'inside out' picture of the young demonstrating their interdependence in protection of those adults having both a collective interest in and responsibility for their care. Here was a snapshot of the reality of mutuality between generations. This was a memorable metaphor or parable going to the heart of what education has to be about – promoting a judicious mix of independence from the reality of our interdependence as social beings.

Yet individually respectful mutuality is continually under siege in our increasingly competitive social and economic environment. The ritual of the school opening ceremony, blessed by the diocesan Bishop, transfixed mutuality for a precious hour. Behind the scenes some of the adults with an interest had sometimes squabbled; community and regional 'politics' had run their course in their varying secular and sacred, and sometimes less than sacred, ways.

But at last these adults had got at least a part of their act together for these and later generations of vulnerable children. And children are vulnerable to parental and teacher conflict, to parental absence and neglect, to less than dedicated holistic teaching, to unsupervised peer and media pressures, to bullying, and much else in a world which is now too often inherently unsafe for children. For a while, though, here there was a unity of purpose – no domestic arguments, no committee posturing, no community or professional backbiting, no battling for time-limited control by intrusive, insecure adult egos.

Sadly in our media-dominated and relationally insecure society the innocence of even 5-year-olds is likely to be short-lived. Indeed, some by the 'infants' stage have already experienced loss of mutuality through family breakdown, and the loss of respect, care, concern and trust which usually accompanies it. Much of such private grief goes unassuaged and tends to impede the educational process. This has a wide range of implications for public policy and personal responsibility in which schools could play a formative part given more opportunity to attend to that vital 'fourth R' – relationships education – now so necessary in a world of greater personal choice and often illusory 'freedoms'.

CHILD-SENSITIVE VALUES

Our dominant social priorities are hugely determined by adults' desires and gratifications. Rarely does our society put children and their needs first. The standards of child rearing and child care are frequently inadequate when assessed against the yardstick of what we now know that children need in order to thrive – biologically, socially, emotionally, intellectually and spiritually. While there are many structural forces undermining children's best interests, there is also widespread ignorance of children's developmental needs, so that decisions about the context and practice of child rearing are frequently less sensitive, coherent or consequential than they might be. The products of this, now clearly visible in most primary schools, include alienation, disruptive or withdrawn social behaviour, and insecure social relationships. Diminished educational achievement is then likely even with good school-based teaching, for education is unavoidably a shared enterprise between home, community and school.

The late Dr Mia Kellmer Pringle, the founding Director of the National Children's Bureau, helpfully summarised the research-based *needs of children* as follows. Given no manifest physical handicaps, a sound diet, appropriate shelter and clothing and sufficient sleep, the optimum development of children depends upon four basic environmental conditions or 'needs' being met:

1 the need for reliable love from and secure attachment to parent figures, reflecting that 'psychological' rather than biological parenthood is crucial; teachers of course may act as parent figures;
2 the need for new experiences – visual, tactile, intellectual, emotional and spiritual – which gradually extend the child's world; these, when explained by patient teaching, in home and school, enable the child to develop structures of meaning and understanding so that the world is experienced more in terms of order than chaos;
3 the need for praise, recognition and affirmation, reflecting the fact that secure identities are jeopardised by overly critical and negative environments; and
4 the need to be given responsibilities appropriate to the child's level of development; this helps in moral development and the establishment of identity through the exercise of constructive social roles.

(adapted from Pringle, 1975)

These basic needs, which transcend cultural differences, set benchmarks for child-sensitive values and policies. They are predicated upon the availability of sufficient material resources, so that addressing circumstances causing child poverty is part and parcel of fulfilling children's needs, viewed as an ethical statement with practical consequences. It is of note that this statement of needs emphasises that the relational, emotional, moral and social components of human functioning are the foundation for intellectual and practical life, and for the growth in personal autonomy and responsibility which characterise sound citizenship.

The next sections elaborate aspects of these four core needs as key aspects of taking children seriously.

PARENT-FIGURE COMMITMENT

A child-concerned society would endeavour to provide every child with dependable and loving relationships with two parents, one of each gender, or equivalent permanent substitutes such as adoptive parents. Through the supportive attention of two complementary parents children come to establish a sense of their own worth, identity and sexuality. Lone parenthood, whether caused by death, divorce or design, is inherently more demanding, and generally a more risky venture for both parent and child, if only because of the usually more limited resources, including time, of the single carer. On the basis of extensive evidence our society should do all it can to encourage biological parents to commit themselves to mutually supportive long-term relationships and active collaboration over the demanding tasks of parenthood. Through both example and teaching, educators can play a part in appropriately re-establishing such norms in communities, without in any way stigmatising children whatever their background.

The crucial characteristic of mature parent-figure love is that it envelops our children in good times and bad. We love our children in commitment regardless of their appearance, personality or abilities; we seek to understand and correct them when their behaviour is unlovable and irritating; taking the time and trouble to correct anti-social behaviour during the years of growing up is an important aspect of helping children to learn about boundaries in the social and physical world, and this promotes their security.

As loving parents or committed teacher parent-figures we are willing to take, and to go on taking trouble with the children in our care. Such love may be viewed as our continuing willingness to extend ourselves in order to foster their social, educational, emotional and spiritual growth while not neglecting our own. This emphasises that love is far more a matter of *will* and *commitment* rather than feeling; indeed love based mainly upon emotion is a poor foundation for all human relationships (Peck, 1987).[1]

The love which children need involves courage, a willingness to attend and to listen as well as to explain. It involves judicious giving and judicious withholding. It recognises the individuality and separateness of the child, and it guards against possessiveness and over-dependency which can perpetuate essentially infantile attitudes into later phases of life.

Novelist Laurie Lee, writing some years ago as a new parent, captures both the dependence and separateness of his baby daughter who, like children at school, is capable of defying our preconceptions (which of course makes both parenting and teaching potentially so fascinating):

> This girl then, my child, this parcel of will and warmth, began to fill the cottage with her obsessive purpose. . . .
>
> I'd been handed twenty odd years wrapped up in this bundle, and hoped to see her grow, learn to totter, to run into the garden, run back, and call this place home. But I realised from these beginnings that I'd got a daughter whose life was already separate from mine, whose will already followed its own directions, and who was quickly correcting my woolly preconceptions of her by being something quite different. She was a child of herself and would be what she was. I was merely the keeper of her temporary helplessness.
>
> (Lee, 1984)

Being a concerned 'keeper' is of course an active, working role in which teachers and parents are cast as both providers and stimulators in the processes of children's becoming.

THE HOME BASE

Children's need for security is met first and foremost by a stable framework of home and family relationships; such stability helps to reflect consistent attitudes and dependable behaviour. Also important, especially for young children, are the security of a familiar place, familiar objects and a familiar routine. Development in childhood is necessarily about change and exploration, some of which can be frightening to the child, whether in toddlerhood or adolescence. Hence a predictable background environment gives continuity, and it encourages safer exploration by the child of its own frontiers. When unavoidable variations in life's pattern occur, it is vital that they are appropriately explained to the child, for a child's security is undermined by randomness or confusion about life's boundaries.

Personal continuity is important for all of us, for in one sense we are no more and no less than our life story. Our identity becomes insecure if we cannot find enough continuity in that story; children in particular need to perceive key events as consequential. For that reason the family stories and other reminders of the past, such as personal photographs, help children and adults alike both to make sense of the present and to give hope for a future in which the necessary risks of being alive can be assimilated without trauma. Confident attachment to and appropriate trust in new people, concerns and places outside the immediate family circle are of course a necessary part of that future hope.

So the child's experience of *attachment*, first and crucially at home, then in mediating institutions like schools, profoundly influences the growth of the individual personality and its educational development. It is the product of cultural forces, which may or may not support its formative processes, and a key determinant of how that culture will be transmitted into the next generation. That transmission, so often better safeguarded in pre-industrial societies, not only includes the culture of attachment itself (e.g. baby's bonding to mother, then later to kin), but all our concepts of social order, authority, control and security. Children entering primary school without secure prior attachments are usually and understandably difficult to handle.

Figure 12.1 (p. 214) summarises the evidence concerning inter-generational pathways for children who have had insecure or stressful home-based attachment patterns particularly with their mothers. This chart has many implications for public policy and personal priorities.

EDUCATION IS INTELLIGIBLE NEW EXPERIENCES

The word 'education' is derived from the Latin verb '*educare*' meaning 'to lead out'. Our temptation as teachers too often is to 'drum in'! Effective learning requires always the child's active and willing engagement and attention.

New experiences for children can be futile or even damaging if they are not explained, and explanation requires someone in the mediating role of a teacher. Thus, for example, allowing children to watch captivating images on TV or video regularly on their own and without explanation can cause them inner disturbance. Tony Charlton focuses on this in Chapter 11. New experiences must be meaningfully related to what has gone before if they are to enlarge the human personality. The child's growth as a person, rather than simply as a body, is dependent upon a gradual exploration of the physical and social environment. Such exploration, based initially upon the child's natural curiosity, requires stimulation (but not over-stimulation), guidance and explanation (but not excessive control and didactic lecturing) from parents and other carers.

From the very early days of life children's educational capabilities, that is their responsiveness to the varied growth tasks which teaching and learning in their widest sense open up to them, are being determined. The emotional and cultural climate of the home is fundamental to the provision of safe and valuable new experiences throughout childhood;

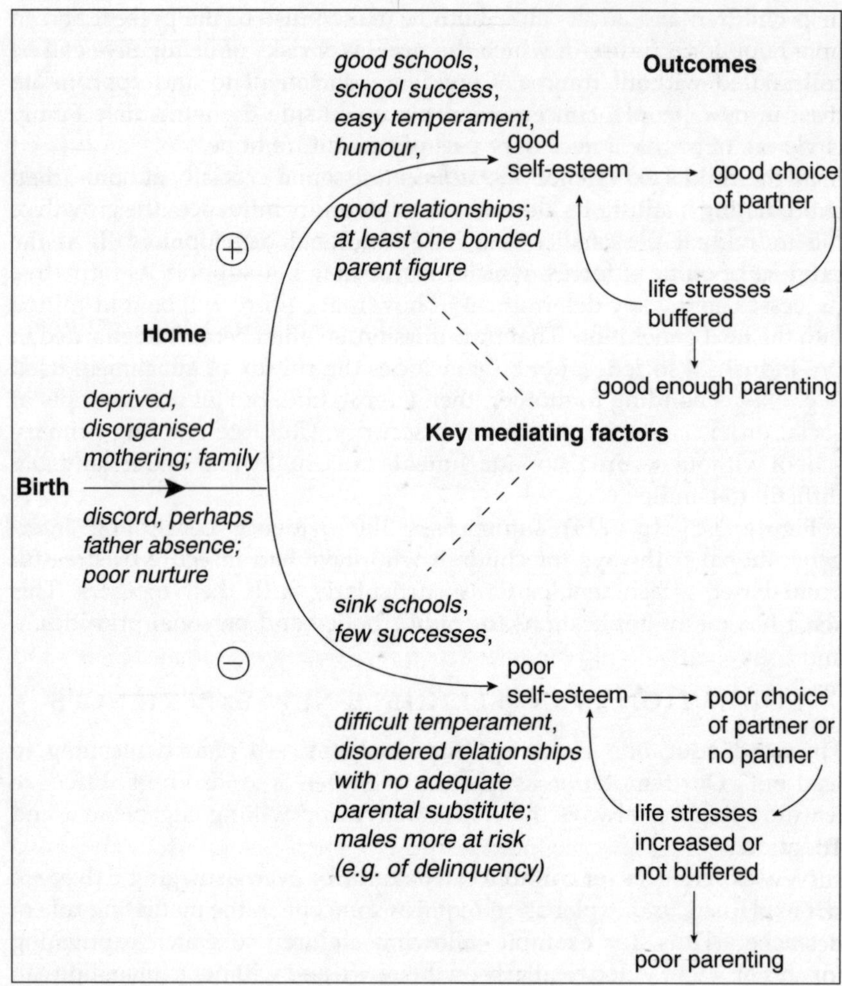

Figure 12.1 Contrasting developmental pathways from early deprivation

these are extended by organised pre-school experience, and later by the formal educational system. Given appropriate explanation by careful teaching, our children's gradually extending experience becomes organised and differentiated so that distinctive forms of meaning and reasoning become apparent to their developing intellects. Children begin to learn that different language and procedural 'rules' apply to thinking and action in mathematics, science, the arts, history, religion and so on.

Fundamentally, the formal educational system exists because there are inevitable limitations to the specialist functions of the home as educator in extending children's understanding and experience of the world, and in providing them with an array of useful skills to enable them, given opportunity, to participate in our complex society. But the school and college systems can only build upon what children and students bring to the classroom from their prior experience, most of which, in terms of time, is derived from home and neighbourhood. Home, school, supervised media and community are thus interdependent agents for providing children with comprehensible and worthwhile new experiences.

The main, specific and irremovable educational functions of the home, extended by school, are concerned with:

1 the development of language – listening, talking and, later, writing;
2 the encouragement of learning through active play; in this the manipulation of toys, body control, sound expressiveness, role play and make-believe each contribute to child development;
3 the fostering of social and relationships skills partly by modelling; and
4 developing an awareness and understanding of a moral order.

Each of these is interdependent, while language is the key to effective communication, to making new experiences intelligible and to understanding different forms of reasoning. The language of homes and schools are parts of their climate, mediating between thought, emotion and behaviour, and linking new experience with the familiar. Parents and teachers have extensive influence upon the ways in which language is used to foster children's growth.

AFFIRMING INCENTIVES

To grow from being a helpless baby into a self-reliant adult, and to be sustained at each stage of that complex and uneven process, requires strong incentives. The will to thrive, and the spirit to stay fully alive are destructible by environmental circumstances. Each of us has the potential for immense psychological strength, but also for delicate vulnerability.

From our very earliest days, we gain the incentive to go on growing from the recognition, praise and affirmation given to us principally by those to whom we are psychologically attached. If those who love or teach us show pleasure at our success, and give us praise, we are affirmed, and our developing identity is thereby confirmed. One of our basic longings is the wish to please those who love or teach us, provided, of course, that we perceive that their expectations of our behaviour are reasonable and sensitive in relation to our innate nature and stage of development. Inappropriate expectations of parents or teachers (whether too low or too high) can make us feel angry, frustrated, and even rejected and unloved; this alone gives us reason to endeavour to understand as much as we can about norms and variations in child development.

Much human learning from the cradle onwards is a matter of trial and error. We can and do learn from our mistakes. Sometimes our errors become clear to us without anyone else intervening to point them out. At other times we are blind or slow to catch on to our failures; on these occasions we need clear correction and explanation from those around us if we are to inhabit the real world. The form in which we are corrected, particularly by those who are close to us, is, however, important to the maintenance of our sense of well-being. Children, and even adults, may become anxious and fearful of making mistakes for fear of personal punitive correction by 'superiors'; this can imply not only that error or misunderstanding is being corrected, but also that personal identity is being demeaned.

There is clearly a balance to be struck between creating a home or school climate which is excessively and unrealistically full of either praise, and possibly bogus affirmation, or of correction and criticism. Genuine, reasonable and consistent encouragement to move forward, involving 'permission' to err, is what both children and adults need to sustain their spirits.

DEVELOPING RESPONSIBLE INDEPENDENCE

The fourth prime need of children concerns their acquisition of tangible contributing roles in the social world, and their moral development. A sense of responsibility, whether to oneself or to others, is essentially an ethical notion involving perception and understanding of the boundaries and interaction between the self and the rest of the world. Early on parents and teachers progressively encourage their charges to take responsibility for their possessions, such as toys and clothes, and also their bodies through health education.

We meet children's need for responsibility by encouraging their personal independence at a pace which they can assimilate without becoming confused, frustrated or simply lonely. The 'Let me do it' urge and the 'Please help me' plaint jostle together throughout life. However, it is in childhood that we begin to learn about the changing boundaries of our dependence and independence.

The fostering of children's independence and responsibility is a delicate balancing act, as concern urges both their protection from harm and their freedom to be. Children need both roots and wings. It is now known that moral development proceeds through a number of inter-related stages, eventually characterised by an ability to act according to our own conscience and principles, duly considering within our actions the rights and feelings of others. Such moral autonomy and 'inner direction' is only achieved if from early childhood we have learned about boundaries to the self and of the likely consequences of our actions upon others. This requires copious illustration.

The framework of social discipline in both home and school is crucial in laying foundations for moral action and responsible behaviour. Wisely, this will progress from accepting that very young children behave to obtain what they need in a relatively egocentric manner, through to a phase of conformity in which there is respect for rules (including rewards and punishments) which are imposed by parents, and teachers, as authority figures. This 'outer directioning' of youngsters by social rules not of their own making is an essential stepping-stone to their later achievement of inner direction. Such transition to mature moral insights is always being assisted by reasoned and reasonable discipline by authority figures.

Table 12.1 summarises the main phases of moral development, understood as being concerned with taking other people's claims and interests into account, that is, learning directly and indirectly to respect others as persons as if the self. Personal action thus becomes based upon reasons rather than whim, impulse or immediate desire. Being able to imagine being 'inside others' shoes' is an aspect of this; working through everyday examples and a good sense of self are essential to achieve this. The phases of Table 12.1 are far from rigidly demarcated in the practical moral development of individuals.

Table 12.1 Phases of moral development (adapted from Piaget, 1965 and Kohlberg, 1984)

Phase 1:	Pre-conventional morality (up to about age 10)	
Principle:	accepts, through fear of harsh consequences, rules prescribed by authority figures.	
	1st element:	child obeys authority figures to avoid punishment
	2nd element:	child respectfully conforms so as to receive rewards
Phase 2:	Conventional morality (up to about age 20 or beyond)	
Principle:	decides that a set of authority figures' rules (e.g. Ten Commandments) are a good code for living even when there is no coercion.	
	1st element:	conforms to avoid disapproval by others
	2nd element:	conforms to avoid guilt from breaking social rules
Phase 3:	Post-conventional 'autonomous' morality (rare before age 16)	
Principle:	adapts set of rules or principles, freely accepted, appropriately to particular situations; understands moral dilemmas.	
	1st element:	guided by principles viewed as good for public welfare and peer/self respect
	2nd element:	guided by self-chosen ethical principles, and can weigh them in situations of potential conflict.

OVERALL DEVELOPMENTAL STAGES

An analysis of children's basic needs, as outlined in the preceding four sections, is however only the 'warp' of the cloth that sensitive parenting and teaching must address. The 'weft' is provided by a framework of time-sequenced, interdependent and interactive phases of child development. There is general agreement about the nature of these phases (Table 12.2), though there are marked individual variations, even in the same family, regarding the pace and extent of each phase; the chronological ages shown are therefore only an appropriate guideline.

Table 12.2 Phases of child development

Stage	*Age guideline*	*Main psychosocial characteristics*	*Main parenthood functions*
Babyhood	–4 months to +12 months	Establishment of trust and feelings of essential goodness of the world.	Mother nurture; father support of both. Accept extreme dependency.
Infancy	1 to 3 years	Beginnings of perception of individuality, gender and social boundaries.	Careful management of distance from child. Encourage play, language, walking, safety.
Early childhood	3 to 6 years	Understanding of separateness of self, mother, father, peers. Happy conformity.	Establish generational and role boundaries and social rules. Confirm gender identity.
Late childhood	6 to 12 years	Acceptable periodic separation from parents. Trust of other carers and peers. Make own plans.	Sharing of caring/ socialisation with teachers and peers. Encourage variety of interests.
Adolescence	13 to 18 years	Life recapitulation; identity exploration in and beyond home; development of self and differentiation from parents.	Tolerate some regression of youngster, along with new expressions of individuality. Provide advisory service and boundaries to kick against.
Young adulthood	19+ years	Establishment of separate lifestyle and domicile; find adult roles; set up enduring relationships; evaluate worldly abilities.	Accept distance and encourage independence of offspring, accepting them as friendly peers.

Each of these phases is characterised by clusters of physical, intellectual and social traits which give indications of the kinds of active parental, teacher and other caregiver responses which are likely to facilitate further development. But similar cues at different ages and with different children need differing interpretations. For example, exaggerated 'bragging' behaviour at 4 represents reality testing and the deciphering of the 'rules' of the social environment; at 12 it more likely reflects underlying feelings of social inadequacy. Temperament and personality variations also lead to varied signs which require individual understanding. Each child is different; there are no unfailing recipes, only guiding principles.

The general personal traits which research suggests as being important for the parental or teaching task can be succinctly summarised as:

1 a generally consistent outgoing *warmth* towards children;
2 a constant *setting of realistic demands* and expectations of them;
3 the *establishment and explanation of a few clear boundaries* for their behaviour; and
4 a *preparedness to be flexible* so as to respect the individuality of each child and to maximise the opportunities provided by new experience.

As schooling progresses, effective teachers need to be able to deploy:

5 skills of *conceptual and 'technical' clarity* within the structure of the particular discourse of different subject and topic areas.

PROMISING FOR CHILDREN: ETHICAL CODES

As implied earlier, adult concern for children is vacuous without commitment. We endeavour to signify our commitments by making implicit or explicit promises. While rituals of commitment are important markers of sincere intention – for example in marriage and other 'initiation' ceremonies – it is on the bumpy road of everyday life that commitments are both put imperfectly into practice and perceived by relevant others as more or less genuine.

Curiously neither our entry into parenthood nor into teaching is marked by visible initiation ceremonies. In neither case do we even have to sign a serious declaration of intent about the implicit duties of guardianship and care. There is no explicit framework of personal and professional ethics for parenthood or teaching, though there may be public consequences arising from serious proven neglect or abuse as enshrined in the Children's Acts, the last major one of which was passed by Parliament in 1989.

This gives an indication of how far Britain is from being a child-sensitive society, for there are relatively explicit codes of business and legal ethics, while for centuries the practice of medicine has been to a large extent safeguarded by the Hippocratic Oath. Of course, ethical codes are always likely to be broken by individuals or groups, but they can and do act as a framework for reference when the appropriateness of human behaviour is publicly questioned and justice is sought.

Governments' signing up to successive United Nations' Declarations of the Rights of the Child, the last version of which became 'law' in 1990 (see Appendix in Miles, 1994), after no less than fifteen years of international ideological manoeuvrings, is relatively painless. Delivering such rights through details of social policy and political priorities is quite another matter, for, unlike the European Convention on Human Rights, there is no legal machinery to enforce the UN declaration nor any right to individual complaint. It is a sad irony that Eglantyne Jebb, who founded the Save the Children Fund in the UK in 1923 after being moved by the plight of refugee children in Europe after the First World War, drafted the first version of the Rights of the Child using far fewer qualifying words than international bureaucrats managed in the 1980s. While actions in terms of mutual care do speak 'louder than words', a few words can focus intentions and, in terms of public policy, sharpen relevant investments.

Some twenty years ago I proposed the establishment of what I then termed a 'pedocratic oath' for teachers (Whitfield, 1976). That notional title, linked to the noun 'pedagogy' (meaning 'the science of teaching'), was intended to convey teachers' fundamental concern for the care of learning. Taking such an idea forward would require the establishment of a General Teaching Council with explicit responsibility for standards in the teaching profession, and in respects similar to the General Medical Council. The GTC idea remains alive, despite government indifference, and would have very different functions from the Teachers' Unions.

Table 12.3 (p. 221) illustrates some potential elements of what could be publicly ratified obligations for both parents and teachers; it will be seen that two of the list of seven categories in this draft are common.

While implementation, let alone enforcement, of the codes of ethics implicit in Table 12.3 would by no means prove easy, wide debate about such ideas is long overdue. It is now, for example, widely agreed that the teachers' strikes of 1986/87 were extremely harmful not only to the children and parents who will long remember them, but also to the public image of teaching as a profession. The political response of an imposed minimum hours contract for full-time service was no less inept in terms of the interests of children, who so often need our time at unpredictable moments; much 'quality time' in child welfare cannot be planned beyond formal curriculum provision.

The seventh entry in Table 12.3 serves to emphasise that the quality and consistency of care which we can give to our children depends upon our own continuing well-being. If we feel over-stressed or depressed or uncared for, our own potential to nurture and stimulate others is harmed. Parents and teachers therefore need to feel secure, affirmed, encouraged and sufficiently stimulated as on-going learners. There remains for us a

Table 12.3 Some suggested basic obligations of parents and teachers

Basic parental duties and obligations	*Core personal obligations for teachers*
1 Strongly supported by wider society, to give our children sufficient of our time, resources and energy so as to deliver consistency of attention, love and care.	1 To prepare my lessons diligently.
2 To ensure that our children's holistic health is safeguarded through sound household routines and eating habits, and regular interaction with local medical services.	2 To set realistic assignments for my pupils, scrutinising and evaluating their resulting work promptly.
3 To safeguard our children's safety in the home and community.	3 To contribute according to my talents and interests to the extra-curricular life of my school.
4 To provide our children with enlarging but monitored opportunities for safe social, educational, emotional and moral growth.	4 To set a good role model for pupils in my life as a citizen in the community.
5 To learn through a variety of avenues as much as possible about parenting.	5 To put the interests of my pupils first, including refraining from withdrawing my labour and my attending to their legitimate needs and expectations.
6 To be sensitive to and endeavour to treat every child as an individual, helping each to grow and to develop to their own potentials as unique whole persons.	
7 To respect, take care of and nurture myself as a person, and others who share responsibility with me for caring for children.	

potentially exciting range of life-course stages beyond our adolescence. However, most of us need significant others around to enable our adult growth, not least if we are giving out to often demanding children. Mutual support of parents by each other inside and beyond the home is vital. Likewise, it is important that teachers in staff rooms and beyond see their work as a collective effort, sharing their insights and difficulties with each other in an atmosphere of collaborative respect. Such mutuality is part and parcel of our being humanely able to deliver in practice any statement of ethical intentions for children.

ADVOCATES FOR CHILDREN

Generally it is only adults who can mess up children's lives – a process which, as we have noted, has a tendency to be inter-generationally transmitted. While there has never been a golden age for children, their fortunes, particularly in terms of secure love and attachment, in most so-called developed economies have in many ways declined over the past thirty years. Adult preoccupations and gratifications, the false presumption that children can easily cope with multiple short-term carers, the collapse of the family wage and along with it much family togetherness, have tended to push the nurture of children towards the back of the queue. That nurturing is a joint responsibility for men and women as mothers and fathers, their extended kin, and the wider community which through its schools symbolises that its pupils are *our* children.

Given the lack of investment in human relationships education (despite coherent schemes such as *Life Foundations*)[2] and the range of now strongly embedded social policies which are hostile to family stability, there is every likelihood of continuing extensive family malformation and major dislocations in relationships. Hence schools, and particularly primary schools, have to be for many youngsters beacons of hope, stability and care, working closely with whatever family supports there are. The staff who work in them must, however, take the children seriously, pressing their insights and knowledge of child development ever more urgently upon a society for which that knowledge will often be uncomfortable.

Gifted and dedicated teachers can only play *a part* in creating a richer psychosocial world for children, and must say so stridently in every community, so that stronger partnerships with parents and other agencies in communities can be formed. Courage and example both in and beyond the classroom are now required of our profession, for social development and other educational accountabilities are far from confined to schools as institutions. The home and family, and the community and media influences (see also Chapter 11) which each household accommodates and tolerates, remain pervasive influences upon all educational outcomes.

Teachers are the largest professional group committed to children's interests. Children are our non-voting 'clients', and we earn our living in their cause. We and their parents are children's advocates, so as we strive for professionalism in every aspect of school organisation and activity we must now also use our influence more assertively within wider public debates which shape children's worlds and life choices. That is an aspect of enfolding them, which is a necessary condition for cultivating mutuality, cultural continuity and a world worth living in.

The myriad of attendant and sometimes tiresome tasks in classroom and beyond are certainly worth sticking at if human life, your own life, is to hold meaning and integrity. These are surely the implicit prizes of your 'keeping at it' – preparing lessons, marking work, giving attention, providing comfort and sometimes castigation and so on – for as long as you choose to remain as a teacher '*in loco parentis*'. Being that 'stand in' for a caring parent has always been the crux of the legal understanding of the teachers' role. It is a noble cause and calling.

NOTES

1 Includes exploration of the nature of love; see also *Life Foundations*, Leader Guide Vol. 2, (Whitfield, 1992).

2 *Life Foundations* is a resource bank for personal, social and family education; 4 leader guides and 2 student journals, NES Arnold/National Family Trust 1992/93. Volume 5 (1996) available from the National Family Trust at 101 Queen Victoria Street, London EC4P 4EP (01242–251583).

BIBLIOGRAPHY

Bettelheim, B. (1987) *A Good Enough Parent*, London: Thames & Hudson.

Bowlby, J. (1988) *A Secure Base: Clinical Applications of Attachment Theory*, London: Routledge.

Fontana, D. (1990) *Your Growing Child from Birth to Adolescence*, London: Fontana Collins.

Kohlberg, L. (1984) *The Philosophy and Psychology of Moral Development*, London: Harper & Row.

Lee, Laurie (1984) *Two Women*, Harmondsworth: Penguin.

Miles, R. (1994) *The Children We Deserve*, London: HarperCollins.

Peck, M. Scott (1987) *The Road Less Travelled*, London: Century Hutchinson.

Peters, R.S. (1981) *Moral Development and Moral Education*, London: Allen & Unwin.

Piaget, J. (1965) *The Moral Judgement of the Child*, New York: Free Press.

Pringle, M. Kellmer (1975) *The Needs of Children*, London: Hutchinson.

Rayner, E. (1986) *Human Development: An Introduction to the Psychodynamics of Growth, Maturity and Ageing*, London: Allen & Unwin.

Whitfield, R.C. (1976) Curriculum planning, teaching and educational accountability, Inaugural Lecture, University of Aston.

Whitfield, R.C. (1980) *Education for Family Life: Some New Policies for Child Care*, London: Hodder & Stoughton.

Whitfield, R.C. (ed.) (1987) *Families Matter: Towards a Programme of Action*, Marshall Pickering/National Family Trust.

Whitfield, R.C. (ed.) (1992–6) *Life Foundations*, London: NES Arnold/National Family Trust.

13

TEACHERS AS PROFESSIONALS

The plight of teaching

Mick Abrahams

This chapter examines changing concepts of the teaching profession and contends that it is very much under threat, at present. Legislation, and its effect on the profession, is analysed and is illustrated through a consideration of personal and social education (PSE) in the primary and middle school curriculum. Developments are proposed to address the needs of the subject which may be extrapolated to the plight of the profession.

INTRODUCTION

Traditionally, professions have been regarded as occupations which differ from others on criteria including specialised knowledge, practitioner autonomy, self-government and a client-centred ethic. Such criteria have been crucial in influencing the public's perception that teaching is a professional activity. Once these criteria are removed, the capacity to deprofessionalise teaching is strengthened.

In recent years, the responsibility for the teaching profession has been devolved, or displaced, among a number of agencies. The School Curriculum and Assessment Authority (SCAA) establishes what should be taught; the Teacher Training Agency (TTA) decides how pre-service training (and, increasingly, in-service training) should be undertaken; the Office for Standards in Education decides the quality of the implementation and delivery of that content; and the School Teachers' Review Body decides the value of the teachers' contribution. Underpinning these agencies is the Department of Education and Employment, appointing members to them as well as delineating their roles and responsibilities. Faced with such a model of government the profession is greatly diluted.

Personal and social education, a non-statutory cross-curricular theme, is underpinned by the client- or pupil-centred ethic. It is usually perceived by teachers as being centrally concerned with the affective role of primary schools (Best, 1989). More specifically, McNiff (1986, p. 14) is of the opinion:

> that academic subjects should be taught against the backdrop of care and support that are the cornerstones of personal and social education; that, ideally, personal and social education should be taught through the whole curriculum.

Such elements may be perceived, therefore, as the glue which bonds the child with the value system of the school. Unfortunately for many teachers, such elements of schooling have never been fully accepted on to the professional agenda. For some teachers the Education Reform Act (1988) has embodied the official marginalisation of the pastoral dimensions of their work. Much of the educational knowledge in primary schools is organised and delivered within subject disciplines. The nature of such transmission acts as a powerful social control mechanism on the practice of teachers. Subject disciplines with high status, such as English, mathematics and science, allow the teachers to enjoy prestige by virtue of association. Organisationally it is not clear what place PSE holds alongside other academic subjects. Hargreaves (1989) contends that curriculum and assessment reform seems oblivious to the personal and social characteristics of teaching and learning (e.g. the value of understanding emotions, self-respect and the commitment to the well-being of others). Furthermore, National Curriculum requirements reassert traditional academic disciplines. More recent government proposals suggest specialist teachers of mathematics and science should be recruited to teach at Key Stage 2. Moreover, anecdotal evidence from primary teachers suggests that assessment patterns have caused PSE programmes to be suspended for weeks to prepare for standard assessment tasks. Personal and social education seems to have less opportunity to be part of the whole curriculum.

There is a glimmer of hope, however. In an article in the *Observer* (15 Nov. 1994) it was reported that:

> The key message Sir Ron [Dearing] delivered on Thursday was that professional responsibility is to be handed back to the teachers with a broad framework, they will decide what goes on in the classroom. This is commonsense; it is what we train them and pay them to do.

THE BACKGROUND

In an attempt to unlock some of the complexities surrounding the changing nature of teachers' work, it is necessary to appreciate the wider context within which teachers operate. Within a period of just over twenty years, teachers have experienced some profound social, economic and political changes affecting the way in which they experience their work. Teachers have been subjected to an ever-increasing amount of criticism. A tradition of 'teacher bashing' and public chastisement of the profession during the present government's term of office has done much to legitimise a subtle and continuing process of political intervention into the structure and nature of teachers' work.

Striding unceremoniously into the curriculum, policy makers have forced teachers to surrender their professional autonomy, to become controlled by outside agencies such as NCC, SCAA and TTA. For some time now, teachers have had to contend with a succession of government-sponsored reforms that are in danger of radically redefining the nature of their work. The consequence has been an intensification of workload within a context increasingly structured by notions of accountability.

In effect, almost an entire redefinition of teachers' work has taken place. Under such strained conditions, the 'art of teaching' has been reduced to the clinical act of craft instruction. Teachers have been demoted to the status of 'deliverers' of a nationally prescribed (and largely externally controlled) curriculum.

Increasing demands and heightened expectations have joined forces with financial restraints and severe compression of time, to threaten the very desire to teach. Teachers are faced with a situation wherein their roles are expanding; the pressures and expectations are increasing, too. Their ultimate challenge becomes one of attempting to meet the needs and demands of a changing society, whilst working within what is ultimately an outdated system of schooling. Juggling with ever-increasing educational reforms, financial and temporal restraints and a fall in public confidence, it is hardly surprising that teachers today are increasingly experiencing 'feelings of disengagement and exclusion' (Hargreaves and MacMillan, 1992, p. 26).

In addition to the far-reaching educational reform that has become so familiar over the past twenty years, the government has enforced some major structural changes within schools. New management systems have been introduced, categorising staff into bureaucratic hierarchies, seen in the job titles of 'curriculum co-ordinators', 'senior management teams' and 'school finance managers'. This organisational reshuffle and consequent redefinition of teachers' roles, points towards a system of education that is increasingly succumbing to the logic of the market.

THE IMPACT OF THE MARKET

One of the most obvious ways in which this ideological shift manifests itself in today's educational climate, is bound up in the promise made by policy makers to hand over financial self-reliance in the form of local management of schools. The overriding irony of this supposed transfer of power is that while such initiatives appear to have reunited teachers with their professional autonomy, the harsh reality is that the government is in effect steering at a distance.

With the introduction of market forces into the nature and structure of schools, a shift has occurred in the power relations operating within the system. This has ultimately resulted in a redirection of power, autonomy and control from teachers to parents. This surrender to the logic of the market has had far reaching implications for the redefinition of teachers' work. As legislation invites open enrolment, parental choice and per capita funding, the place of personal and social education becomes even more marginalised and jeopardised. Teachers' worth is evaluated through outcomes and cost (Ball, 1994). Key elements within the market ideology, including production costs and efficiency strategies, image and competition have all found their way into the value systems of contemporary education. Each teacher, like the pupils they teach, has a price tag attached. In such a market-driven society, the onus is placed upon schools today to attract 'clients' and therefore maximise income.

Such a dramatic shift in terms of the power relations within which teachers' work has also encouraged a split between the management structures within schools, and the class teacher. Senior staff have been decorated with a kind of 'superficial superiority', which purposely sets them apart from the main body of the teaching staff. The intention here is to convince all involved that their interventionist policies are implemented from within the school. In this way any protagonists are made to look as though they are trying to upset the system. Paradoxically then, teachers are forced to contend with a hypocritical situation wherein there is more centralisation than decentralisation.

A further example of this appearance of autonomy can be seen in the actions of the present government. In keeping with the market ideology of attracting clients to their schools, teachers are submitting to the demands of the consumer. Traditional and academic views have been forced to the fore as parents are led to believe that 'back to basics' will raise educational standards. Mathematics, science and English retain their position of superiority in what has been described as 'a curriculum of the dead' (Ball, 1994, p. 361). Thus, while the conditions of the post-industrial age call for flexible working skills and more diverse definitions of intelligence, which include interpersonal and intra-personal intelligence, teachers are forced to deliver what is, at best, a pre-packaged curriculum loaded with messages of national strength and old-fashioned, restricted definitions of intelligence. The introduction of standardised testing has restricted teachers' professional autonomy and limited their imagination in classroom practices as they are increasingly compelled to 'teach to the test'. A standardisation of practice and a reaffirmation of subject specialists has resulted, and the possibilities for diversity and integration within teaching, themselves prerequisites of the post-industrial age, are reduced. In addition, this standardisation of the practices has done much to legitimise and reaffirm subject specialisms, which consequently isolates subject departments into 'balkanised' units, distanced and separated from the rest of the school. Ball (1994, p. 64) goes further in claiming that:

> Teachers' careers, institutional micropolitics, and state power and policies are intertwined in a complex process of changes in patterns of control, relationships and values in schools. The meaning of 'the teacher' and the nature of teaching as a career are at stake, as is, in general terms, the future of education as a public service.

The place of personal and social education becomes even more jeopardised. Teaching, therefore, is being defined as a labour process and articulated more and more in technicist terms in which efficiency, delivery and the perpetuation of an instrumental rationality are constantly being advanced as performance indicators. Thus, there has been a preoccupation with the measurable, objective, productive and instrumental dimensions of schooling at the expense of the subjective, experiential, intrinsic and moral agenda that is central to any critical pedagogy. It goes without saying that, despite its imputed curricular marginality, personal and social education has not been immune to these forces of change. On the contrary, one could argue that because of its marginal status, this area is particularly prone to the pressures that have attended this period of intensification. For instance, consider the manner in which the actions of teachers seeking access to a share of finite resources are increasingly being shaped by the market principles and economic expediency that pervades contemporary schooling. For those members of marginal occupational groups, the allocation of resources has come to represent a key 'site of contestation'. The concern has to be the extent to which teachers of personal and social education's capacity to acquire a shared depth of knowledge, sensitivity and consensus of the subject's contribution to the development of the whole child is being compromised by forces that seem to have little to do with meeting the real needs of the youngsters. Coming to terms with prevailing conditions will not only require teachers to engage the institutional micro-politics of schools but also demands the resolution of tensions generated from within a subject area that has not always been at ease with itself.

Not only are these conditions contributing to increases in teachers' workload but they are also in danger of radically reshaping the nature and purpose of pastoral care itself with consequences for the professional identity of teachers. Drawing upon his analysis of curriculum developments in physical education, Hoyle (1986) identified 'the decade of innovation' (1966–1975), and 'the decade of accountability' (1976–1985) which did much to advance our appreciation of this unsettled period of radical education reform. An analysis of the present 'spirit of the time' would suggest an extension of Hoyle's fundamental analysis towards what may be proposed as 'the decade of intensification' (1986–1995).

Teachers face the constant struggle of keeping their heads above a relentless stream of policy changes and curriculum reform. In the contemporary educational climate, such transformations manifest themselves within what have been categorised as two levels of change (Armstrong and Sparkes, 1991). Primarily, superficial change can be seen in the introduction of the subject-by-subject, stage-by-stage National Curriculum and the quick-to-follow nationwide system of standardised testing. Teachers may choose to develop, or not to develop, such changes. Alternatively, real changes are regarded as deeper transformations of the beliefs and values of how teaching is defined and organised. Examples here might include the introduction of performance appraisal schemes, the shift from centralised management of schools to local management and financial self-reliance, and the introduction of new management systems in schools, including 'senior management teams' and 'line managers'. Clearly, it is the cumulative impact of these multiple reforms that serves to create the intense pressure within the working conditions of teachers today.

PROFESSIONALISATION AND INTENSIFICATION

Hargreaves (1994) proposes two main, yet opposing beliefs to the meaning and significance of the changing nature and structure of teachers' work. These are bound up in what he refers to as 'professionalisation' and 'intensification'. Briefly, arguments based around the principle of professionalisation emphasise the emergence of a greater teacher professionalism through extensions of the teachers' role. Such a theory of 'extended teacher professionalism' (Hoyle, 1986) can be seen to have been generated through role expansion, increased involvement in collaborative cultures of mutual support and professional growth, experiences of teacher leadership and engagement with processes of extensive school-wide change. This somewhat optimistic view sees teaching as becoming more complex and more skilled and therefore increases the professional aspect of teachers' work, and their public image.

However, several educationists have suggested a theory of the labour process that points towards a general 'de-professionalisation' of teachers' work, wherein the nature of the job has become increasingly 'routinised' and 'deskilled' (Smyth, 1991; Mac an Ghaill, 1992; Ball, 1994; Hargreaves, 1994). Indeed, in reference to this general deterioration of teachers' work and professional status, Hargreaves (1994, p. 117) suggests that their work is becoming more like: 'the degraded work of manual workers and less like that of autonomous professionals trusted to exercise the power and expertise of discretionary judgement in the classrooms they understand best'. Intensification is one of the most tangible ways in which the work privileges of educated workers are eroded. Increased preparation time, and recognition of professional status and autonomy, are just some of the work privileges that teachers have had taken away from them to make room for the constant reforms and initiatives that have become commonplace in their working lives today.

In 1995, this intensification of teachers' work manifested itself in the prospect of increasing class sizes, decreasing staff numbers, performance-related pay schemes, public accountability via the publishing of school league tables and the ever-present curriculum reform. Teachers today are often left demoralised, de-professionalised and generally depressed by the bleak prospect of improvement to their 'intensified' work loads. As Hargreaves (1994, p. 6) is keen to point out, such extreme educational reform, and more specifically the imposers of such change, have had very little respect for teachers themselves. He contends that:

> In the political rush to bring about reform, teachers' voices have been largely neglected, their opinions overriden, and their concerns dismissed. Change has been developed and imposed in a context where teachers have been given little credit or recognition for changing themselves, and for possessing their own wisdom to distinguish between what reasonably can be changed and what cannot.

As in every profession, some teachers are of poor calibre (up to 5 per cent is suggested). Regrettably, publicity often focuses upon the weak practitioners obscuring the good works of the great majority who remain largely ignored and devalued. From this view, it is clear to see that the notion of 'extended professionalism' becomes what Hargreaves (1994, p. 118) refers to as a 'rhetorical ruse, a strategy for getting teachers to collaborate willingly in their own exploitation as more and more effort is extracted from them'.

A solution to the problem of intensification is obviously overdue. However, this is no easy task and may in fact require a complete 'restructuring' and 'reculturing' of the school (Hargreaves, 1994, p. 254). As a result of the surfeit of reforms and initiatives and a heightening of public expectation, the culture of teaching has undergone transformation over the years. The intensification of teachers' working conditions has done much to bring about a 'culture of individualism' within teaching (Hargreaves, 1994, p. 163). In this forum, most teachers are still seen to be teaching in isolation, within the privacy of their own classrooms.

Such isolated cultures can be seen as inconclusive to a healthy work ethic in which shared planning and decision-making can flourish. In order to reduce the fragmentation and restriction imposed on teachers in such working environments, there is a real need to develop cultures of collaboration among teachers in today's schools. With the prevailing trends of many schools towards school-based management or local management, teachers find themselves responsible for collectively implementing a centrally defined curriculum. In order to avoid 'top–down' implementation strategies, teachers must strive towards a collective involvement in curriculum and pedagogical decision-making. In an environment of this kind, the sharing of resources and ideas can greatly reduce some of the immense feelings of stress and guilt experienced by teachers. In this way, collegial support can only serve to raise the standards of education and therefore heighten the experiences and achievements of both teachers and pupils.

If collaboration amongst teachers is not properly and purposefully integrated into the administrative systems of the school, in terms of consistent and planned preparation time for teachers, then it becomes what Hargreaves (1994, p. 17) refers to as 'contrived collegiality', a 'bolt-on' afterthought that is not recognised as useful by either the practitioners or the administrators who plan for it. Timetables must be reorganised to incorporate routinely co-ordinated planning times. In this way, protected periods of time can be used to bring together teachers who teach the same year or pastoral group. This may help to break down the barriers of self-contained sub-groups like subject departments, behind which specialist teachers have retreated over the years. Such teaching cultures are too preoccupied with their own 'personal troubles' to have the time to take a whole-school view of the 'public issues' in teaching necessary for personal and social education to thrive within the schools, and for the school ethos to become effective.

It is only when teachers are provided with the analytical space in which to stand back and reflect, that such a heightening of educational practice can be fostered. Reflecting on the entire structure and nature of teachers' work requires a great deal of that most precious resource 'time', and time is exactly what teachers do not have.

PROPOSALS

Drawing upon the work of Hargreaves (1995), Sammons *et al.* (1995) and Reynolds (1994), this chapter makes proposals with regard to developing personal and social education in schools at the threshold of a new century.

First, schools should know the direction they wish to take with regard to personal and social education. There should be a limited range of curriculum goals with strong clarity and a sense of primary mission, not multiple goals which paralyse teachers because of the need for so much information. Effective leadership in this aspect of the curriculum is essential to present a vision and purpose, which will encourage participation amongst the staff. This implies involvement in, and knowledge about, content, pedagogy and evaluation. Typically, teachers are isolated, professionally lonely and unlikely to seek or accept help from their colleagues. A leader proposing 'unity of purpose, consistency of practice' and 'collaboration' will break through such an egg crate culture of norms of isolation (Sammons *et al.*, 1995, pp. 11–12).

The use of knowledge produced from outside the school and implanted wholesale is to be avoided. Decisions about subject material, teaching strategies and assessment should be determined at the immediate level where teachers will have to realise them. Detailed documents become dated and are overtaken as they are written. Schools should, therefore, produce highly individualised programmes which are context-specific, take imported materials but enquire into their content, and reformulate them bearing in mind pupils, teachers and circumstances of the school.

By reculturing the school to create such collaborative cultures among teachers it is important to encourage communication outside the school to the partners beyond the school walls. Schools will need more help from parents if the messages with regard to pastoral care and PSE are to be successfully understood. Teachers attempt to place education about sex, drugs and wider personal issues in a firm moral context. They will not succeed without greater support from parents. The relationship between parents and the school has a crucial bearing on progress and the effectiveness of any PSE programme. Their wishes, feelings and knowledge of the child should always be taken into account, and they should be encouraged to work in partnership with teachers. Parent skills should be appreciated and employed where appropriate, and provision made for two-way communication. More time devoted to such issues should involve attempts to offer moral perceptions and avoid moralistic tones. Schools should be underpinned by a set of shared values which are recognised and aspired to by everyone within the community of the school (e.g. pupils, teachers, governors and parents).

Extended links with colleges and universities may provide the exchange of a wealth of expertise; they may produce, also, more practical contextualised theory and more theoretically grounded practice. Networks between schools will help teachers overcome content problems, and rethink teaching and learning strategies. Collaborations between schools and the business sector may well go some way to addressing the habit of valuing the academic over the vocational in the curriculum. Teachers may recognise a new learning resource, be able to select aspects relevant to PSE, and develop learning activities and support materials which go beyond the use of the business sector, as merely a context for learning. There is a value in teachers working with associates from the business sector to gain expertise in communications, problem-solving, team-building, project work and conflict-management.

Schools should strive to become learning organisations. At one level, teachers should be learning from their colleagues. When best practice is discovered it should be made available to all. Schools need to build more time and incentives into the system through staff development reviews for professional learning. Comprehensive and effective in-service opportunities can enhance staff competence and morale.

Good primary and middle schools for teachers are invariably good places for pupil learning. During personal and social education lessons, pupils should be presented with varied and active approaches to their learning such as problem clarification, idea generation, swot analysis, games, simulations and role play. The potency of peer tutoring should not be ignored (see Charlton, 1996). Placing infant and junior classes in adjacent rooms can bring together children to share experiences. Their lessons should be filled with information, be knowledge-rich and well-resourced. Risk and innovation should be encouraged.

In conclusion, as we move into a postmodern society, schools should be demanding more awareness of the pupil as a whole being, and requiring more originality in addressing his/her needs; teaching, not by whips and chains, but through innovation and sensitivity. The twenty-first century will have an increasing need for new ideas and skills, which can only be provided by the children of today. This chapter contends that primary and middle schools are bound by command and control which are elements in conflict with creativity. Young children need a model of the personal and social traits of an effective thinker and learner. Such development will support the growth from dependency on clarity and definitive answers, the modern society, to the application and management of ambiguity in the postmodern age. Let us be judged not by the weak elements in the profession, but by the majority of first class teachers who await the leadership to bring out greater professionalism.

BIBLIOGRAPHY

Armstrong, N. and Sparkes, A. (1991) *Issues in Physical Education*, London: Cassell

Ball, S. (1994) *Education Reform. A Critical and Post-structural Approach*, Milton Keynes: Open University Press.

Best, R. (1989) Pastoral care in education: some reflections and a restatement, *Pastoral Care*, 7, 4, 7–14.

Charlton, T. (1996) Peer support practices in classrooms and schools, in K. Jones and T. Charlton (eds) *Overcoming Learning and Behaviour Difficulties (5–16): Partnership with Pupils*, London: Routledge.

Department of Education and Science (1988) *Education Act*, London: HMSO.

Department of Education and Science (1989) *Personal and Social Education from 5–16*, London: HMSO.

Hargreaves, A. (1989) *Curriculum and Assessment Reform*, Milton Keynes: Open University Press.

Hargreaves, A. (1994) *Changing Teachers, Changing Times*, London: Cassell.

Hargreaves, A. (1994) Development and desire: a postmodern perspective, paper presented at American Educational Research Association.

Hargreaves, A. (1995) Working with paradox: why we have to reinvent educational change, paper presented at Roehampton Institute, London, 'Re-thinking UK Education: What next?'

Hargreaves, D. and Hopkins, D. (1991) *The Empowered School*, London: Cassell.

Hargreaves, A. and MacMillan, R. (1992) Balkanised secondary schools and the malaise of modernity, paper presented at American Educational Research Association.

Hoyle, E. (1986) Curriculum development in physical education 1966–1985, in *Proceedings of the VIII Commonwealth and International Conference on Sport, PE, Dance, Recreation and Health*, London: E. and F.N. Spon Ltd.

Mac an Ghaill, M. (1992) Teachers' work. Curriculum restructuring culture, power and comprehensive schooling, *British Journal of Sociology of Education*, 13, 2, 177–199.

McNiff, J. (1986) *Personal and Social Education*, Cambridge: CRAC.

National Curriculum Council (1990) *Curriculum Guidance 3: The Whole Curriculum*, York: NCC.

Pring, R. (1985) *Personal and Social Education in the Curriculum*, London: Hodder & Stoughton.

Reynolds, D. (1994) *School Effectiveness and Quality in Education*, Melbourne: IARTV.

Sammons, P., Hillman, J. and Mortimore, P. (1995) *Key Characteristics of Effective Schools*, London: Ofsted.

Smyth, J. (1991) International perspectives on teacher collegiality, *British Journal of Sociology of Education*, 13, 2, 323–346.

Part IV

AN AGENDA FOR DISCUSSION

14

AN AGENDA FOR DISCUSSION

Kenneth David and Tony Charlton

PART I

Part I of this book included four topics from among the many themes that make up pastoral care. This choice identifies major themes that we think should loom very large in planning pastoral care with younger pupils. The chapters are by experienced practitioners, and stand in their own right, and after introducing and commenting on them in turn we offer other ideas which are associated with them. These ideas are presented as a series of topics and questions that we think will reinforce and extend the views of our Part I contributors. They can also be used in initial and in-service training discussions.

In **Chapter 1** Kenneth David attempted the difficult task of guessing what the future lives of our pupils may be like, giving consideration to the equally controversial debate as to how much influence schools and teachers have upon pupils' development. We believe schools and individual teachers can be good models for many children, and have considerable influence. A co-ordinated approach to pastoral care and personal and social education can shape and strengthen this influence, and may help in preparing pupils for their lives in a partially understood future. More than ever before in education, the need to strengthen children's personal skills and competences, with the aid of pastoral approaches, is vital, for work, careers, relationships and family life are now massively challenged.

How do we keep up with the changing world?

(see also Chapters 11 and 12)

Dedicated teachers often find it difficult to look up from demanding daily tasks, but they must make occasional assessments as to whether their teaching and curricula are relevant to life in our society (see also Chapter 2). Pastoral matters need especial care for they often lack priority, though their relevance is increasingly obvious.

In considering pupils' future needs we suggest that leadership in schools keep points like the following in mind, and under regular review.

1 What practical efforts can be made by class teachers to reduce passivity in school work? How do we usefully increase active involvement by pupils?
2 What can be done to improve support for, and reduce stress among staff, and how can we encourage pupils to deal sensibly with anger and violence, now and in the future? Is it only by exhortation?
3 Does the curriculum include up-to-date examples of work and leisure pursuits?
4 How far is it practicable for young pupils to be taught study and learning skills, and what do the terms precisely mean? What resources can we call on?
5 Are there practical ways of teaching about respect for age, knowledge, achievements or accomplishments and experience? What community links are really worth developing?
6 Does the curriculum include teaching about personal relationships and family life, and how is their relevance in everyday life emphasised?
7 Are environmental issues commonly discussed, obligations as well as rights?
8 It has been suggested that teachers and students are drowning in facts, spending more than 80 per cent of their time finding information, 10 per cent putting it in order, and only 5 per cent in making decisions. Does this apply with young children, and could classroom procedures and modern technology change the proportions?
9 Children learn nowadays in a way totally different from their parents, unable to conceive or accept a world without ever-increasing excellence in electronic media, interactional technology, graphics and colour. Is this suggestion linked with pupils' view that 'School's boring'?
10 The speed of change and complexity in our pupils' lives is increasing. How can teachers keep up to date? How far can teachers be 'street-wise' about the lives of their pupils?

Speaking up (see also Chapters 7, 9, 10 and 11)

Part of passivity might be something termed oral impoverishment. The English Speaking Board[1] provides advice, materials and examinations aimed at improving children's clarity, tone, confidence, and the verbal fluency to communicate ideas and information effectively. There are costs involved which may be met by parents, school or LEA.

Ninety per cent of all communication is oral, and personal and work relationships depend on our ability to say what we think and feel. Being an inarticulate person means you may have limited self-regard, and cannot always easily manage situations. Listening to TV street interviews can be saddening proof that talking clearly is not a well-developed skill.

Is learning too passive? (see also Chapters 2 and 11)

John Abbott (1994) a former head of Manchester Grammar School, and Director of the charitable trust Education 2000, thinks that we need to change the way we educate our young or we are doomed. He argues that teachers have to teach children how to learn, as well as teaching facts. People need to be taught to think for themselves and to develop confidence in their judgement. Education needs to be more interactive and less teacher-oriented, and more priority should be given to developing quality in nursery and early primary education. Should we fail to change, he predicts a society 'torn apart by frustration, manifested in helplessness and criminality'. He quotes Dryden (1994) who claims that 50 per cent of a person's ability to learn is developed in the first four years of life, and suggests infant classes of four to six children, with classes becoming progressively bigger as children get older. Michael Green, chairman of Carlton Communications, Microsoft's Bill Gates and Virgin's Richard Branson, all achievers, all found school boring, he notes, as he emphasises motivation as crucial, and 'argument' to make sense of what is being learned.

Can any practical points come from theorists like this? Would 'discussion' be better than 'argument', and how skilled are teachers in true discussion skills? Can young children 'discuss' their learning?

Effective teachers (see also Chapters 2, 8 and 13)

Can we reduce teacher stress? Dyfed Education Department (Dyfed County Council, 1994) suggest these individual coping strategies, with outside help sought whenever there is an effect on health: recognition of a stress problem; identifying the systems and cause of stress; selection of a course of action; monitoring the outcome.

Their six major factors within schools associated with job satisfaction and the creation of an ideal working environment conducive to high levels of performance from teachers are: improved communications; approaches to time, deadlines and workload; staff welfare; morale and motivation; building effective teams and negotiating conflict.

They suggest school working groups to attempt an audit of stress generation and means of alleviating stress levels, a helpline and voluntary counselling services, clustering of small schools for mutual help, extended pastoral advisory support, and LEA stress management courses.

Are teachers under siege? Len Barton (1991) in an article in *Support for Learning* argues that teachers are central in the process of schooling, and their well-being is important. He suggests that teachers' accounts of stress should be taken more seriously. More than ever, teachers now need to collaborate and support each other, to liaise more effectively with parents, and to involve pupils in school processes far more than is often the case. In illustrating an increasing business mentality in education Barton quotes a *Times Educational Supplement* item in 1989 where a Midlands comprehensive school, trying to boost its first year intake, offered parents a pack including school tie, stationery, sports insurance, plus a discount on shower units. He suggests that much educational reform is based upon distrust of teachers, and points to a lack of administrative, technical and ancillary support for teachers. Teachers are leaving the profession, he believes, because of work overload, poor pay, loss of autonomy, lack of status, poor working environments and pupil misbehaviour. Which, if any, of these suggested reasons for teacher loss are unfair or exaggerated?

Signs of breakdown. We have been told that the outward signs of adult breakdown are: increasing irritability; increasing difficulty in concentrating; a growing incapacity to delegate; and the persistent taking home of work which is then often not attended to. Can all of us feel concern in considering these factors, and what other signs of breakdown might be noted?

In **Chapter 2** Kevin Jones and Mayling Quah wrote of the learning process, our fundamental task as teachers, which pastoral care exists to serve in all schools. We note their emphasis that pastoral care must inevitably be part of the process of pupils' learning. So much remains to be improved in schools in the way we enable children to learn, to memorise, to summarise – the whole range of study and learning skills. In a thorough and constructive chapter we value their suggestions on collaborative learning. We note, however, the need for tight control of 'discussion' to prevent it meandering.

Study skills (see also Chapter 10)

Douglas Hamblin (1981) suggests ten areas of skill for secondary pupils. They apply in our consideration of middle school pastoral care matters, and some clearly apply in primary education.

- Listening, linked with recall.
- Reading, the mechanics, recall and the development of inferences.
- Presentation of work, associated with competence and self-respect.
- Active methods of homework, with consistent practice.
- Planning and target-setting, with essential peer support.
- Essay writing and answering questions.

- Revision and examination techniques.
- Note taking.
- Raising the level of aspiration.
- Evaluation of work.

Another measure of study skills suggests four principal areas: reading, notes, memory and study techniques.

Reading. We usually concentrate on comprehension and style, once pupils manage to make sense of word recognition and various sentence structures. It is strongly suggested that speed of reading is also important. Most children (and students) read at a speed below their potential, largely because of reading habits which have not been challenged. Once the basic mechanics of reading are grasped children can be trained to speed up their reading while still retaining comprehension. The reading of groups of words, the avoidance of constantly going back over words, the avoiding of 'reading to themselves' or sub-vocalising can be taught. Comprehension falters at first as reading is speeded up, but as the child's brain responds and accepts a new habit, comprehension returns.

Note-taking. With older primary and lower secondary pupils this can be taught as a valuable aid to learning, a habit of combining sight, sound and hand. Children can learn the habit of choosing personal 'key words' which link with the material. Relationships between parts of the material being taught, or the concepts put forward by the teacher can be linked with lines between key words. Some children can be encouraged to add colour to their notes to link points in the material.

Memory. Many children can be helped to understand the difference between short- and long-term memory, and the aids of repetition, of having material to be memorised available visually where it can be seen regularly and of reciting material. Some pupils can learn to use mnemonics.

Study techniques. Although applying more to older pupils, some teachers may choose to consider: methods of writing essays or longer accounts, the physical conditions necessary for efficient study, time-limits on efficient study, breaks in study learning, organising revision, and ways of dealing with tests or examinations.

Is there fair criticism of teachers? (see also Chapter 13)

The Office for Standards in Education reported in May 1995 that teachers have persistent weaknesses in knowledge and expertise. In English, there is emphasis on failings in formal aspects of language, particularly grammar and syntax. Standards were lowest in junior schools, and in the first three years of secondary education: 20 per cent of schools failed to teach the subject adequately. In writing standards they reported only one junior school in seven performing well, with little attention being given to the skills of handwriting and spelling. In mathematics, they report that teachers showed a good command of their subject in only one primary school in ten. A quarter of junior school teachers did not have sufficient understanding to teach the subject properly.

If correct, these reports are heartbreaking, and explain the constant criticism of our work as teachers by both public and employers. Are they true? Could it be true that children working individually can 'coast along' more easily, and might whole-class teaching be edging back?

Are weak teachers still with us? How can we help them more?

Gender differences

Girls are doing better than boys in many parts of education. In 1993, 39 per cent of girls taking GCSE mathematics obtained A–C grades, compared with 38 per cent of boys. There appears to be a growing superiority of girls in GCSE. Reports of 1995 results in newspapers indicate that 43 per cent of pupils (48 per cent of girls and 39 per cent of boys) passed at least five subjects at grades A–C in GCSE.

- Are girls more responsible by nature?
- Is adolescence tougher on boys?
- Is it mainly boys who regard school as 'uncool'?
- Have girls had more attention in maths in recent years?
- Is there a social class dimension in this?
- Is the increasing reduction of lower-skilled male jobs and greater likelihood of unemployment relevant?

The effect of divorce on pupils (see also Chapters 1 and 12)

The Centre for Family Research at Cambridge University has studied 17,000 children from the National Child Development Survey who were born in one week in 1958, and were followed up at ages 7, 11, 16 and 23. They compared children whose mother or father had died with those whose parents had split up, in terms of education, career, health and wealth. The harmful effects of divorce are apparent across all social classes but the effects on middle-class children are striking, particularly for girls. Parental death before the age of 16 has an effect, of course, on a child's life, but divorce appears to cause much more damage. The latest figures on divorce in England and Wales for 1993, show that 165,000 decrees were made absolute, the highest annual number of divorces recorded. There were 176,000 children aged under 16 whose families were affected by divorce.

Middle-class children born in 1958 whose parents were divorced before they reached the age of 15, compared with their more fortunate peers:

- were twice as likely to leave school without any qualification;
- had only two-thirds the chance of going to university;
- were a third more likely not to have a full-time job at age 23 (boys);
- were two-thirds more likely not to have a full-time job at age 23 (girls);
- were four times more likely to be living in a council house at age 23;
- were two-thirds more likely to be a regular smoker by age 23.

Taking children of middle- and working-class parents together, children of divorced parents were:

- twice as likely to have a child before age 20;
- twice as likely to be married or living with someone before age 20.

The research also claims that children whose parents had divorced were on average less emotionally stable, left home earlier, and divorced or separated more frequently. They had more behavioural problems in school and did less well at reading and arithmetic.

What can we criticise about this research? How much of it is likely to be correct? If it is likely to be correct, can schools do anything about it?

In **Chapter 3** Jean-Pierre Kirkland and David Hammond described, as a case study, the development of a 'pastoral school', which means, of course, an efficient and caring school, but one in which there must be deliberate pastoral planning by the headteacher. Schools planning to improve the abilities of their teachers in pastoral matters have a template they may seek to follow. Chapter 4 also discusses the influence of Heads.

A checklist for pastoral care (see also Chapters 4, 5 and 7)

The following checklist has been used in in-service teacher training.

1 Pastoral care should be *positive*, *planned* and *professional*.
2 It is *not*:
   - primarily disciplinary;
   - intended to cover up school faults;
   - an occasional happening;
   - just concerned with welfare;
   - only intended to remedy deficiences in individual pupils.
3 It *is*:
   - about learning processes;
   - about creating a sense of order and clarity;
   - about creating routines for diagnosing problems;
   - about reviewing action taken and results obtained;
   - continuous through a pupil's career in the school, and after;
   - for all children, not a few;
   - a committed partnership with parents;

- not only intuitive and incidental;
- preventive.

4 It includes:

- a test of the quality of the leadership of the school;
- a test of the quality of staff relationships and team-work;
- questioning the status of pastoral care among staff and governors;
- staff skills of counselling and group discussion, knowledge of child development, study skills and learning methods;
- carefully developed liaison with other agencies;
- good communication systems within the school;
- good record keeping;
- good welfare contacts and arrangements;
- constant evaluation and assessment of the effects of pastoral care arrangements.

In **Chapter 4** Anita Ryall and her colleagues review their research into pastoral care and the co-ordination of personal and social education with younger pupils. There is a need to develop and sustain such co-ordination; without it our efforts with younger pupils can be well-intentioned but incidental. *Curriculum Guidance 5* (NCC, 1990b) illustrates such Health/PSE co-ordination. The evidence Anita Ryall and her colleagues provide from their schools is heartening. We note their reference to the need for the head teacher to lead and co-ordinate PSE whenever possible, to avoid the haphazard presentation of PSE which can occur where there is a lack of status.

Life skills (see also Chapters 3, 7, 9 and 10)

There are numerous schemes for teaching life skills, mostly for secondary pupils. A recent scheme developed for pupils aged 9 to 11, sponsored by British Telecom and supported by the Police, has been successful with some 20,000 children a year in the Metropolitan Police area. Children are in groups of three or four, accompanied by an adult guide, and face situations such as fire, water and road safety, stranger danger, phone vandalism, litter, first aid, use of the underground, a gas leak and dangerous products in the home. Situations are staged with appropriate effects and children are challenged on what action they take, and then what they might have done.

Material for discussion

Many secondary schools use published material for tutorial periods, the daily or occasional discussion periods which form teachers hold with their forms. Schemes provided by Baldwin and Wells (1979–83), Button

(1982) and others continue to provide appropriate material for a co-ordinated and developing series of topics and activities which can make tutorial periods more purposeful than they often are. Material from such schemes can also be selected as appropriate for primary school pupils.

Material from Charlton and David *Supportive Schools* (1990, pp. 58–74) can also be used by primary schools preparing their own lists of topics for discussion in personal and social education.

Further assessment and evaluation (see also Chapters 2, 3 and 13)

Ungoed-Thomas (1994), writing on the inspection of spiritual, moral, social and cultural development in schools, describes how inspectors may attempt to assess the success of a school in these areas. He refers to discussions in an Ofsted (1994) paper, and definitions in the Ofsted *Handbook*, revised in May 1994. Inspectors may 'indicate strengths which a school too readily takes for granted and which could usefully be built on', and can point out 'certain overall imbalances'. Whilst he writes of continuing negotiations with staff as evaluations proceed, we can see, from experience, the possibility of considerable misinterpretations between school and inspectors in this area.

Fletcher-Campbell (1995, p. 26) usefully points out that, 'There must be some content to care. We can't just drift around the world generously caring.' She adds that it may well be that, 'an evaluation of a school's care may only be done by those within it'.

PART II

Part I considered what children's future lives might be like, the process of learning and its link with pastoral care, the practicalities of creating a 'pastoral school', and the way personal and social education can be co-ordinated into the curriculum.

In Part II we considered the whole range of pastoral care again, and chose experienced contributors who had something purposeful to say on six particular pastoral themes, selected because we think they require emphasising and are often requested in in-service training.

In **Chapter 5** Kate Wall, an experienced practitioner, dealt with a wide range of welfare matters and support systems for schools, as well as summarising legislation which affects schools. This chapter reminds us of the essential and everyday welfare part of pastoral care, which in some schools is the major part of pastoral care as they understand it. She rightly emphasises the need for very good liaison with helping agencies, and we suspect her case study could be matched in many schools.

Special educational needs (see also Chapters 2 and 4)

Operative from 1994, the Special Educational Needs Code of Practice has major implications for schools. If any child is failing to learn properly or performing significantly below his/her potential in any part of the curriculum, including bright children who are insufficiently stretched, the school must set in motion a process of assessment leading to recommendations to deal with the child's needs. This can be requested by a parent. The class teacher investigates the problem, taking into account the parents' and child's views, and a plan of action must be developed, with a review six to twelve weeks later. If the plan has not worked teachers, parents and child develop a fresh plan. When this is reviewed later an 'external specialist' (usually an educational psychologist) is brought in if the first stages have been unsatisfactory, and planning moves into stage 3, again involving parents and child. The effectiveness of each stage is reviewed, and eventually the local authority may be involved in providing extra resources to help the child, perhaps in the form of a specially trained 'support teacher'. The code emphasises that 'the knowledge, views and experiences of parents are vital', and it forces the school to respond to the individual needs of the child. The quality and methods of a school's teaching may be reviewed as part of the required response.

Critics note that the code may lack teeth: local authorities are merely required to 'have regard' to the Code, and the law still requires councils to have regard to the 'efficient use of resources' in all decisions they make.

Jean Price in **Chapter 6** writes on the school health service. The details of Chapters 5 and 6 are sometimes only sketchily understood by students and teachers, and we feel they provide a useful checklist of these topics.

Sex education

David and Wise (1987, p. 193) write:

> One has to accept the freedom of choice which young people have on a range of sexual matters, but encourage them to make responsible informed decisions that are in the best interest of themselves and others.

Since such sexual freedom of choice occurs normally in the late teens, the foundations of responsible informed decisions will certainly lie in the primary and lower secondary school sex education teaching, hopefully complementing the teaching and example youngsters have from their parents. Where that family teaching or example is weak, the school's responsibility is the greater.

David and Wise also recommend that sex education should be subsumed in a broader programme of personal and social education or health education, agree that schools should not challenge or seek to undermine family relationships, and emphasise the importance of personal integrity and the significance of moral values within schools' sex education. Matters upon which many people have strong and deeply held views should not be avoided.

Bibby (1945) expressed the aims and objectives of sex education clearly:

> that our people should grow up learning the appropriate facts in the best possible way; that their general attitude to sex should be a completely healthy one; that they should draw up for themselves a code of conduct after a careful consideration of all the issues involved and should endeavour to behave according to this rationally determined code; and that they should react to the behaviour of others with sympathy, tolerance and charity, but without spineless acquiescence in a code inferior to their own.

One LEA expressed the following aims for sex education for 11–12-year-old pupils.

- To give a simple account of the facts of reproduction, in a setting of family life or of caring relationships.
- To prepare pupils for the changes of puberty so that they will appreciate that what is happening to them is perfectly normal.
- To encourage a sense of wonder in the creation of a new life, and to help them to develop a proper attitude towards reproduction.
- To satisfy the natural curiosity of pupils as far as it can be done at this age, and to give reassurance by emphasising normality.

The following summary indicates the range of discussion that will arise as schools continue to revise their sex education programmes.

1 Sex education is more than a transmission of biological facts.
2 It may appear in many places within the curriculum.
3 It is a continuing process throughout primary and secondary schooling.
4 It should not cause personal hurt or offence.
5 It is for boys and girls, and emphasises the likelihood that young people will experience differing rates of physiological, psychological and social development.
6 It should be responsive to the felt needs and emotional level of young people, and will take account of the influences on young people.
7 It is seldom to be expressed in clear terms of 'Do' and 'Don't'.
8 It can be well taught by prepared teachers who are familiar to the pupils, not necessarily by 'experts'.

9 It is often best taught by less didactic teaching approaches, aided but not replaced by appropriate visual and TV material.

David and Wise (1987, p. 212) comment finally:

> One should see a programme (of sex education) not as a 'cure-all' recipe, but as an aid to the promotion of personal and social development. The caring school does have an important role to play in the healthy sexual development of young people.

Children growing up (see also Chapters 6, 7, 8, 9 and 10)

A teachers' seminar produced the following checklist of health and growth topics that often arose in primary and lower secondary classes.

- A rapid growth 'spurt' can arise during adolescence, varying greatly with individuals, and earlier in girls than boys.
- Apparent clumsiness can arise from physical growth and a lack of co-ordination.
- Extremes of emotion and moodiness are not uncommon in early adolescence, as are self-consciousness and embarrassment.
- Facial blemishes and spots are common.
- Acne, eczema and asthma are very common, often requiring medication.
- Hay fever can be distressing for some pupils.
- Eyesight and hearing problems can be noted by the way pupils react in class.
- Overweight children are more common now in classrooms.
- Epileptic and diabetic children have to be dealt with in classrooms on occasion.
- Abnormal or unusual bruising can indicate bullying or abuse.
- Children with medical problems have special educational needs, and their classmates may need to be taught understanding.

The teachers emphasised that schools must ensure that staff are fully briefed on such topics, and the part that teachers play *vis-à-vis* other professionals must be clear.

Philip Carey in **Chapter 7** looked afresh at the whole theme of counselling children, and we value a fresh voice on the subject. He usefully combines theory and practice, and compares and clarifies harmful and constructive coping strategies. Two of his comments can be repeated; they are very simple and apparently obvious truths, which are basic in pastoral attitudes. First, the available evidence is that young people are more receptive to learning if they feel they are listened to; and, second, teachers must integrate the skills of counselling into their day-to-day teaching.

Helping pupils to accept responsibility for their behaviour is an important aspect in most counselling processes. This desired state is often referred to as an internal locus of control. By comparison, those who do not accept this responsibility can be termed externals. However, there is no such thing as an internal/external dichotomy; rather a continuum situated between the two. Progress from externality to internality may be a slow – yet important – stage in some pupils' development.

Do people listen? (see also Chapter 3)

(The following is based on notes from conference papers of some years back, regrettably with no source of origin, and frequently amended since.)

1 Listening is an art, a skill and a discipline. It requires control – intellectual, emotional and behavioural. The individual must understand what is involved in listening and in developing the necessary self-mastery to be silent and listen.
2 Listening is based on hearing and understanding what others say to us. Hearing becomes listening only when we pay attention to what is said and follow it very closely, without working out what we are going to say next.
3 We should try to create a situation in which people can:
   - discuss frankly matters which are important to them;
   - give without embarrassment as much information as possible;
   - gain insight and understanding of their problem as they talk;
   - try to see the causes and reasons for their problems;
   - work out for themselves what action to take.
4 Listening responses may include:
   - clarification of what is being said – 'Do you mean . . . ?';
   - encouraging comments to show interest – 'I see', 'Uh-huh';
   - showing understanding of how a child feels about what he is saying – 'You feel that . . . ?'; ' . . . as you saw it then . . . ';
   - summarising the discussion periodically – 'If I understand it then . . . '; 'These seem to be the key ideas you have expressed . . . '.
5 There are well-known blocks to careful listening.
   - Preoccupied listening (open ears and closed mind).
   - Stereotyping and consciousness of status preventing understanding.
   - Physical conditions precluding careful listening.
   - 'Wandering mind' and 'on–off' listening.
   - Past experience and prejudices affecting what we are hearing.
   - Hostility and defensiveness put up barriers.
   - Personal anxieties and overwork preventing understanding.
6 Does anybody know what anybody really says? Most individuals

think about four times as fast as the average person speaks. Thus the listener has three-quarters of a minute spare thinking time in each listening minute.

Material for counselling courses?

Wallis (1973) suggests that personal counselling is characterised by:

- Lack of pressure from the counsellor.
- Acceptance of a valid difficulty.
- Clarification of meaning for the client.
- A recognition of the validity of feeling.
- A tolerance of conflict.
- Personal acceptance.

Hughes (1971, p. 33) defines counselling as:

> an interview characterised by an absence of moralising, by sympathy without sentimentality, concern without interference and with no strings attached, where one person sets out to enable another to examine confusion in thinking and feeling, reach his own diagnosis and perhaps formulate workable plans for the immediate or even more distant future.

Taylor (1971, pp. 103–4) suggests:

> Individual counselling in schools can be defined as a way of offering an opportunity to the young person to experience a one-to-one relationship which is accepting and tolerant yet relatively free from moralising, directing, advising or judging. In this way the hope is that enough understanding will be gained of themselves so that they can stand on their own two feet without support.

Everyday school counselling

Few schools have the luxury of trained school counsellors. In our experience it is possible to offer short training courses for primary or secondary teachers (and even ancillary staff) which will prepare them better to cope with what we might term first level counselling, the type of support which almost all teachers are likely to provide as part of their everyday work. Such courses also appear to enrich teaching skills.

A proportion of the staff of a school may well be selected by head teachers to take more extensive in-service counselling training, to provide second level counselling support in schools – cases taking more time than usual, and with the potential for major problems to develop. Teachers of this counselling level can be supportive with their colleagues, particularly in warning them of the potential risks in trying to deal with problems which should go to more experienced colleagues or to specialised agencies. Third level counselling requires more professional training, and normally lies outside the school's expertise.

It is interesting that Samaritans report that young children increasingly telephone them for help, and Young People's Advisory Services give similar accounts. Whilst teachers will normally 'befriend' or counsel their pupils at a basic level, perhaps providing even more professional support within the school, young people, including those of primary school age, will often seek help from voluntary bodies, or from other adults that they have learned to trust. We know of a school caretaker who is a particularly valued member of his school's pastoral staff.

Behaviour management was dealt with by the editors in **Chapter 8**, and this is a major consideration in pastoral care. The chapter summarises some aspects of our *Managing Misbehaviour* (Charlton and David, 1993), the wide distribution of which in many countries perhaps confirms the fact that teachers worldwide have a continuing concern with pupils' behaviour. We are referring to attempts to develop techniques, strategies, skills and attitudes which can be used effectively to manage pupils' behaviour in school.

Discipline (see also Chapters 7, 8 and 9)

The following quotes have provided discussion points on Inset courses.

- 'Schools can easily avoid questioning about their practice as long as they keep focusing the blame on students for classroom disruption.'
- Canter is quoted in Render *et al.* (1989, p. 618) as saying, 'fear can cure a kid of craziness, deprivation, and poor parenting'.
- Curwen and Mendler (1989, p. 83) state, 'a truly effective discipline plan must include, but go beyond rules, rewards, consequences and punishments. It must send a message of respect, dignity, belief and hope.'
- A journalist wrote the other day that perhaps we should not always regard learning as fun, something to be enjoyed, since life is not like that, and children ought perhaps to learn a tolerance of tedium. To be obliged to learn by rote at times might be good preparation for life?
- In Charlton and David (1993) we discuss research evidence that shows that much misbehaviour in school is caused by school-based factors, over which schools have considerable control.

'Killer' statements by teachers (see also Chapters 7, 10 and 13)

These were recalled from their schooldays by postgraduate teachers attending a training day on self-concepts.

- . . . belittled me for doing badly in the class history test. I took the test after a weekend when our house had been burgled and my mother was taken suddenly into hospital. When I explained all this I was given an aspirin and told to stop crying.
- . . . who had taught me French for the previous four years, asked me what my name was, and if I was new to the school.
- . . . kept me in class after a lesson, and punched me in the stomach with the text book for doing badly in a test.
- . . . said, 'You won't get your 'O' levels, let alone go to university'.
- . . . laughed about me (in front of me) with the Headmaster, when my mother had just been to school.
- . . . remarked that my low test score was just what he expected from a 'council house' child.
- . . . said, 'You're nearly as stupid as your brother, if that's possible.'
- . . . told me to stand on the stage and show the school the long stockings I was wearing (they were not allowed). He said that I looked like a wrinkled, old woman. He then got the whole school to clap at his 'joke'.
- . . . said I didn't need to learn to swim. I was so fat I'd float anyway.

Chapter 9 continued the examination of behaviour problems, and Sonia Sharp contributes a helpful and authoritative viewpoint on bullying, using her considerable experience with a major DES project.

Bullying and child abuse[2] (see Chapters 5, 7 and 9)

It is suggested in a paper circulating in Victim Support training that parents could look for the following possible signs of bullying in their children:

- coming home with disordered or torn clothing or damaged books;
- bruises, cuts and scratches without reasonable explanation;
- varying their route to school;
- do not bring classmates home and do not visit any;
- few or no friends to play with in leisure time;
- not invited to parties, and do not seek to have parties;
- reluctant to go to school and morning illness excuses;
- restless sleep and bad dreams;
- lower grades and lack of interest in school work;
- start stammering and become withdrawn;
- appear unhappy or sad, unexpected mood shifts, and sudden tempers;
- memory and concentration problems;

- often 'losing' their dinner money or pocket money;
- returning home starving because dinner money was taken;
- seeking or stealing extra money to accommodate the bullies.

It is also suggested that parents:

- should understand their child may not admit to being bullied;
- question their child directly, or encourage them always to talk to someone trusted about problems;
- check that their child is not inviting bullying by unpleasant habits;
- keep a written diary of signs and events, and photograph bruises and injuries;
- contact other parents as well as the school;
- contact school and school governors about policy on bullying.

Tattum and Lane (1989) list much practical help on bullying. They also comment (1989, p. 112):

> there is a growing awareness of the importance of listening to and talking with children. Many schools are recognising that the ability to 'get on with others' is not just a natural talent which some have and others do not, and are actively promoting concepts which educate children in 'learning for life'.

Charlton and David (1990) give a case study and supportive information and material on child abuse, including useful addresses, types of abuse, indications of possible abuse, responsibilities and procedures, estimates of abuse, the teacher's role, considerations for parents and teachers, the Children Act 1989, and useful publications. They quote Maher (1988, p. 282):

> there will never be an understanding or acceptance of the importance of the teacher's role in detecting, and helping pupils who are being abused as long as a teacher contends that, 'this is a minor problem and the numbers of abused children that I come into contact with is small'.

Teachers need to be aware of possible physical, sexual and emotional abuse, and of neglect. Signs may include those listed for bullying, and particularly:

- unexplained changes in behaviour, including unusual dependence or attention seeking and precocity or withdrawal;
- unexplained bruises or burns;
- physical neglect indicated by inadequate clothing, poor growth and unusual hunger.

Teachers will obviously be wary of misinterpreting such signs. They are not proof, but they merit suspicion, discussion with colleagues and possible referral to other professionals.

Peter Maher (1988) cites research enquiries which indicate that some one in ten of children are, or have been, the subject of some form of child sex abuse. He refers to another study which suggests the rate may be as high as one in three. Official figures such as those given by the NSPCC are unlikely to provide helpful data in terms of the incidence of such abuse, and may seriously underestimate the true extent of abuse. For every case reported there may be many others which go unreported. How many we still do not know.

To round off these six chapters on specifics we invited David Frost in **Chapter 10** to write on his research into the transfer of pupils from primary to secondary school, which we consider is often insufficiently considered and planned. His account is down to earth, we feel, and, as he says, 'I hope . . . this will help other groups who may wish to undertake a similar journey.'

Other methods of easing transition to secondary school

We read with interest Daniel Tabor's (1993) article in *Pastoral Care in Education*. He surveys the theoretical background and then describes the arrangements at his secondary school. From his English Faculty one teacher pairs with a teacher from a contributing primary school. Each pair of teachers plans a joint project involving primary pupils usually in Class 6 and secondary pupils from Years 7 to 9, over one to three terms, usually based at the secondary school, but also in the primary school concerned. The children worked in pairs and groups, with a sense of audience as an important feature. Subjects have included poetry, environment, soap operas, media studies and IT. His article reports favourably on the result of some 1,800 pupils involved so far.

Changing schools

Moore and Wade (1994) asked children experiencing special educational needs about the primary–secondary transfer experience. Over half the children experienced fears about being lonely, not being able to make friends, being bullied or picked on, not coping with academic work or meeting harsh teachers. Pupils suggested that before pupils move, teachers should:

- tell you what it is like;
- have things ready;
- show you around;
- be aware that you're coming;
- let you meet the teachers;
- know what a difficult and painful experience it is.

PART III

This part of *Pastoral Care Matters* contains three personal viewpoints, again associated with pastoral care and the work of teachers. In **Chapter 11** Tony Charlton reflected on the influence of television. We are personally convinced that television has a considerable effect on children, and is an influential counter-balance to what we do in schools, sometimes aiding our work, frequently negating it.

He argues that viewing television violence does not always result in behaving aggressively. The effects of viewing violence are likely to be lessened where:

1 children have a well-developed value system;
2 parents exercise prudent censorship over their children's viewing;
3 parents view programmes with their children, and discuss them;
4 schools and parents help pupils to become 'mediate' by:
- encouraging pupils to become critical viewers of television;
- showing differences between television fantasy and reality;
- drawing attention to, and encouraging, pro-social behaviour on television;
- incorporating aspects of children's television viewing into personal and social education lessons.

Clearly there are obligations on the part of parents and teachers to help their children to benefit from their television viewing. It is worthwhile for schools to make a checklist of ways to help pupils in these areas. We know that children are likely to imitate behaviour on television where the behaviour has prestige. Potential role models such as sportspersons, pop stars, actors and politicians have a responsibility to display behaviour which we wish to encourage in our children. Teachers and parents also have important responsibilities.

Richard Whitfield has been a major influence on family life education for many years, and in **Chapter 12** he considered some of the core values that could underpin the influence of teachers and parents. His writing is important in this book, reviewing as we are the whole range of personal and social education, and the associated and implicit links with moral education. We find the phrase 'advocates for children' a good one for our profession, as is the down-to-earth reminder about 'keeping at it' in the last paragraph.

What are essential needs and values? (see also Chapters 1, 7 and 11)

How much of what follows is family-based in childhood, and how much can be contributed by others?

1 Are the following adult personal needs?
- health;
- giving and receiving affection;
- ambition and drive;
- personal and social skills
- security and privacy;
- feeling worthwhile;
- knowledge and qualifications;
- personal values and maturity.

2 Are these the basic needs of children?
- to feel secure in family and environment;
- acceptance by and of others;
- sensitivity about their own and others' feelings;
- to be competent in observing, listening, talking and learning skills;
- health, proper sleep and food, enjoyable activity and friendship;
- some aesthetic appreciation of music and art;
- some lifelong curiosity about people and things;
- affection from and for others;
- some self-awareness of personal abilities and potential;
- some comprehension of society and their place in it;
- standards, giving values to live by and a philosophy for their existence;
- gradual responsibility and co-operation with the efforts of others;
- a lively and stimulating education.

3 Are these the measures of maturity? At what age do primary- and lower secondary-age children begin to develop some of them?
- the capacity to accept and depend on oneself;
- to stop constantly identifying with others;
- to rely on and justify one's own standards;
- to aspire towards a personal ideal;
- to be capable of detaching oneself from social demands, to stand outside our customary setting.

4 Are these commonly agreed values in society?
- appropriate care of the young;
- knowledge of the need to share and co-operate with others to preserve social order;
- understanding the need for love and respect in relationships;
- acceptance of the need to value and control sexual feelings;
- the maximising of unselfish happiness.

The following have also been suggested by students as commonly accepted values: fairness and justice, pleasure, development and fulfilment through knowledge and education (enabling choices to be rational), personal sensitivity and creativity. Are they generally agreed?

5 The following have long been suggested as the qualities men and women admire and do not admire in others. Are they slowly becoming outdated now?
   - admired: love, patience, faithfulness, sacrifice, courage and faith;
   - not admired: hatred, prejudice, greed, revenge, sloth and cowardice.

6 Goggin (1994, p. 20) suggests in a reasoned article on basic values that education can, and should, aim to achieve the three 'basic values' (self-discipline, knowledge of right and wrong, and family values) provided these values are understood in a broadly informed way rather than tied to a partisan model of man, the family, or society.

7 NCC (1993, p. 4) suggest that school values should include:
   - telling the truth;
   - keeping promises;
   - respecting the rights and properties of others;
   - acting considerately towards others;
   - helping those less fortunate and weaker than ourselves;
   - taking personal responsibility for one's actions;
   - self-discipline.

School values, they suggest, should reject bullying, cheating, deceit, cruelty, irresponsibility and dishonesty.

Fears and concerns of children

A listing of fears and concerns of children in a *Sunday Times* article (6 August 1995) suggests:

What children are frightened of today	*Children's concerns today*
War	Crime (murders, burglars, thieves and vandalism)
The dark	
Killing animals	Bullying
Bullying and being picked on	Baby and child abduction
Bombs and the IRA	Unemployment
Dying and being killed	Homelessness
Guns	
Losing a parent or member of family	
Spiders	
Wild or fierce animals	

The article also comments that:

- nearly a third of children are collected from school by car, four times the proportion of German children, the great majority of whom walk home.

- children appear to be more home-centred, with television and computer games taking up to 30 hours a week.

It appears that many caring parents are very concerned with dangers to their children in the world outside their home. Home Office researchers say, 'children are not becoming more vulnerable to homicide, and . . . the evidence of homicide by strangers on children has been consistently low'.

To what extent are parents and schools spoiling childhood by too great an emphasis on dangers and fears?

National Curriculum

National Curriculum Council (1990c), *Curriculum Guidance No. 8: Education for Citizenship* makes the following suggestions.

Attitudes. Promoting positive attitudes is essential if pupils are to value democracy and its associated duties, responsibilities and rights. The attitudes and personal qualities listed below contribute to this process.

- independence of thought on social and moral issues
- an enterprising and persistent approach to tasks and challenges
- a sense of fair play, including respect for the processes of law and the rights of others
- respect for different ways of life, beliefs, opinions and ideas
- a willingness to respect the legitimate interests of others
- respect for rational argument and non-violent ways of resolving conflict
- a constructive interest in community affairs
- an active concern for human rights
- appreciation of the paramount importance of democratic decision-making.

Moral Codes and Values. Pupils should be helped to develop a personal moral code and to explore values and beliefs. Shared values such as concern for others, industry and effort, self-respect and self-discipline, as well as moral qualities such as honesty and truthfulness, should be promoted and the opportunity be provided for pupils to:

- compare values and beliefs held by themselves and identify common ground
- examine evidence and opinions and form conclusions
- discuss differences and resolve conflict
- discuss and consider solutions to moral dilemmas, personal and social
- appreciate that distinguishing between right and wrong is not always straightforward

- appreciate that the individual's values, beliefs and moral codes change over time and are influenced by personal experience (e.g. of the family, friends, the media, school, religion and the cultural background in which an individual is raised).

The third viewpoint was by Mick Abrahams in **Chapter 13** where we asked him to review the professionalism of teachers, and the links with pastoral care, and initial and in-service education. He feels strongly that teachers are being deskilled. We find strong feelings among teachers that because there are weak schools and poor teachers (as there are poor politicians, plumbers or doctors) the profession is being judged on them, rather than on the greater numbers of dedicated and hardworking teachers. We find that while there is only limited disagreement with many of the recent educational innovations in testing and curriculum, there is bitter disagreement and some despair at the devaluing of the professionalism and work of the majority of good teachers.

Primary heads and pastoral care

Professionalism must include continuing in-service education. A brief account follows of day conferences held with groups of primary head teachers, under the heading 'Learning and Pupil Development'. These notes may provide ideas for others in their endeavours to provide for staff Inset needs in pastoral care matters.

The setting was informal with a changing pattern of groups. Short talks based on handouts introduced topics, with frequent breaks for discussions and questions. Similar conferences for their deputy heads accompanied by a member of staff were held a few weeks later. The following themes were discussed.

1 Adult and children's needs.
2 Some definitions: health education, personal and social education, family life education and moral education, and the place of these in the curriculum. Adult recollections of childhood. Definitions of: temperament, personality, reference groups and models of behaviour. The effect of the environment, and the fundamental family blueprint.
3 Changes in society: materialism, secularism, egalitarianism, new technology and changed job and career expectations, media power, changing sex roles multi-cultural changes, divorce and changing family life, and challenges to authority. Pressures on the schools as they try to meet the needs of children.
4 Can schools develop the greater range of personal competences children need to function in a competitive society: language to say what they mean and what they feel; knowledge about human behaviour;

social competence skills; learning to live comfortably with oneself; learning to be both an individual and a co-operative member of groups; learning and study skills to use throughout life; decision-making skills.

5 The varying influences of family, environment and school. Heads' own experiences and approaches discussed. Relations with Governors and Authority.

6 Various PSE and other syllabuses and checklists distributed and reviewed. Such work can be implicit in the curriculum, timetabled periods, occasional courses, taken by all staff, by selected staff, by visitors. The value of co-ordination of who does what and when.

7 Seven questions about such co-ordination: what problems often occur, what is 'normal' behaviour, what can be an invasion of privacy, what is only a family's business, what is the link with learning, what exactly is the school's role, and what evaluation and assessment is possible?

8 The preparation of staff, use of other agencies, visual aids and books, and parental involvement.

9 Sex education, including national and local guidelines, and involvement of governors and parents.

10 The primary school's work in preparing children for entry to secondary school, and for adolescence.

11 In concluding emphasis was placed on:
- the understated social power of the teacher in influencing children;
- the effect of the leadership of the school, and of the quality of the teachers;
- the effect of the hidden and informal curriculum;
- the effect of the ethos of the school, and of the total curriculum;
- experience shows that – 'life skills' can be taught; that children's attitudes can be varied, challenged or reinforced; that positive habits can be encouraged; that values can be suggested; that teachers and schools do provide models for children, whether they realise it or not.

A primary school head's account

We invited Colin Harding the headmaster of a popular and successful primary school to give us his personal views on pastoral care. His account follows.

The primary school is uniquely placed to fulfil a crucial pastoral role which benefits children, parents and staff. It is often, by its small size and easy accessibility to parents, supremely good at providing an apparently safe haven of friendliness and involvement in the local community.

The sympathy with which schools cope with the huge variety of family problems can only be significant if the staff are sympathetic by nature, and have the ability to empathise with the problems families are facing. We have to create an atmosphere where parents and children feel sufficiently comfortable to discuss their concerns or ask advice from a teacher who is not a close friend, but who is linked to the family by the important fact that they care for the child daily. This sympathetic concern does not just happen, it is a positive action by a team of people who consciously plan to create this ethos, which then provides a thread of care and support for each member of the school, woven into the fabric of school and National Curriculum policies. The school's Teaching and Learning Policy underpins everything that is taught. Great stress is laid upon relationships, and how these relationships interrelate and support the required ethos. Children are taught to listen, respect different views and empathise with others.

We have seen our pastoral role developing at a frightening pace as more families seek support from teachers, who try to help them make sense of personal tragedies, discord in the home, and children who are no longer quiet and acquiescent but are the products (and victims) of a selfish and materialistic society.

Scarcely a day passes without such help being sought, and the following list is neither exhaustive nor given in priority. It simply represents the kind of things we have dealt with recently.

- Children being difficult at home.
- Children disobedient and refusing to be co-operative in the mornings.
- Children beginning to steal and lie for no apparent reason.
- Children showing jealousy when a new child is born into the family.
- Poor classroom performance, leading to difficult behaviour at home.
- Sexual abuse.
- Children without friends.
- Breakdown of marriage where there is considerable bitterness between parents, who use the children in their battle to hurt each other.
- Health concerns of one person in a marriage relationship.
- Family break up caused by service life, and a distraught mother concerned because of her husband being in danger in service life.
- Death of twins in a fire, and a subsequent court case.
- Death of a child, and its effect on a close-knit family.
- Death of a parent, and the effect on a 5-year-old.

Many problems arise from unkindness and thoughtlessness, and the children are often the recipients. Our relationships with the children, the parents and each other must, therefore, counter these attitudes. Our school worship is an important occasion when one can teach stories of unselfishness, kindness, concern and generosity which percolate into a child's mind and hopefully promote the skills of building good relationships. 'Circle time' is an opportunity for children to share their experiences. Each class teacher organises 15–20 minutes of such discussion during each day, sometimes using points of common concern raised in the staffroom. Children can express their unhappiness about others being unkind or thoughtless. Children learn to be sympathetic listeners as well as being made aware of the lack of consideration of their peers. Discussions and role play provide ways of working through problems.

Helping bereaved children and parents is a harrowing experience, but total support must be given. A written message, attendance at funerals and face-to-face support must be part of the pastoral role. I can listen, understand the changes of behaviour, support the child when school work suffers, and if necessary refer the child to a local Gloucestershire Grief Support Programme, which organises holiday programmes for bereaved children and parents. Recently we set aside a small garden to remember a former pupil of the school, and the brother and sister still at this school planted a rose tree to help them come to terms with the death.

We use the usual supportive agencies, and have found our educational welfare officer very helpful, as are the school nurse and medical officer. The doctor and nurse help the deputy head and myself with the sex education programme based on a TV series. Parents are offered the opportunity to withdraw their children from the programme, but none do so.

To sum up, our school approach is threefold. First, a team of able adults committed to the ideal of pastoral care has been formed, and we expect newcomers to the staff to be part of that caring team. Second, our teaching obligations outlined in the National Curriculum must be underpinned with a strong pastoral identity. Third, the children are encouraged through our curriculum model to become involved in pastoral care themselves, aware of each other's needs, aware of each other's personalities, and fully aware of their actions and what those actions mean in the context of their own families and the wider community.

Parents and teachers (see also Chapters 4, 5, 10, 11 and 12)

This book has necessarily concentrated on teachers and their part in pastoral care. As a postscript to Chapter 13 it may be useful to remind ourselves that it is parents in families of varied types who shape the early years of the children who are our clients. Children's personality, habits and attitudes can be formed in these early years. It is obviously common sense for teachers to know the families of their pupils, and to work in co-operation with parents in continuing their children's development in school, for pastoral care lies in homes as well as schools.

Croll and Moses (1985, p. 47) show that teachers see behaviour problems in the main as deriving from the home and parental circumstances of the child. Jones and Lock (1993, p. 173) writing on 'Working with parents' comment as follows.

Misunderstanding between teachers and parents, and the apportioning of 'blame' for certain behaviours may come about because of:

1 a lack of understanding of the role and intentions of each other;
2 a failure to appreciate the constraints under which the other person is working;
3 an insufficient awareness that certain behaviours may be specific to particular situations, occurring, for example, in school but not in the home, and vice versa (Rutter *et al.*, 1971; Hanko, 1985).

They describe four stages of parent–teacher involvement, and conclude that a sharing of educational responsibility towards behaviour problems can result in a change in the total environment in which the child finds him or herself. We suggest this must be good for pastoral care in the widest sense, including successful learning and personal development as well as for behaviour. Pastoral care planning must obviously include constant efforts to involve parents as partners.

NOTES

1 English Speaking Board, 26a Princes Street, Southport, PR8 1EQ; tel. 01704 501730.

2 Useful addresses:
Children's Legal Centre, 20 Compton Terrace, London, N1 2UN. Advice Line – 0171 359 6251.
Advisory Centre for Education (ACE), 18 Aberdeen Studios, 22–24 Highbury Grove, London, N5 2EA. Advice line – 0171 354 8321.
Kidscape, 152 Buckingham Palace Road, London, SW1W 9TR. 0171 730 3300.
Anti-Bullying Campaign (ABC), 44 Priory Drive, Reigate, Surrey; tel. 01737 242880.
Childline – 01800 1111.

BIBLIOGRAPHY

Abbott, J. (1994) *Learning Makes Sense*, Letchworth: Education 2000.

Baldwin, J. and Wells, H. (1979–83) *Active Tutorial Work*, Oxford: Blackwell.

Barton, L. (1991) Teachers under siege: a case of unmet needs, *Support for Learning*, 6, 1, 3–7.

Bibby, C. (1945) Sex education: aims, possibilities and plans, *Nature*, 156, 6 Oct., p. 413, and 13 Oct., p. 438.

Butterworth, C. and Macdonald, M. (1985) *Teaching Social Education and Communication: A Practical Handbook*, London: Hutchinson.

Button, L. (1982) *Group Tutoring for the Form Tutor*, London: Hodder & Stoughton.

Canter, L. (1989) Assertive discipline: A critical review, in G. Render, J. Padilla and H. Crank (eds) *Teacher College Record* 90, pp. 607–30.

Croll, P. and Moses, D. (1985) *One in Five*, London: Routledge.

Charlton, T. and David, K. (1990) *Supportive Schools*, Basingstoke: Macmillan.

Charlton, T. and David, K. (1993) *Managing Misbehaviour in Schools* (2nd edn), London: Routledge.

Curwen, R.L. and Mendler, A.N. (1989) *Discipline with Dignity*, Alexandria, USA: Association for Supervision and Curriculum.

David, K. (1983) *Personal and Social Education in Secondary Schools*, London: Longman for Schools Council.

David, K. and Charlton, T. (1988) *The Caring Role of the Primary School*, Basingstoke: Macmillan.

David, K. and Wise, C. (1987) Challenges for sex education in schools, in K. David and T. Williams (eds) *Health Education in Schools* (2nd edn), London: Harper & Row.

Dryden, G. (1994) *The Learning Revolution*, London: Associated Learning Systems.

Dyfed County Council (1994) *Stress Support for School Staff*, Education Department, Carmarthen.

Fletcher-Campbell, F. (1995) Caring about caring, *Pastoral Care in Education*, 13, 3, 26–28.

Goggin, P. (1994) Basic values in education, *Pastoral Care in Education*, 12, 4, 16–20.

Hamblin, D.H. (1974) *The Teacher and Counselling*, Oxford: Blackwell.

Hamblin, D.H. (1981) *Problems and Practice in Pastoral Care*, Oxford: Blackwell.

Hamblin, D.H. (1983) *Teaching Study Skills*, Oxford: Blackwell.

Handy, C. (1981) *Understanding Organisations*, Harmondsworth: Penguin.

Hanko, G. (1985) *Special Needs in Ordinary Classrooms*, Oxford: Blackwell.

Hopson, B. and Scally, M. (1981) *Lifeskills Teaching*, Maidenhead: McGraw-Hill.

Hughes, P. (1971) *Guidance and Counselling in Schools*, Oxford: Pergamon.

Jones, K. and Lock, M. (1993) Working with parents, in T. Charlton and K. David (eds) *Managing Misbehaviour in Schools* (2nd edn), London: Routledge.

Kirby, N. (1981) *Personal Values in Primary Education*, London: Harper & Row.

Lang, P. (1988) *Thinking about Personal and Social Education in the Primary School*, Oxford: Blackwell.

Maher, P. (1988) Lessons for teachers from Cleveland, *Children and Society*, 2, 3, 279–288.

McGuiness, J.B. (1982) *Planned Pastoral Care*, London: McGraw-Hill.

Moore, N. and Wade, B. (1994) Good for a change? The views of students with special educational needs on changing school, *Pastoral Care in Education*, 12, 2, 23–27.

National Curriculum Council (1990a) *Curriculum Guidance: 3 The Whole Curriculum*, York: NCC.

National Curriculum Council (1990b) *Curriculum Guidance: 5 Health Education*, York: NCC.

National Curriculum Council (1990c) *Curriculum Guidance: 8 Education for Citizenship*, York: NCC.

National Curriculum Council (1993) *Spiritual and Moral Development: A Discussion Paper*, York: NCC.

Office for Standards in Education (1993) *Handbook for the Inspection of Schools* and *Supplement* (1994), London: HMSO.

Office for Standards in Education (1994) *Spiritual, Moral and Cultural Development*, London: HMSO.

Office for Standards in Education (1995a) *Subjects and Standards*, London: HMSO.

Office for Standards in Education (1995b) *Inspection of Schools*, London: HMSO.

Pring, R. (1984) *Personal and Social Education in the Curriculum*, London: Hodder & Stoughton.

Pringle, K. (1974) *The Needs of Children*, London: Hutchinson.

Rutter, M., Tizard, J. and Whitmore, K. (1971) *Education, Health and Behaviour*, London: Longman.

Schools Council (1977) *Health Education 5–13 Project*, London: Nelson.

Stonier, T. (1983) *The Wealth of Information – A Profile of the Post-industrial Society*, London: Thames/Methuen.

Tabor, D. (1993) Smoothing their path: transition, continuity and pastoral liaison between primary and secondary school, *Pastoral Care in Education*, 11, 1, 10–14.
Tattum, D.P. and Lane, D.A. (1989) *Bullying in Schools*, Stoke on Trent: Trentham Books.
Taylor, H.J. (1971) *School Counselling*, Basingstoke: Macmillan.
Ungoed-Thomas, J. (1994) Inspecting spiritual, moral, social and cultural development, *Pastoral Care in Education*, 12, 4, 21–25.
Wallis, J.H. (1973) *Personal Counselling*, Hemel Hempstead: Allen & Unwin.
Whitfield, R. (1985) *Families Matter*, Basingstoke: Marshall Pickering.
Williams, K. (1973) *The School Counsellor*, London: Methuen.

INDEX